California
HMH SCIENCE DIMENSIONS®

Grade 4

Watch the cover come alive as you move the car with solar energy.
Download the HMH Science Dimensions AR app available on Android or iOS devices.

This Write-In Book belongs to

_____

Teacher/Room

D1614062

Houghton Mifflin Harcourt

Consulting Authors

Michael A. DiSpezio
Global Educator
North Falmouth, Massachusetts

Marjorie Frank
*Science Writer and Content-Area
 Reading Specialist*
Brooklyn, New York

Michael R. Heithaus, PhD
*Dean, College of Arts, Sciences &
 Education*
*Professor, Department of Biological
 Sciences*
Florida International University
Miami, Florida

Bernadine Okoro
Access and Equity Consultant
S.T.E.M. Learning Advocate & Consultant
Washington, DC

Cary Sneider, PhD
Associate Research Professor
Portland State University
Portland, Oregon

All images ©Houghton Mifflin Harcourt, Inc., unless otherwise noted
Front cover: model car ©GIPhotoStock/Science Source
Back cover: Mars Rover ©NASA/JPL/Cornell University/Maas Digital

© Houghton Mifflin Harcourt Publishing Company

Program Advisors

Paul D. Asimow, PhD
Eleanor and John R. McMillan Professor of Geology and Geochemistry
California Institute of Technology
Pasadena, California

Eileen Cashman, PhD
Professor
Humboldt State University
Arcata, California

Mark B. Moldwin, PhD
Professor of Space Sciences and Engineering
University of Michigan
Ann Arbor, Michigan

Kelly Y. Neiles, PhD
Assistant Professor of Chemistry
St. Mary's College of Maryland
St. Mary's City, Maryland

Sten Odenwald, PhD
Astronomer
NASA Goddard Spaceflight Center
Greenbelt, Maryland

Bruce W. Schafer
Director of K–12 STEM Collaborations, retired
Oregon University System
Portland, Oregon

Barry A. Van Deman
President and CEO
Museum of Life and Science
Durham, North Carolina

Kim Withers, PhD
Assistant Professor
Texas A&M University-Corpus Christi
Corpus Christi, Texas

Adam D. Woods, PhD
Professor
California State University, Fullerton
Fullerton, California

English Language Development Advisors

Mercy D. Momary
Local District Northwest
Los Angeles, California

Michelle Sullivan
Balboa Elementary
San Diego, California

Classroom Reviewers & Hands-On Activities Advisors

Julie Arreola
Sun Valley Magnet School
Sun Valley, California

Pamela Bluestein
Sycamore Canyon School
Newbury Park, California

Andrea Brown
HLPUSD Science and STEAM TOSA
Hacienda Heights, California

Cynthia Sistek-Chandler, PhD
Associate Professor
National University, Sanford College of Education
San Diego, California

Leslie C. Antosy-Flores
Star View Elementary
Midway City, California

Stephanie Greene
Science Department Chair
Sun Valley Magnet School
Sun Valley, California

Kimberly Ann Huesing
Carlsbad Unified
Carlsbad, California

Rana Mujtaba Khan
Will Rogers High School
Van Nuys, California

George Kwong
Schafer Park Elementary
Hayward, California

Imelda Madrid
Bassett St. Elementary School
Lake Balboa, California

Susana Martinez O'Brien
Diocese of San Diego
San Diego, California

Craig Moss
Mt. Gleason Middle School
Sunland, California

Isabel Souto
Schafer Park Elementary
Hayward, California

Emily R.C.G. Williams
South Pasadena Middle School
South Pasadena, California

UNIT 1

Engineering and Technology ...1

© Houghton Mifflin Harcourt Publishing Company • Image Credits: ©Tom Grundy/Alamy

Earthquake Engineering **311**

© Houghton Mifflin Harcourt Publishing Company • Image Credits: ©FRANKHILDEBRAND/iStockPhoto.com

Claims, Evidence, and Reasoning

Constructing Explanations

A complete scientific explanation needs three parts—a claim, evidence, and reasoning.

A **claim** is a statement you think is true. A claim answers the question, "What do you know?" **Evidence** is data collected during an investigation. Evidence answers the question, "How do you know that?" **Reasoning** tells the connection between the evidence and the claim. Reasoning answers the question, "Why does your evidence support your claim?"

Suppose you're investigating what combination of baking soda and vinegar will produce the largest "volcanic" eruption. Specifically, you are increasing the amount of vinegar but leaving the amount of baking soda the same.

The largest amount of vinegar will react the most.

You have three containers of vinegar—50 mL, 100 mL, and 200 mL—and one tablespoon of baking soda for each container. Before you begin, you make a **claim**.

Then you add the baking soda to each container and observe. The data you gather is your **evidence**. You can use data to show if your claim is true or not. Now you're ready to construct a scientific explanation with a claim, evidence, and reasoning.

50mL   100mL   200ml

Claim	I think the largest amount of vinegar will react the most.
Evidence	The container with 200 mL of vinegar made more bubbles than the containers with 50 mL and 100mL.
Reasoning	The evidence showed that more vinegar makes a larger reaction than a little vinegar.

Evidence used to support a claim can be used to make another claim.

You decide to try a different type of investigation. Describe it below, then record your possible claim, evidence, and reasoning.

Warm vinegar will produce a larger reaction than cold vinegar.

My investigation is

_____

_____

_____

Claim	
Evidence	
Reasoning	

Safety in the Lab

Doing science is a lot of fun. But, a science lab can be a dangerous place. Falls, cuts, and burns can happen easily. **Know the safety rules and listen to your teacher.**

☐ **Think ahead.** Study the investigation steps so you know what to expect. If you have any questions, ask your teacher. Be sure you understand all caution statements and safety reminders.

☐ **Be neat and clean.** Keep your work area clean. If you have long hair, pull it back so it doesn't get in the way. Roll or push up long sleeves to keep them away from your activity.

☐ **Oops!** If you spill or break something, or get cut, tell your teacher right away.

☐ **Watch your eyes.** Wear safety goggles anytime you are directed to do so. If you get anything in your eyes, tell your teacher right away.

☐ **Yuck!** Never eat or drink anything during a science activity.

☐ **Don't get shocked.** Be careful if an electric appliance is used. Be sure that electric cords are in a safe place where you can't trip over them. Never use the cord to pull a plug from an outlet.

☐ **Keep it clean.** Always clean up when you have finished. Put everything away and wipe your work area. Wash your hands.

☐ **Play it safe.** Always know where to find safety equipment, such as fire extinguishers. Know how to use the safety equipment around you.

Safety in the Field

Lots of science research happens outdoors. It's fun to explore the wild! But, you need to be careful. The weather, the land, and the living things can surprise you.

- ☐ **Think ahead.** Study the investigation steps so you know what to expect. If you have any questions, ask your teacher. Be sure you understand all caution statements and safety reminders.

- ☐ **Dress right.** Wear appropriate clothes and shoes for the outdoors. Cover up and wear sunscreen and sunglasses for sun safety.

- ☐ **Clean up the area.** Follow your teacher's instructions for when and how to throw away waste.

- ☐ **Oops!** Tell your teacher right away if you break something or get hurt.

- ☐ **Watch your eyes.** Wear safety goggles when directed to do so. If you get anything in your eyes, tell your teacher right away.

- ☐ **Yuck!** Never taste anything outdoors.

- ☐ **Stay with your group.** Work in the area as directed by your teacher. Stay on marked trails.

- ☐ **"Wilderness" doesn't mean go wild.** Never engage in horseplay, games, or pranks.

- ☐ **Always walk.** No running!

- ☐ **Play it safe.** Know where safety equipment can be found and how to use it. Know how to get help.

- ☐ **Clean up.** Wash your hands with soap and water when you come back indoors.

Safety Symbols

To highlight important safety concerns, the following symbols are used in a Hands-On Activity. Remember that no matter what safety symbols you see, all safety rules should be followed at all times.

Dress Code

- Wear safety goggles as directed.
- If anything gets into your eye, tell your teacher immediately.
- Do not wear contact lenses in the lab.
- Wear appropriate protective gloves as directed.
- Tie back long hair, secure loose clothing, and remove loose jewelry.

Glassware and Sharp Object Safety

- Do not use chipped or cracked glassware.
- Notify your teacher immediately if a piece of glass breaks.
- Use extreme care when handling all sharp and pointed instruments.
- Do not cut an object while holding the object in your hands.
- Cut objects on a suitable surface, always in a direction away from your body.

Electrical Safety

- Do not use equipment with frayed electrical cords or loose plugs.
- Do not use electrical equipment near water or when clothing or hands are wet.
- Hold the plug when you plug in or unplug equipment.

Chemical Safety

- If a chemical gets on your skin, on your clothing, or in your eyes, rinse it immediately, and tell your teacher.
- Do not clean up spilled chemicals unless your teacher directs you to do so.
- Keep your hands away from your face while you are working on any activity.

Heating and Fire Safety

- Know your school's evacuation-fire routes.
- Never leave a hot plate unattended while it is turned on or while it is cooling.
- Allow equipment to cool before storing it.

Plant and Animal Safety

- Do not eat any part of a plant.
- Do not pick any wild plant unless your teacher instructs you to do so.
- Treat animals carefully and respectfully.
- Wash your hands throughly after handling any plant or animal.

Cleanup

- Clean all work surfaces and protective equipment as directed by your teacher.
- Wash your hands throughly before you leave the lab or after any activity.

Safety Quiz

Circle the letter of the BEST answer.

1. At the end of any activity you should
   a. wash your hands thoroughly before leaving the lab.
   b. cover your face with your hands.
   c. put on your safety goggles.
   d. leave the materials where they are.

2. If you get hurt or injured in any way, you should
   a. tell your teacher immediately.
   b. find bandages or a first aid kit.
   c. go to your principal's office.
   d. get help after you finish the activity.

3. Before starting an activity, you should
   a. try an experiment of your own.
   b. open all containers and packages.
   c. read all directions and make sure you understand them.
   d. handle all the equipment to become familiar with it.

4. When working with materials that might fly into the air and hurt someone's eye, you should wear
   a. goggles.
   b. an apron.
   c. gloves.
   d. a hat.

5. If you get something in your eye you should
   a. wash your hands immediately.
   b. put the lid back on the container.
   c. wait to see if your eye becomes irritated.
   d. tell your teacher right away.

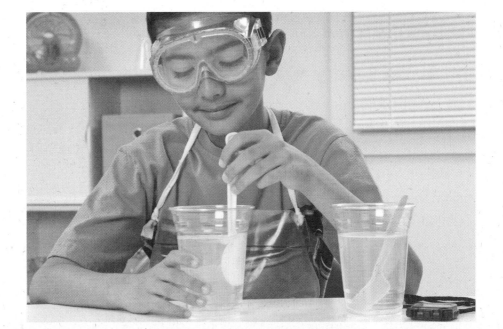

Engineering and Technology

Explore Online

You Solve It: Keeping It Warm and Cool
As you learn about engineering, you will apply the design process. You'll evaluate building materials and consider cost constraints while finding a solution to a problem.

When a new rocket is designed, it must be tested.

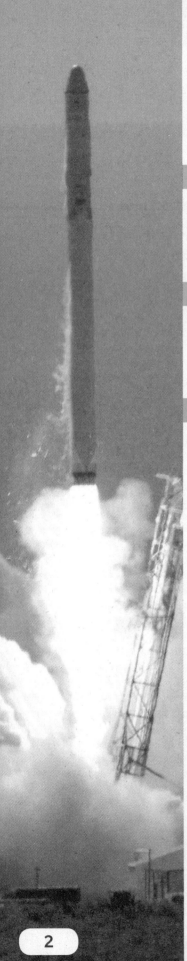

At a Glance

UNIT PROJECT • Engineer It!
Extend a Sense

Think of the many different senses you have. If you could improve any of your senses to a superpower level, which sense would it be? How would your sense work differently and be better? For this project, you will work with your team to come up with a design for a device that can be used to enhance your sense of sight, smell, or touch. Then you will present your design concept to the class.

Binoculars are devices that allow users to see items from a long distance.

Write a question that you will consider as you come up with your sense-enhancing designs.

_____

_____

_____

Materials Think about how you will perform this investigation. What materials will you need?

_____

_____

_____

As a team, decide on the sense you wish to focus on. Think about selecting a sense based on your interest. Which sense did you select, and why?

_____

_____

_____

Research and Plan Plan your research.
Consider the following:

- What is the problem that you are trying to solve?

- What is the solution?

- What are the criteria?

- What are the constraints?

Make a plan before starting your research.

_____

_____

_____

_____

_____

_____

_____

_____

_____

Review your design with your team, and look for possible areas for improvement. Will you make any modifications to your design? Why or why not?

_____

_____

_____

_____

_____

Analyze Your Results Using your design, make two observations about how your selected sense will be enhanced.

_____

_____

_____

Restate Your Question Write the question you investigated.

_____

_____

_____

Claims, Evidence, and Reasoning Make a claim that answers your question.

_____

_____

_____

What evidence from your analysis supports your claim?

_____

_____

_____

Discuss your reasoning with a partner.

Language Development

Use the lessons in this unit to complete the network and expand
understanding of the science concepts.

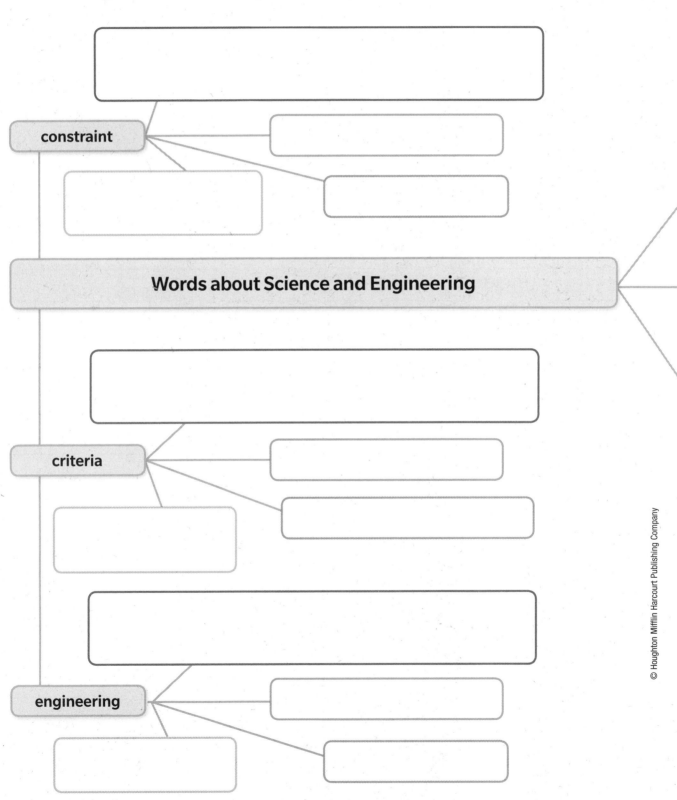

constraint

Words about Science and Engineering

criteria

engineering

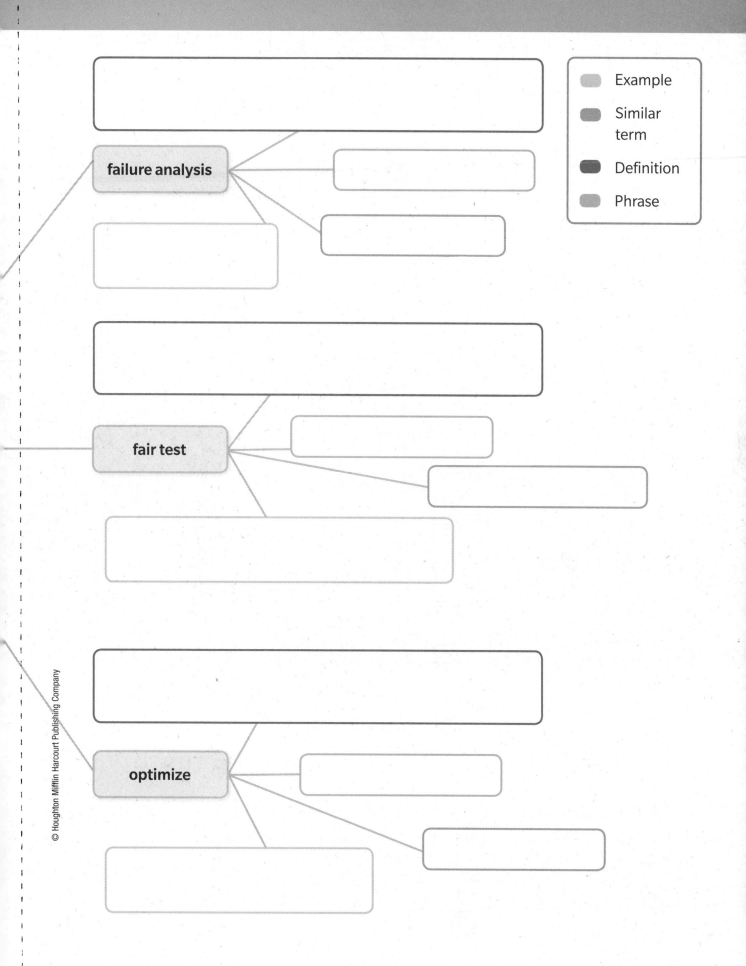

failure analysis

fair test

optimize

Example
Similar term
Definition
Phrase

How Do Engineers Define Problems?

Animals that live in the wild have to catch their own food if they want to eat. A hunter often can hear the prey. The prey often can hear the hunter coming. Think about the ways in which these animals hear the world around them.

Explore First

Hear Here! Think about what is involved in hearing. What would happen if a sound was very quiet? How could you find where a sound is coming from? As a group, think of ways you could pinpoint the location of a quiet sound.

Can You Solve It?

Explore Online

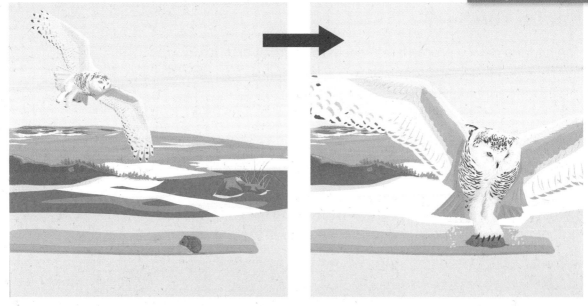

What sounds do you think the vole makes that the owl could hear? What helps the animals on these two pages find food? What helps them protect themselves from being eaten?

Think of the sounds living things make. Imagine that your class is going on a nature hike to observe and identify these sounds. You need to design a lightweight hearing-enhancing device that you can wear. It can't use batteries. How would you define this problem?

_____

_____

_____

_____

_____

_____

 EVIDENCE NOTEBOOK Look for this icon to help you gather evidence to answer the questions above.

What Is Technology?

What Do You See?

The hearing device problem may seem too hard at first. It's easier if you tackle it in an organized way. First, though, you need to learn a little about technology.

Kitchen Tech

Think about how each technology you see meets a want or need. How did engineers play a role in the technology shown in the picture? Match the engineering contributions with the technology in the picture.

a. designed tools to melt and form glass; made a process to cut glass and assemble a frame

b. designed tools to cut, fold, and glue sheets of cardboard into containers

c. designed electric circuits, mechanical parts, and an easy-to-use control panel

Technology is how humans change the natural world to meet a want or a need. **Engineering** is the process of designing new or improved technology. Engineers are the people who do engineering.

The first part of designing a solution is describing what it must do. How will it meet a want or need? Examining familiar technology can help you learn to design a solution.

Apply What You Know

Engineered?

In the first column, write the name of six nonliving things you see in your classroom that are engineered. In the other column, write the name of six nonliving things you see in your classroom that are not engineered. With a partner, explain your choices for each column.

Engineered	Not engineered

Look at the kitchen scene again. Identify three more examples of technology and the problems they solve. How do you know that these are examples of technology?

_____

_____

_____

_____

_____

_____

What Is the Problem?

View the image of the kitchen again. After you think about the specific technologies in the kitchen, pick three items that you think best meet a want or need.

Write the name of each item in the left-hand column. Write the need or want that is met by the item in the right-hand column.

Technology item	Need or want met
1.	
2.	
3.	

You have learned that when a need or want is met, engineers have worked to meet the criteria. **Criteria** are desirable features of the solution. For example, you want rags that can soak up liquids. Paper towels were considered an improvement on rags. Paper towels meet a new criterion—they are made to be thrown away. They still soak up liquids.

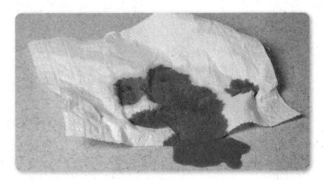

A paper towel is designed to be absorbent and strong so it can soak up liquids without ripping.

 EVIDENCE NOTEBOOK What are the criteria for your hearing enhancer?

 Language SmArts
Cite Evidence for Criteria

Pick an everyday object, such as a backpack or lunchbox, that you would like to improve. Give the criteria for a successful improvement.

_____

_____

_____

_____

© Houghton Mifflin Harcourt Publishing Company

Menu Planning

Objective

Collaborate Engineering solutions can be a plan or process, too. Suppose that you need to plan three main dishes for dinner on three different nights, nine meals altogether. Each night, you must analyze your meal options in order to meet a constraint. A **constraint** is a limit on possible solutions. On the first night, you have a constraint that the budget is $35.00.

For each night, choose a main dish from the recipe cards. The constraints for each set of meals are listed in the steps below. Your goal is a set of three main dishes that meet all the constraints.

Think about when you are faced with a problem or situation that needs a solution. How can thinking carefully about the criteria and constraints help you develop a solution?

Materials
• recipe cards

_____

_____

Procedure

STEP 1 Think of what you would consider a good meal. It may be that the meal is healthy for you, contains well-balanced ingredients, or looks and smells tasty. Write down three criteria for what makes a good meal.

Criteria

1.	
2.	
3.	

STEP 2 Plan out the first set of meals. Choose from the list of recipe cards that meet the constraint of a budget of $35.00. Make a table to record the recipe cards and costs. Don't forget to check your math.

STEP 3 Now apply the three criteria you picked to the three meals you have put together. Evaluate the quality of the meals using the three criteria. Enter your evaluation below.

_____

_____

STEP 4 Now plan out a second set of meals for the next three nights, choosing from all 12 recipe cards. For this set, your constraints are that your budget is $35.00 and you have 100 minutes to prepare the meals. The meals must be prepared one at a time. Make another table to record the recipe cards, costs, and preparation times. Check the totals.

STEP 5 Now apply the three criteria you picked before to the three meals you have put together. Evaluate the quality of the meals using the three criteria. Write your evaluation below.

_____

_____

STEP 6 Finally, plan out a third set of meals for the last three nights using all 12 recipe cards. Your constraints are that you have a budget of $35.00 and you have a total of 100 minutes to prepare the meals. In addition, some of your guests are vegetarians. Make a table to record the recipe cards, costs, preparation times, and vegetarian options. Check the totals.

STEP 7 Now apply the three criteria you picked before to the three meals you have put together. Evaluate the quality of the meals using the three criteria. Enter your evaluation below.

_____

_____

Which constraint was easiest to plan around? Which constraint was hardest? In both cases, tell how you might have planned differently. Enter your answers in the table below.

Best	
Worst	

What was the goal of the activity? How did your solution help achieve that goal?

_____

_____

_____

Say that another student wants to complete this activity for the first time. What are two things you would tell this student to guide him or her during the activity?

_____

_____

_____

Change one of your criteria. How would this change your recipe selections?

_____

_____

_____

What other questions do you have about how criteria and constraints may affect solutions?

_____

_____

_____

Real-World Limits

Limited Limits

Part of defining engineering problems is identifying constraints. A constraint is a limit on possible solutions. Examples of constraints include money, time, and materials. Some safety constraints are required by law.

Bike Tech

Explore Online

Match the safety constraints described to the bike parts.

a. It helps control speed. Safety rules say that a 68 kg (150 lb) bicycle rider moving at 24 km/hr (15 mph) must be able to use it to stop within 4.5 m (15 ft).

b. It undergoes great force as you pedal. Grit from the road causes wear, and water rusts it. Safety rules say that it must withstand a pull of 818 kg (1,800 lb) before breaking.

c. This part supports your weight while you ride. Its height is adjustable. Safety rules say that it must support a weight of 68 kg (150 lb) without moving down.

Paper Building 10 • 10 • 10

You have 10 index cards and 10 cm of tape. In 10 minutes, work as a team to build the tallest structure you can. It should support at least one book. In the space below, list the constraints and tell which was the hardest to meet and why.

_____

_____

Do the Math

Safety Check!

Many states require bicycle helmets for individuals under 18. The table shows the numbers of bicycle deaths in the United States for people wearing, or not wearing, helmets.

Year	No helmet	Helmet	Total
2012	469	123	592
2013	464	127	591
2014	429	118	547
2015	440	139	579

Solve In 2012, there were 592 bicyclist deaths. What fraction of these deaths was of people not wearing helmets?

_____

Evaluate What do you notice about the number of deaths of riders wearing helmets versus the number of deaths of riders not wearing helmets?

_____

_____

Apply Describe another possible constraint for a bicycle. List your answer below.

_____

_____

Improvements

Engineers improve solutions all the time. A new solution may not work for everyone, though. Some people may have constraints, such as money or available space, on the solutions they can decide to buy or use.

laundry basket

three-bin laundry basket

Language SmArts
Interpret Information

Look at the laundry baskets. How is the three-bin basket an improvement? What constraints might a buyer have that would keep them from using the improved solution?

_____

_____

_____

 EVIDENCE NOTEBOOK Think back to your hearing enhancer. What constraints are there on your solution?

Putting It Together

Remember, criteria are features of a desirable solution, while constraints are limits that must be met in order to be acceptable. In the following lists of criteria and constraints, draw a star next to each constraint.

A new pair of shoes	A homework assignment
comfortable	neatly written
resists water	shows originality
attractive	completed by tomorrow's class
costs less than $35	good grammar

18

Discover More

Check out this path . . . or go online to choose one of these other paths.

People in Science & Engineering

- **Writing Within Constraints**
- **Limits in Nature**

Marion Downs

Marion Downs was an audiologist, a doctor specializing in hearing. She helped many thousands of children to speak and hear better by noticing and solving a problem.

Infants born with hearing problems can't hear their own voice or the voices of others. This means that they can't develop language skills. Infants can't talk, so before the 1960s, it took two or three years to notice a child's hearing problem.

Dr. Downs pioneered the release of a hearing testing program that didn't require infants to talk. A doctor watched them respond to sounds, such as rattles. A second part of the solution was to change what doctors do nationwide. Now, doctors screen all six-month-old infants to see if they might need hearing aids.

One type of hearing aid infants receive is a cochlear implant. This hearing aid is implanted under the skin, behind the ear. It converts sounds to electrical signals that are sent to the inner ear.

Although Dr. Downs was not an engineer, she engineered a solution to a serious gap in our nation's health system.

Explore Online

Marion Downs, audiologist

Cochlear implant

Protecting Hearing

Noise is a major cause of hearing loss later in life. The loss can be temporary after being exposed to a loud noise, such as a firecracker. It might take a day or more to recover. A person can have permanent hearing loss if he or she is exposed to loud noises for long periods of time. Loud music, jet engine noise, and gunfire can cause permanent hearing loss.

Musicians, construction workers, and others who have jobs in loud noise environments can protect their sense of hearing from permanent damage. Devices such as over-the-ear hearing protectors block loud noises from damaging the sense of hearing.

Dense foam earplugs also protect the ear from loud noises. They are flexible and fit snugly in the ear canal.

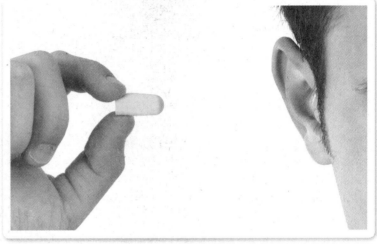
Dense foam earplugs

Over-ear hearing protectors

Explain What are some criteria for hearing aids? Is the criteria for hearing protectors different or the same? What are constraints for hearing aids and hearing protectors?

_____

_____

_____

_____

_____

_____

Gather Evidence Research how people have their hearing tested. Summarize what you find below. Include an idea that you want to explore more. Be prepared to share your findings.

_____

_____

_____

Lesson Check

Name _____

Can You Solve It?

1. In the next lesson, you will develop a device to enhance your ability to hear sounds in the wild.

   • What does your hearing enhancer need to do? What are the limits on its design?

   • Make sure to use the words *criteria* and *constraints*.

Explore Online

EVIDENCE NOTEBOOK Use the information you've collected in your Evidence Notebook to help you cover each point above.

_____

_____

_____

_____

_____

_____

_____

Checkpoints

Answer the questions that follow about how engineers define problems.

2. Choose all the statements that are correct.

   a. Solutions meet a want or need.

   b. Solutions are separate from engineering.

   c. Solutions are the technology all around us.

   d. Solutions come in different forms because they help solve problems.

   e. Solutions must be complicated in order to work.

3. Janet is trying to improve the design of her lunchbox. Choose all of the following statements that are good criteria for her to keep in mind.

    a. The lunchbox can't be too heavy to hold for a long time.

    b. The lunchbox should have sharp corners and rough edges.

    c. The lunchbox could use a special pocket for water bottles.

    d. The lunchbox could keep food colder.

4. Identify all the likely constraints faced when designing and building a two-room treehouse.

    a. time   **d.** sunlight

    b. budget   **e.** tree size

    c. materials   **f.** number of rooms

5. Draw lines to match each word to its description.

engineering	desired features of a solution
constraints	identification of a want or need
criteria	using technology to design solutions to solve problems
problem	absolute limits on a solution

6. Write the name of the item from the picture that uses technology to fill each need or want.

    a. keep warm _____

    b. protect the head _____

    c. improve vision _____

    d. adjust speed and force _____

Lesson Roundup

A. Choose the best words from the word bank to complete the sentences.

> **a specific weight**   **limitations**   **requirements**
> **criteria**   **solutions**

Good criteria tell what _____ an engineering solution should meet.

Constraints are the _____ on an engineering solution.

B. Choose the best words from the word bank to complete the sentences.

> **solutions**   **criteria**   **constraints**   **weather and day of the week**
> **a budget and a time limit**   **brand of bike and criteria**

Omar is going to try to improve his bicycle. He first looks to see what his

limitations, or _____, are. He knows that the biggest limit is

how much money he can spend. He also must have the bike ready to ride in a race

in two weeks. His constraints are _____.

C. Choose the best words from the word bank to complete the sentences.

> **solutions**   **other materials**   **books**   **design**
> **solution**   **requirements**   **limitations**   **criteria**

Engineering _____ have different criteria and constraints.

These criteria describe _____. The constraints describe the

_____ for the engineering solution.

How Do Engineers Design Solutions?

Think about the bird calls and other sounds you might hear on a nature walk. Observing and identifying those sounds can be a challenge.

Explore First

Problems in Nature Scientists often wish to record audio or video of birds and other animals in nature. Can you think of some problems that scientists may encounter when trying to capture these recordings? Work as a group to think of ways these problems can be solved.

Recall the nature hike scenario that you read about in the last lesson. You thought about the criteria and constraints for a hearing-enhancing device. This device would help you and others better hear the wildlife on your walk.

What might your hearing-enhancing device look like? Why? How will the constraints and criteria affect its appearance? Enter your answers below.

_____

_____

_____

_____

_____

_____

_____

_____

EVIDENCE NOTEBOOK Look for this icon to help you gather evidence to answer the questions above.

Research Matters!

Ears to You!

Designing a solution can be tough. Depending on the situation, there can be many different steps. One important first step is to learn more about the problem before you start to design a solution.

Your challenge is to design a hearing-enhancing device to use on a nature walk. Where should you start? You might want to start by learning how different animals use hearing to solve their problems. View each image below to explore how some animals use hearing to solve different problems.

The red fox is an excellent hunter. It uses its hearing to locate small mammals that burrow underground. When the red fox figures out where an animal is, it will dig it up.

Mule deer are common in the western United States. These animals have large ears that allow them to hear sounds, such as those made by predators that can pose dangers.

Aye-ayes live on Madagascar. They tap on tree bark with their long fingers and use their ears to listen for moving larvae. When they hear the larvae, aye-ayes use their fingers to pry the larvae out of the bark and eat them.

Wild rabbits live in many temperate environments. These animals can independently rotate their ears to pick up the softest of sounds. Rabbits use their hearing to identify possible predators.

Look again at the photos on the previous page, and recall what you read. Use this information to complete the table below. Then answer the questions to compare the animals' ears and explain how looking at their ears can help you design a hearing-enhancing device.

Ears, Ears, Ears

In the table, make a detailed drawing of each animal's ear.

Type of animal	Shape of ear
red fox	
mule deer	
aye-aye	
wild rabbit	

Compare and Contrast How do the ears of these animals differ? How are they the same? How can looking at these animals' ears help you design your hearing-enhancing device?

_____

_____

_____

Targeting Sounds

Explore Online

Hearing is an important sense for many animals. It helps them to survive in their environments. It helps them find food and avoid predators or other dangers. View the photos on these pages, and think about the sounds each songbird makes. How could your hearing enhancer help you hear differences between the songs?

North American Songbirds

The black-capped chickadee is a songbird often found near wooded areas. Its most often heard song is a short whistled two or three note "fee-bee" or "fee-bee-bee."

The American robin is a common songbird. It often sings just before daylight. Some describe its song as "cheerily cheer-up cheer-up cheerily cheer-up."

The northern cardinal is often found near dense bushy areas. Its song can be described as a quick and lively "birdie birdie birdie." It signals danger with a loud, short "chip."

The yellow warbler lives in dense woody areas and swamps. Its song sounds like, "sweet sweet sweet, I'm so sweet."

 EVIDENCE NOTEBOOK Apply what you read on this page to possible features of your hearing-enhancing device.

Wildlife, including songbirds, use sounds to communicate and survive in their environments. Use the similarities and differences between the songs of the North American songbirds to answer the questions below.

 Language SmArts
Comparing and Contrasting

What is the same about the birds' songs? What is different? What else might you need to help you determine what type of bird you are listening to?

_____

_____

_____

_____

_____

_____

_____

Past Hearing Helpers

Looking Back to Look Forward

Many hearing-enhancing devices have been made over time. Most are not perfect solutions, though. Engineers continue to build on and work to improve solutions such as these hearing aids from the past and present.

This early ear trumpet collected and directed sound waves to the listener's ear. The device worked best when the sounds were nearby. The small end is held near the ear.

Ear trumpets with longer tubes helped amplify sounds, too. They were easier to hold and direct toward the sound.

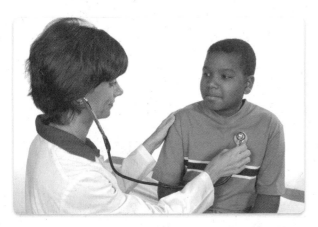

A stethoscope is often used in medicine. Sound travels from the patient to the cup, which increases the volume of the sound. The sound moves through the tubes to the user's ears.

This concrete listening post collects and focuses sounds like a curved mirror. Before radar, it was used to listen for approaching enemy planes.

Solutions to problems can have many different parts. Looking at others' solutions can often help improve an existing design. In other words, we can learn from past solutions to help us with new and better solutions.

Listen and Learn!

Look again at the photos on the previous page. In the table below, describe each device in your own words. Then tell how you think you could change the device to improve it.

Description	How I might improve device
ear trumpet	
ear trumpet with a long tube	
stethoscope	
British acoustic mirror listening post	

Language SmArts

Connecting Ideas

How might you use what you've learned to design your hearing-enhancing device?

_____

_____

_____

_____

Hearing Here

Work with a partner. Stand about 3 m apart. Turn so that your ear is pointing toward your partner. Close your eyes. Have your partner whisper your name. Have your partner whisper your name again, but cup your hands to your ears. Compare the two sounds. Trade roles with your partner so that he or she can observe your whispering. Describe the sounds below. Why did they sound different? Can cupping your hands to your ears make it easier to locate a faint sound? Test and see.

_____

_____

_____

_____

_____

_____

EVIDENCE NOTEBOOK How can your results from this activity help you design your device?

Putting It Together

How does studying others' hearing-enhancing solutions help you with your possible design? How does looking at different types of animals' ears help you with your design?

_____

_____

_____

_____

Passing the Test

Testing, Testing, 1, 2, 3

Engineers design many things that people depend on. It's not enough for an engineer to say that a design works. It needs to be tested to ensure it solves the problem. Each design starts out as a prototype, or early version for testing. Prototypes must be thoroughly tested to be sure they're safe and work correctly. Often, it takes many prototypes to get one that is ideal. Most types of engineering solutions are like this. They need to be tested and improved many times before they meet criteria and satisfy constraints of safety, time, money, or materials.

Anechoic means "no echoes." An *anechoic chamber* is used to test speakers, headphones, and microphones. The walls in the chamber are designed to absorb sound waves.

Do the Math
Measuring Sound

Human hearing is amazingly sensitive. We can hear sounds from a pin dropping to a landslide. Sound is measured in decibels (dB). A sound that you can barely hear is 0 dB. A quiet whisper that is 10 times louder is 10 dB. A sound that is 100 times louder is 20 dB. A sound that is 1,000 times louder is 30 dB. Complete the table.

Sound	Decibels	Times louder
whisper	10 dB	10 times
country sounds	20 dB	100 times
city sounds	30 dB	
big truck	90 dB	
rock band	100 dB	

More Testing

Look at the photos below. Then read the captions to learn more about some other engineering designs and how they are tested.

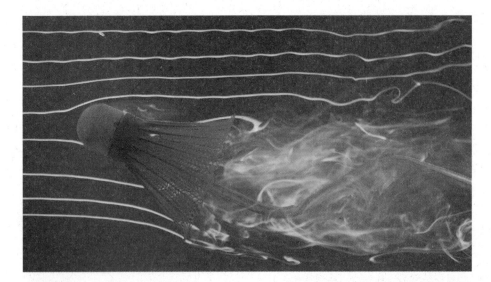

An *aquadynamic* testing facility is similar to a wind tunnel. It is used to test vehicles and objects that move through water to make sure they are safe and do not leak. It is also used to model movement through air.

This is an eye-tracking rig. It keeps a record of eye movements while a person uses software or a webpage. Portable, wearable devices are used in sports to see if players are really keeping their eyes on the ball!

Identify Choose the word or words that complete each sentence.

anechoic chamber	eye-tracking rig	final design
improve	prototype	

A _____ is an early version of a design solution. These versions

are tested to help _____ a design solution. An _____

might be tested by a rock band to help with their recordings. Video gamers

might use an _____ to test and improve their gaming skills.

© Houghton Mifflin Harcourt Publishing Company • Image Credits: (t) ©Rob Bulmahn; (b) ©Phillippe Psalla/Science Source

Fair Tests

Testing and retesting solutions is important. A **fair test** is one that doesn't give any advantage to the conditions or objects being tested. For a fair test, engineers observe and measure the effects of changing only one thing, or *variable*, at a time. Changing many variables at once seems faster. However, you don't know what causes the results.

Here's an example of a fair test. Suppose you want to find the fastest way to walk home. You'd need to time each route walking at roughly the same speed on similar days. You would not compare walking the first route, running the second, and carrying a heavy backpack on the third. The same is true for the results on a slippery, icy day and on a warm, dry day.

Learn More about Sound Tests

Look at the sound system test room below. You may have seen one like it in a store. Read each caption to find out more about different parts. Then answer the question on the next page.

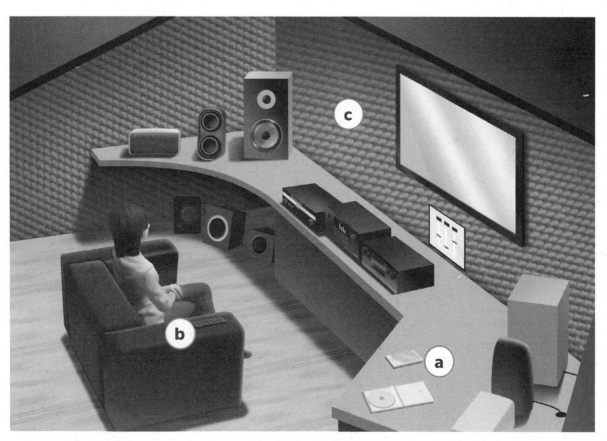

a. **Sound source**
A CD, smartphone, TV, or radio is a possible source of test sounds.

b. **Remote control**
A remote control adjusts loudness and chooses the speakers being tested.

c. **Wall lining**
The wall lining helps keep outside sounds from interfering with the music.

Language SmArts
Your Fair Test

What steps would you take to make a fair test of the speakers shown in the sound system test room?

_____

_____

_____

_____

_____

_____

 EVIDENCE NOTEBOOK Explain how the criteria for your hearing-enhancing device affect what you will test.

Putting It Together

What factors will your team need to think about and address to make a fair test of your hearing-enhancing device?

_____

_____

_____

_____

_____

_____

_____

HANDS-ON ACTIVITY • ENGINEER IT
Design It!

Objective

Collaborate with a team to design your own hearing-enhancing device. The device should not have a battery and should not go in your ear. Make sure you use the design criteria and constraints as you construct your device. Also use what you've learned about past solutions, animals' ears, and fair tests. Be safe—don't put *anything* in your ears.

Form a question: What problem will you solve to meet this objective?

_____

_____

Possible Materials
- plastic cups
- paper cups
- cloth scraps
- duct tape
- masking tape
- wire clothes hangers
- string
- rubber tubing
- plastic headbands
- scissors
- baseball or painter's cap

Procedure

STEP 1 Handle and examine the materials available to you. Brainstorm ideas with your team. Choose the best one. Then make a rough sketch in the box of how you think your device will look and work.

What are the constraints? _____

_____

What are your criteria? _____

_____

STEP 2 Identify the materials from those available that you will use to make your design come to life. Write your list in the first box below. Also write how the materials will help to meet the criteria.

First Design Notes

STEP 3 With your team, build and test your device. Make sure to not put anything in your ears. Use the test results to improve the device. Stop testing and improving when you are satisfied that it meets the constraints and criteria. In the space below, keep a record of the design changes you make. Include a reason for each change.

Additional Design Notes

STEP 4 When you are satisfied that the device meets the constraints and criteria, think of a different design that might work even better. If there is time, build and test a second device that is different in some way.

STEP 5 Use the final design and your notes to answer the questions in the table below.

a. Why did you choose each material? How did they help your design?	
b. Why did you pick this design?	
c. How well did your design meet the criteria and constraints? Explain.	

Did your design meet the goals of this activity? Support your **claim** with **evidence** and **reasoning**.

_____

_____

Explain why you chose two of your materials.

_____

_____

If other students looked at your final design, what improvements did they suggest? Why?

_____

_____

What is one new question you have about designing hearing-enhancement devices?

_____

_____

Discover More

Check out this path . . . or go online to choose one of these other paths.

Careers in
Science &
Engineering

- **Hearing Aid History**
- **Don't Make a Move . . .**
- **People in Science & Engineering**

Acoustic Engineer

Engineers work in many fields. An acoustic engineer solves problems related to sound or hearing. From concert halls to quiet cars, acoustic engineers design sound-related objects and systems. They study engineering, physics, and math to be successful. The tools of their trade are microphones, computers, and their ears.

Acoustic engineers can design concert halls so that the sounds coming from the stage sound great no matter where you sit. Like all engineers, acoustic engineers make and test multiple solutions. Acoustic engineers find the best solutions that work within the design constraints and criteria.

An acoustic test lab

William Cumpiano is a guitarmaker and luthier (guitar repairman). He learned about acoustics at several colleges and through apprenticeships with two master guitarmakers in the 1970s. Later, he received a patent for a carbon-fiber board that optimizes guitar design.

William Cumpiano uses his knowledge about acoustics to build guitars. His instruments are highly prized and have been on display at the Smithsonian Institute in Washington, D.C.

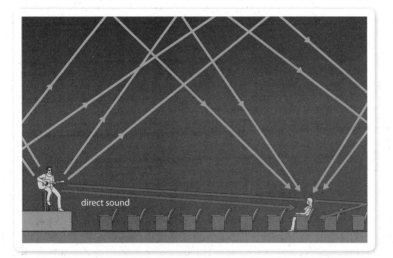

direct sound

This shows the paths of sound reflection in an auditorium.

Explain Describe two or three problems that an acoustic engineer might help solve.

_____

_____

_____

_____

_____

Make Some Sound Observations

Look around the room you are in. List at least five different materials that the room itself and objects within it are made of. Write the materials on the lines in the table. Speak softly with your mouth about 3 inches (in.) away from the material. Listen for differences in the sound of your voice. Record your observations.

Material	Observations

Infer Which materials would you use in a music hall to keep the sound in? Base your answer on your observations of how the materials affected the sound of your voice. Which would you use if there were not enough sound reflected? Why?

_____

_____

_____

_____

Apply Which materials would you use in an anechoic chamber? Which materials would you avoid? Why?

_____

_____

_____

© Houghton Mifflin Harcourt Publishing Company

Lesson Check

Name _____

Can You Solve It?

1. Recall the imaginary nature hike and your proposed solution for a hearing-enhancing device. Use what you've learned to do the following:

   • Explain the importance of researching previous solutions to the same problem.

   • Explain how solutions are designed.

   • Describe how and why potential design solutions are tested.

Explore Online

EVIDENCE NOTEBOOK Use the information you've collected in your Evidence Notebook to help you cover each point above.

_____

_____

_____

_____

_____

_____

_____

Checkpoints

2. Choose the word or words that correctly complete each sentence.

solutions	problems	audio
acoustics	fair tests	old prototypes

Engineers design _____ to help solve problems. They perform

_____ to help them design new devices.

3. Draw lines to sort each of the following descriptions of the engineering design process into the correct category.

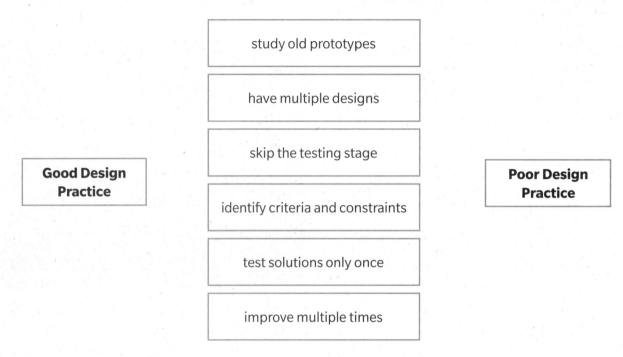

| study old prototypes |
| have multiple designs |
| skip the testing stage |
| identify criteria and constraints |
| test solutions only once |
| improve multiple times |

Good Design Practice

Poor Design Practice

4. Circle all of the choices that correctly complete this sentence.

Engineers _____
   a. test solutions to design problems more than once.
   b. don't waste time learning about other solutions to their problems.
   c. don't try to improve others' solutions or their own solutions.
   d. create more than one solution to the same problem.

5. You've learned that animals use their hearing to solve problems. Which of these problems can they solve using this sense? Circle all that apply.
   a. finding food
   b. swimming faster or slower
   c. locating dangerous predators
   d. sleeping well at night

6. Choose words from the word bank to complete the sentences.

| many tries | retest | retesting |
| test | testing | one try |

Engineers _____ designs because it's important to be

sure a solution works. Usually _____ happens because it takes

_____ to get a working prototype.

Lesson Roundup

A. A new student just joined your class and needs to get caught up on this lesson. What should she do to begin designing her hearing-enhancing device?

  a. research careers in acoustic engineering

  b. study the devices already made by other students

  c. learn how different birds sing different types of songs

  d. ask for materials other than those available

B. Which of these should the new student learn more about at this point? Circle all that apply.

  a. ear trumpets

  b. light and mirrors

  c. stethoscopes

  d. sound waves

C. It's your job to tutor the new student so that she quickly catches up. Suppose that you will give her the paragraph below to help her. Choose the words to correctly complete the sentences that she will read.

| one part | many parts | no prototypes |
| multiple prototypes | test them only once | retest them many times |

Like actual engineers, we are solving a problem. Thus, we should create

_____ of our hearing-enhancing devices. Then we should

_____. During our tests, we should change _____

of the design at a time.

D. What do professional engineers do during the design process? Select all that apply.

  a. use prototypes

  b. test each design only once

  c. come up with a single solution

  d. research on existing solutions

  e. change multiple things when testing

  f. meet all of the constraints and as many criteria as possible

How Do Engineers Test and Improve Prototypes?

Crash dummies test what happens to humans in car crashes. Since the 1950s, the dummies have gotten smarter! Some early dummies were much smaller than average humans. Others didn't collect good data. Testing and redesign have made today's crash dummies more effective than those in the past.

Explore First

Build a Boat Cars aren't the only kind of technology that can get people from one place to another. Can you build a boat that can float on water and carry a small load? With a partner, use the materials your teacher gives you to design and test a boat.

Can You Solve It?

Early rocket designs often failed with their first tests. They ended with crashes and fiery explosions. Future designs were improved to solve those problems.

How can collaboration and communication lead to improving your hearing-enhancing device prototype?

_____

_____

_____

_____

_____

_____

 EVIDENCE NOTEBOOK Look for this icon to help you gather evidence to answer the question above.

Class Collaboration

Objective

In the past two lessons, you learned how to define engineering problems and design engineering solutions. You have also learned how to apply these skills to designing a hearing-enhancing device. Recall that the purpose of this device is to help someone observe and identify natural sounds during a nature walk.

Collaborate Work with your class to further improve your team's design from the previous lesson. First, collect your team's device or gather the materials you need to rebuild it.

Form a question: What problem will you solve to meet this objective?

_____

_____

_____

Possible Materials

- safety goggles
- plastic cups
- paper cups
- cloth scraps
- duct tape
- masking tape
- wire clothes hangers
- string
- rubber tubing
- plastic headbands
- scissors
- baseball or painter's cap

Procedure

STEP 1 Recall your design criteria and constraints. List them on the lines below. Rank the criteria in order of importance. Remember them as your class works to improve your designs.

_____

_____

_____

_____

_____

_____

STEP 2 Demonstrate and explain your team's design for your class. Tell which features and materials worked best. As the other teams demonstrate their designs, take notes below. List features that you might use to improve your team's design.

Notes from demonstrations

STEP 3 Choose one feature to improve based on your notes in Step 2. It should support one of your top-ranked criteria. Plan and build your improved device.

STEP 4 As a team, plan a fair test of your improved design. Write down the test procedure you will use in the table below. Test your design. Record your test results. If you need to, keep revising and testing your design until you are satisfied with the improvement.

Test plan and results
Test plan
Test results

What improvement did your team add, and why did you choose it?

_____

_____

Did your team's design pass your test? Explain.

_____

_____

If you could add or change another feature to improve your design, what would it be? Why?

_____

_____

_____

State a **claim** about your improved design and how it tested. Cite **evidence** from the activity to support your claim.

_____

_____

_____

If you could start over with designing your hearing-enhancing device, how would you do it? Explain your **reasoning.**

_____

_____

_____

What questions came to you about the task of designing and testing prototypes?

_____

_____

_____

Things Fail and Improve

Try, Try Again!

You've learned that engineering solutions are designed and built to solve a problem. Often, perhaps like what happened with your hearing-enhancing device, a first design doesn't work. For example, a design might work okay, but testing suggests that it can work a lot better. Or the design might meet almost all of the criteria but be unsafe. When this happens, engineers head back to the drawing board to improve their designs.

 HANDS-ON Apply What You Know

Tissue Rope

Look at the rope shown here. Suppose you need to make your own, but out of toilet paper.

- Your goal is to work with a partner to find the best toilet paper rope-making technique you can. You are limited to 15 minutes to explore and build. A loop of your product will be tested to see how much weight it will support.

- Get two arm-lengths of toilet paper from your teacher.

- Wait for your teacher to say "start." Then, with your partner, figure out the best way to turn the paper into a rope.

- Try lots of ideas! When you are happy with your technique, get more paper from your teacher and make your test sample. Be sure to budget time for this.

Was your final product better or worse than your first try?
Tell how your rope-making technique changed as you tried different ideas.

_____

_____

_____

Designs can also improve bit by bit as engineers learn more about the materials they're using. Small positive changes build up as engineers test and add them to the design. The result is the ideal, or best, design possible within the constraints of time, materials, and budget.

Cakes Done Right!

Engineers test their designs many times to get the best solution. Tests help them figure out what went wrong and why. This process is called **failure analysis**. It requires thinking carefully about causes and effects, especially for more complex devices or systems.

Language SmArts
Doing Research

Review the process of testing your hearing-enhancing device. Use your testing and results to complete a failure analysis on your solution. Use the table below to record your thoughts and ideas.

What didn't work?	Why I think it didn't work	How can I fix or improve it?	How critical is it to fix the solution?

Engineers improve designs by careful testing, one system part at a time. They work this way to find an ideal solution for given criteria—the best bicycle, or even the best tasting cake. Read below about recreating Grandma's famous yellow cake.

Explore Online

Too High, Too Low, Too Dry . . .Just Right!

Look at the test bake pictures and the information for each test cake. Then write in the likely ideal recipe choices below.

Grandma's Ideal Cake

You're trying to match this cake's taste and look. Based on the test cakes, what are these recipe details?

Use _____ of baking powder.

Bake for _____ minutes.

- This test cake tastes about right. It has 3 teaspoons (tsp) of baking powder to make it puff up. It baked for 30 minutes at 350 °F.
- How does it compare to the ideal cake you're trying to match?

- This test cake also tastes okay, although it's a little chewy. It has 1 tsp of baking powder and baked for 25 minutes at 350 °F.
- How does it compare to the ideal cake you're trying to match?

- This test cake tastes about right. It's dry and crumbly, though. It baked for 35 minutes at 350 °F. It used 2 tsp of baking powder.
- How does it compare to the ideal cake you're trying to match?

 EVIDENCE NOTEBOOK Summarize your response in your Evidence Notebook.

Putting It Together

Choose the correct word to complete each sentence.

| destroy | failure | imperfect | improve | problem solving | perfect |

Most prototypes are _____. When testing a design solution, it is critical to go through a _____ analysis. This helps _____ a solution.

Getting Better

Talking to the Team

Explore Online

When engineers work on design solutions, team members often communicate with one another. They share their observations to help improve what they are working on and to perhaps gain insight on future solutions.

Communication is an important part of most situations. Like an engineering team, a volleyball team needs to communicate. By talking or giving one another signals during practice, players work as a team and will likely play better during a game.

a. Players communicate what the next play will be. The player who plans to hit the ball first calls, "Got it!"

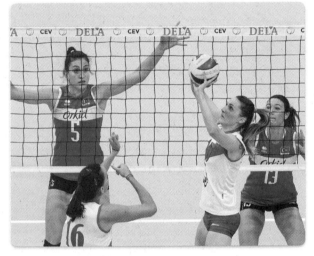

b. Players signal so that everyone knows where the ball is going. The second player is ready and waiting to make the second hit.

c. The third player is in motion and ready to return the ball over the net.

Do the Math

Teamwork!

When playing volleyball on a team, players usually want the closest teammate to get the ball first.

Sophia is 4 m away from the ball and can travel 2 m/s. How long will it take her to reach the ball?

_____

Kaius is 6 m away from the ball and can travel 2 m/s. How long will it take him to reach the ball?

_____

Analyze Considering how quickly each player can get to the ball, which one should call "Got it!"?

_____

After a game, volleyball players may talk about what worked well and what didn't work so well. They also may talk about what they plan on doing better during their next practice or game. Likewise, engineers communicate after testing solutions to try to **optimize,** or make as good as possible, their solutions and designs. Good communication and teamwork help improve any team's final results.

Explain How is communication important to both sports and engineering?

_____

_____

Identify Which of these do you think are ways to improve communication among team members? Circle all that apply.

a. Tell a team member that her design is good, and suggest improvements.

b. Tell a team member that her project is bad.

c. Give a team member some suggestions for other materials.

d. Yell at a team member until he agrees with your viewpoint.

e. Talk to others about the way they tested their project, and suggest more good tests.

f. Tell a team member that he used the materials wrong, even though his design tested well.

Sharing Feedback

You now know about the importance of communication. Team up with two other students and take turns giving feedback on each of your designs. After you have considered one another's feedback, make a plan to retest and improve your hearing-enhancing device.

Process These steps show a process for designing solutions. Write an *A* by steps you learned about in Lesson 1, a *B* for Lesson 2, and a *C* for Lesson 3.

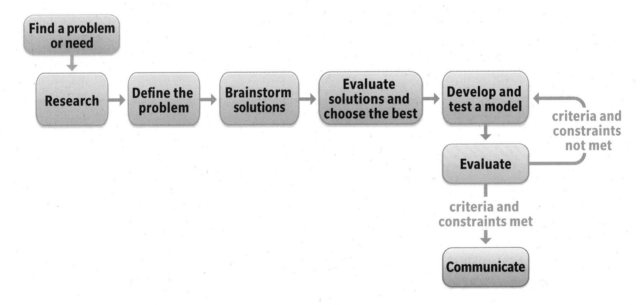

 EVIDENCE NOTEBOOK Use what you've learned in this lesson to describe how you can optimize your solution.

 Language SmArts
Recalling Relevant Information

Think about what you learned during the testing of your device. Also think about the feedback you got from others. Use this relevant information to explain what you've learned about the last few steps of an engineering design process.

_____

_____

_____

_____

Discover More

Check out this path . . . or go online to choose one of these other paths.

Sense Extenders for Science

- **Ear Areas**
- **High or Low?**
- **Careers in Science & Engineering**

Sense Extenders for Science

Scientists and engineers use many different types of tools to extend their senses. Some tools enhance the user's ability to see objects that are very far away or too small to see with the unaided eye. Other tools amplify sound or allow their users to see what's inside the human body. Some tools produce images that can be studied at a later time.

All of the tools shown on these two pages have been redesigned over time to extend human senses.

Explore Online

The first telescopes were invented in the early 17th century. **Refracting telescopes,** such as this one, use lenses to magnify objects. Over time, these tools were improved to make their lenses larger and clearer.

Hydrophones are underwater microphones. The earliest ones were used in the 1920s by ship captains to communicate. Today, hydrophones have many uses, including listening to whales communicate.

In 1667, Robert Hooke used a simple **light microscope** to observe tiny living things. Today, complex light microscopes are used in many fields of science, including biology and geology.

Thermographic cameras produce images using infrared radiation. Such cameras were first used in the early 1900s to help soldiers see at night. Today, these cameras are used to study rocks that could cause earthquakes. Astronomers use these cameras to study far away galaxies. Veterinarians can use these cameras to determine if farm animals are sick. The cameras can also be used to identify pollutants in the environment, and to inspect structures for damage or poor construction.

Explain How would you use a thermographic camera?

_____

_____

_____

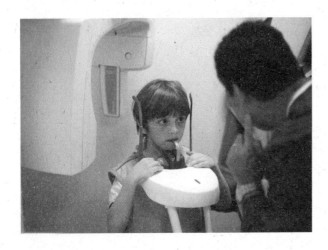

X-rays were discovered in 1895. These rays can pass through skin and tissue but not denser materials, such as teeth and bones. X-rays are used to determine if teeth are healthy, bones are broken, or tumors are present in the body. They can also be used to treat some cancerous tumors.

X-rays are also used at airports to screen for dangerous materials inside suitcases. They can also be used to research the minerals that make up rocks, and to study objects in space.

Describe Research one of the tools on these pages. Or find another tool that extends other senses. Draw the tool, and show how it works. Describe how an engineer might use the tool to solve a problem or test a solution.

Lesson Check

Name _____

Can You Solve It?

1. Now that you know about the importance of testing prototypes, apply what you've learned to the rocket example. Be sure to do the following:

   • Explain why multiple solutions should be developed and tested.

   • Discuss the importance of identifying failure points.

   • Describe why communication is critical to any team of people working together.

EVIDENCE NOTEBOOK Use the information you've collected in your Evidence Notebook to help you cover each point above.

_____

_____

_____

_____

_____

_____

_____

_____

Checkpoints

2. How is communication an important part of designing solutions? Choose all of the statements that are correct.

   a. Communication helps people talk about improvement.

   b. Communication helps identify problems.

   c. Communication only causes arguments.

   d. Communication builds a sense of teamwork.

   e. Communication is critical only if everyone agrees.

3. Choose the correct words to complete each sentence.

not build	test	throw away
multiple times	once	once and then stop
mistakes	testing	original problem

When building and designing an engineering solution, it is always

important to _____ the solution. Good engineers will

always try to test a solution _____. It is important to keep

in mind the _____ that the solution was meant to solve

when designing and testing a solution.

4. Circle the letter of each correct statement.
   a. Making good observations is important.
   b. Making good observations helps to figure out what needs to be improved.
   c. Making good observations shows you what to test next.
   d. Making good observations is not important because it slows down the process.
   e. Making good observations can be distracting and should be stopped when it happens.

5. An engineer is testing a solution. The solution is failing. What should she do? Select all that apply.
   a. She should consider using other materials for the same design.
   b. She should figure out what didn't go right with her design.
   c. She should understand that sometimes things don't work as planned.
   d. She should not try to develop other solutions to this problem.

6. Feedback is important in solving any problem. Select the best example of how to give good feedback.
   a. Tell the other person that his or her project is a good example of what not to do.
   b. Tell the person that his or her design is poorly built. Do not suggest any improvements.
   c. Tell the person that his or her design is built well, but still suggest some possible improvements.
   d. Ignore the person if he or she isn't listening to you.

60

Lesson Roundup

A. Which of these describes a good approach to solving an engineering problem? Select all that apply.

    a. Research, revise, and repeat.

    b. Give up if your first solution fails so that you don't waste any more of your time.

    c. Failure marks the end of the process.

    d. If at first you don't succeed, try, try again.

B. Explain why an engineering design solution that does not pass testing can be considered a successful solution.

_____

_____

_____

_____

C. Below are steps that you might follow to solve an engineering problem. Add numbers to put them in order.

    a. Test the prototype. _____

    b. Perform failure analysis. _____

    c. Identify criteria and constraints. _____

    d. Test final design. _____

    e. Create the prototype. _____

    f. Identify the problem that needs solving. _____

    g. Choose materials for the prototype. _____

    h. Improve the prototype. _____

    i. Research information about the problem. _____

Designing a Portable Chair

You work for a company that builds seating for large events. Clients are complaining that the portable chairs you make are not comfortable. It is your team's task to learn about portable chairs and design one that your clients will like.

Clients don't like sitting on this.

STATING YOUR GOAL: How will you know that you have completed your assignment?

_____

_____

Review the checklist at the end of this Unit Performance Task. Keep those requirements in mind as you proceed.

RESEARCH: Study the portable chairs that are currently on the market. Find out which are the most popular. Note their features. Examine several online or library resources, and cite them.

_____

_____

_____

BRAINSTORM: Brainstorm three or more ideas with your team that might fit with your goal. Evaluate the ideas, and choose the best based on the criteria of the project.

_____

_____

_____

_____

MAKE A PLAN: Plan a design for your chair by considering the questions below.

1. What materials will you use for your chair, and why?

2. What are your standards for using or rejecting materials or features?

3. What features from other chairs, if any, will you use for your chair?

4. What original features, if any, will you use for your chair?

_____

_____

_____

_____

_____

_____

VISUALIZE: Draw a sketch and make a construction paper model of your chair. Name and describe all of your chair's parts and features.

EVALUATE AND REDESIGN: How close have you come to reaching your goal? Are there ways to improve your design? If so, what are they?

_____

_____

COMMUNICATE: Make improvements if necessary, and present and describe your chair to your class.

☑ Checklist

Review your project and check off each completed item.

_____ includes information about considered features and why each was included or rejected

_____ includes citation of multiple sources used in your research

_____ includes a sketch and model of your completed chair, along with written descriptions of its parts and features

_____ includes an evaluation of the chair's design and descriptions of any improvements made

Unit Review

1. Which statements are true of the object shown here?
   Circle all that apply.

   a. It meets a want or need.

   b. It can be found in nature.

   c. It meets no specified criteria.

   d. It was designed by engineers.

   e. It is an example of technology.

2. Which pair of factors defines any engineering problem?
   Circle the correct choice.

   a. wants and needs

   b. time and expense

   c. nature and technology

   d. criteria and constraints

3. Fill in the blank with the correct word or phrase to complete each sentence.

A set of criteria	A budget	materials
A list of constraints	criteria	constraints

   _____ states the desirable features

   of a solution.

   Limits on solving a problem are called _____.

4. You are faced with the situation shown here, a filthy pet, and decide to confront it using technology.
Using the numbers 1–8, arrange these steps to show one way you could proceed.

_____ Evaluate test results.

_____ Design a prototype to solve the problem.

__1__ Identify the problem to be solved.

_____ Retest the modified prototype.

__8__ Construct a final design.

_____ Research existing related technology.

__4__ Build and test the prototype.

_____ Modify the prototype.

5. Which steps from the previous exercise are likely to be taken more than once? Circle all that apply.

a. Evaluate test results.

b. Improve the prototype.

c. Construct a final design.

d. Retest improved prototype.

e. Identify the problem to be solved.

6. Fill in the blank with the correct word or phrase to complete each sentence.

a single thing	**several things at once**
improve their designs	**develop their criteria**

Testing a prototype works best when the engineer observes

and measures the effects of changing _____.

Engineers test and retest to _____.

7. What makes crash test dummies useful substitutes for human beings? Circle the correct choice.

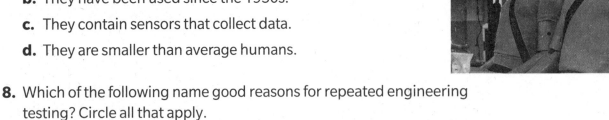

    a. They are able to avoid collisions.

    b. They have been used since the 1950s.

    c. They contain sensors that collect data.

    d. They are smaller than average humans.

8. Which of the following name good reasons for repeated engineering testing? Circle all that apply.

    a. to ensure safety

    b. to solve problems

    c. to reduce feedback

    d. to eliminate criteria

    e. to develop a final product

9. Fill in the blank with the correct word or phrase to complete each sentence.

failure points	**results**	**prototypes**
working solutions	**design difficulties**	**breakthroughs**

An engineer can find things needing improvement by isolating

_____.

That term refers to _____.

10. Fill in the blank with the correct word or phrase to complete each sentence.

collaboration	**failure**	**research**
a prototype	**peer pressure**	**brainstorming**

_____ gets you a lot of ideas quickly.

However, we say that "_____ leads to optimization,"

because sharing successes often helps make the best engineering solution.

Energy and Motion

Explore
Online

You Solve It: Crash Course As you learn about energy, you'll discover how it can make objects move. You'll play a game that you will use to determine the optimum speed a toy car needs to scatter foam bricks.

Bumper cars show how physical contact transfers energy.

At a Glance

Name _____

UNIT PROJECT
Truck Pull

What makes things move? How can you move an object, such as a toy? You can use energy to move a toy truck. You can design ways that test how collisions affect the truck and other objects.

For this project, you will work in teams to design a way to move a toy truck across a surface. You'll also see what happens to the energy when two things bump into each other.

Think about how energy makes objects move. Write a question that you will consider as you work on your designs.

You will design a way to move a toy truck across a surface.

_____

_____

Materials

Think about how you will make your design work. What materials will you need?

_____

_____

_____

For your design, start by thinking about the type of energy you will use. What kind of energy will you use to move the toy truck?

_____

_____

_____

© Houghton Mifflin Harcourt Publishing Company

Plan and Design

Make a plan for the research you will need to do and how you will test your model. As you make your plan, consider the following:

- what type of energy will transfer between objects

- the amount of energy used to move the toy truck

- the way a truck collision can cause another object to move

Use what you know about energy and collisions to start planning your research.

_____

_____

_____

_____

_____

_____

Use your design to see what happens when the truck collides with another object. Describe any improvements or changes you would make.

_____

_____

_____

_____

_____

_____

Analyze Your Results

Analyze the results of your test. Focus on what happened when your truck collided with other objects. If your truck moved the other objects during a collision, did the objects move far? Why or why not?

_____

_____

_____

_____

_____

_____

Restate Your Question

Write the question you investigated.

_____

_____

_____

Claims, Evidence, and Reasoning

Make a claim that answers your question.

_____

_____

_____

Review your design. What evidence from your design supports your claim?

_____

_____

_____

Discuss your reasoning with a partner.

Language Development

Use the lessons in this unit to complete the network and expand understanding of the science concepts.

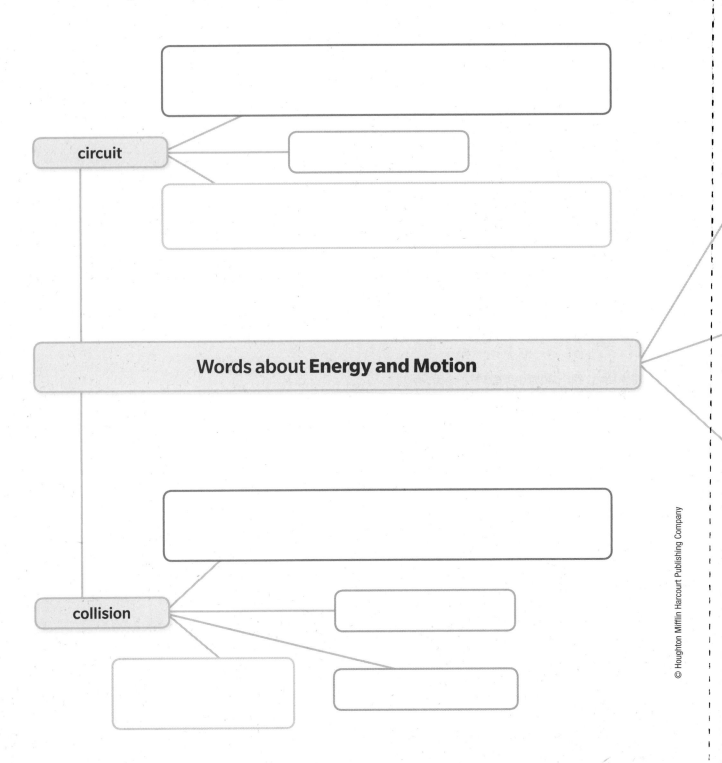

circuit

Words about **Energy and Motion**

collision

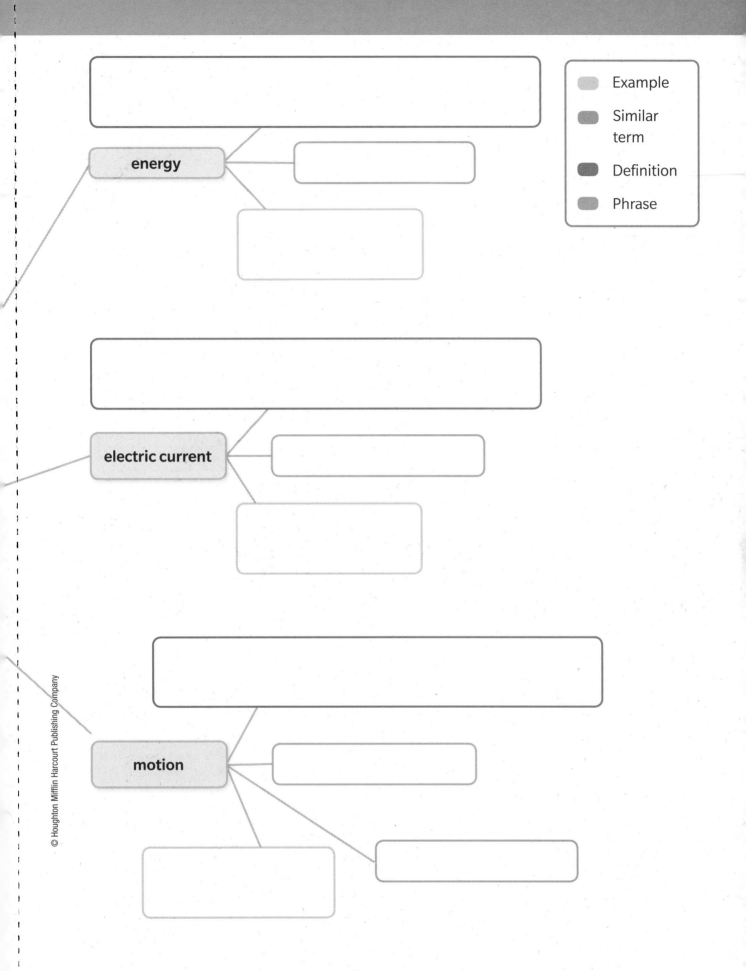

energy

electric current

motion

Example

Similar term

Definition

Phrase

What Are Energy and Motion?

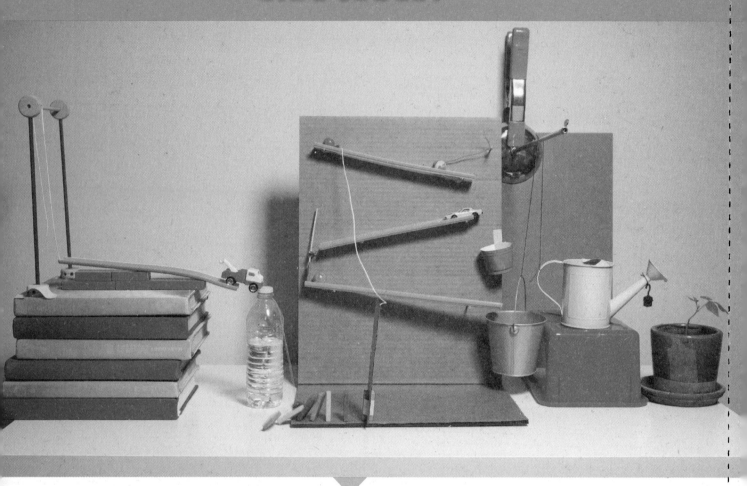

This machine is made up of many parts. It begins to work when one part is set in motion. The energy from one part's movement moves to the next part until the energy has moved through the entire machine.

Explore First

Moving Energy Place two pencils a few inches apart on a flat, hard surface. Gently push one into the other. Do this several more times, varying the strength of your push each time. What happens to the first pencil? What happens to the second pencil? Why?

Can You Explain It?

Energy makes things change. Energy in a toaster produces heat, and the heat toasts a slice of bread. Your body's energy might pedal a bicycle so that it goes faster or slows down. Heavy trains need energy to stop and go.

Where did the energy come from to make the heavy train speed along the track? When the train stopped, where did the energy go?

_____

_____

_____

_____

_____

_____

_____

 EVIDENCE NOTEBOOK Look for this icon to help you gather evidence to answer the questions above.

Energy and Motion

Energy and Things that Move

Objects do not start to move unless energy is applied to them. **Energy** is the ability to cause change in matter.

Explore Online

If an object starts moving or changes direction, it is receiving energy. This object is at rest, meaning that energy is not being applied to it.

Evaluate What does this toy car need to begin moving?

a. gasoline

c. light

b. energy

d. sound

Analyze There are many ways to make the toy car move, including pushing it with your finger or with another object. What are some other ways to make the car move?

_____

_____

 EVIDENCE NOTEBOOK Think about the ways you brainstormed to get the car moving. Compare your ideas with those of your classmates. How are they similar? How are they different? Write your ideas in your Evidence Notebook.

Energy and Motion

When objects are in **motion**, they are moving. When objects are motionless, they are at rest.

Explore Online

For an object to go from a resting state to being in motion, energy has to be applied to it.

Resting objects cannot move on their own. They need energy. Consider the carnival ride above. When you first get into a carnival ride, it is at rest. Once the ride is full of people, a switch is flipped and the ride begins to move. That's because energy has been applied to the ride.

Language SmArts Make a list of objects in motion that have energy. Write a description of each, using words you have learned in this exploration.

_____

_____

_____

_____

_____

_____

_____

Moving Energy, Chain Reaction

Explore Online

A chain-reaction machine is a machine with many parts. But each part will only move if the part before it moves first. Why? Because energy is moving from part to part. Once you move the first part, a reaction occurs. Each part moves, one after the other, until the energy has passed through the entire machine.

Design your own chain-reaction machine.

- Work in small groups to brainstorm a chain-reaction machine. The machine can turn off a light, shut a door, pop a balloon, or something else.

- Select your materials. These should be a mix of items such as marbles, tubes, string, and so on.

- Design your machine on paper.

- Build your machine.

- Test it. If it doesn't work, make changes to it, then test it again.

Once your machine works, record in your Evidence Notebook why each part stopped when it did.

Explain Why do objects that are in motion come to a stop?

_____

_____

Putting It Together

Apply Select all that apply. What causes objects to change motion?

- a. energy from one object affecting another object
- b. energy remaining the same in two objects
- c. the material an object is made of
- d. the starting positions of two objects

Infer How can one moving object cause another resting object to move?

- a. Energy moves from one object to the other.
- b. Energy remains constant in both objects.
- c. Energy increases in both objects.
- d. Energy remains the same in one object but increases in the other.

Energy Is All Around

Sound? Light? Heat? Motion? ENERGY!

You use energy every day. With energy from your muscles, you move. You pick up a book, open a door, and toss a ball. Using energy from devices, you might talk on the phone, watch a program, or go to school.

There are different kinds of energy. Motion energy can cause objects to move or change direction. Heat energy can cook food in an oven. Energy stored in a battery can run a computer. Wind energy can push a sailboat.

Ways Energy Moves

Explore Online

The picture shows different forms of energy. What objects do you think are moving? What energy makes those objects move? What sends out sound energy? Where is there light or heat energy? On the next page, label each image *energy* or *not energy*.

a. brightly shining sun

_____

d. radio

_____

c. empty shell on the beach

_____

b. rolling water waves

_____

Evaluate Name another example of energy that you see in the picture. What kind of energy is it?

_____

Describe Choose the best words to complete the sentences.

light	sound	heat

Energy is a measure of the ability to cause change in matter. You

can see _____ energy, you can hear _____

energy, and you can feel _____ energy.

Language SmArts

Cause and Effect

Choose one of the energy examples above. Describe the effect the energy causes.

_____

_____

Apply What You Know

Energy Near You

Find five examples of energy in your classroom. Write them below.
Group them by the kind of energy they show.

_____

_____

_____

Where Does Energy Come From?

When you turn on a television, you see pictures and hear sound. Where do the light and sound energy come from?

You can see a wire connecting a wall socket to the television. That wire carries electric current. **Electric current** is a flow of electric charges along a path. Each photo shows one step in how the energy gets to your home.

Hundreds of millions of years ago, plants took in the sun's energy, just as they do now. After the plants died, a long, slow change turned them into a material called coal. Some of the energy the plants got from the sun is now in that coal. That stored energy is called chemical energy.

a. At the energy-generating station, the coal is burned. Burning changes the coal's chemical energy into heat energy.

b. Next, that heat energy makes water become steam, and the expanding steam makes a turbine spin.

c. The spinning of magnets in the generator produces electrical energy from the stored energy within the coal.

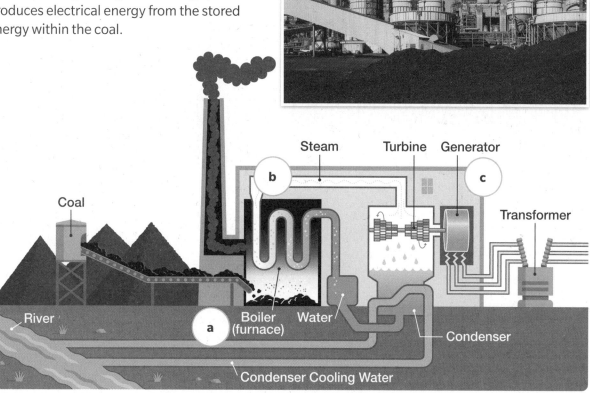

How does electrical energy get to your home?

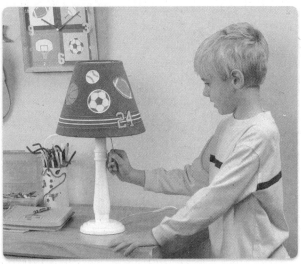

How do you use electrical energy?

Summarize How is the energy we use produced?

_____

_____

Engineer It!
Energy from Algae

Scientists and engineers are always **brainstorming solutions** for alternative forms of energy. A new source of energy being developed is the harvesting of algae.

Algae use a gas to make energy and release a clean gas as a byproduct. Algae farmed for this purpose become an oil that is then converted into fuel. These renewable algae fuels are an alternative to fossil fuels such as coal or oil.

Algae are grown in this farm facility.

Explain How does algae farming help make air quality better?

_____

_____

 EVIDENCE NOTEBOOK Describe alternative energy, and explain why it is important to have different forms of it.

Saving It for Later

A battery stores chemical energy. When a device uses the battery, the chemical energy inside the battery changes into electrical energy. The device changes the electrical energy into motion, sound, or other forms of energy. There are many types and sizes of batteries for different purposes.

Explore Online

Batteries

Learn more about different types of batteries. Then answer the question below.

Button batteries are named for their size and shape. They are small and reliable for devices that use small amounts of energy very slowly.

AA batteries are used in many devices. They come in both single-use and rechargeable forms.

9V batteries are useful in devices that change stored energy into other energy. They are a reliable energy source for safety devices.

Apply Which type of battery goes in these devices?

Do the Math

Calculate Energy Units

Your portable DVD player uses rechargeable AA batteries. They last 48 hours before needing to be recharged. In the space below, calculate how many 2-hour movies you can watch on your DVD player with fully charged batteries. How many times will the batteries need to be recharged in a 30-day month?

Apply What You Know

Testing, Testing

Suppose you have a battery and you want to know whether it still has energy stored in it. Design a way to test whether the battery still works. Describe your design below.

_____

_____

_____

Putting It Together

Choose the words that make the sentences most correct.

sound	matter	batteries	current

Energy is a measure of the ability to cause change in _____. You

can feel some heat energy and hear some _____ energy. An

electric _____ is a flow of electric charge. Two ways that energy is

stored are coal and _____.

Light the Bulb

Objective

In a flashlight or other electrical device, a battery may be connected in a circuit. A **circuit** is a closed path or loop that an electric charge flows through.

Form a question: What question will you investigate to meet this objective?

_____

_____

Materials
- battery (size D) with holder
- light bulb with holder
- three lengths of wire
- switch

Procedure

STEP 1 Start by asking questions and sharing ideas. How should you connect the materials you have to make the bulb light up? Plan a simple investigation to find out. Write your plan below, and show your plan to your teacher.

_____

_____

_____

_____

STEP 2 Lay out the parts in the order you think will make the bulb light up.

STEP 3 Connect the parts to test your plan. How did you connect the parts?

_____

_____

_____

_____

_____

STEP 4 Does the bulb light up? If not, keep working until you "see the light"! What did you change about your arrangement?

_____

_____

After you've built a circuit that works, draw a picture of it. Show how the parts are connected.

┌──┐
│   │
│   │
│   │
│   │
│   │
│   │
│   │
│   │
└──┘

What occurred when the battery was connected to the light bulb and switch?

_____

What caused the bulb to light up?

_____

Use **reasoning** to make a **claim** about bulbs. Cite **evidence** to support your claim.

_____

_____

What questions do you have about circuits?

_____

_____

_____

_____

Energy and Its Effects

Action/Reaction

When too much energy passes into a person or object, it can cause serious harm or damage. Why? Because the person or object may not be able to handle that much energy.

Have you ever burned yourself by touching something hot?

Infer How do you think energy is involved when something gets burned?

_____

_____

_____

_____

_____

Energy and Injury

Have you ever caught a speeding ball in your hand? When someone gently throws a ball, catching it usually doesn't hurt. However, when someone throws a ball hard, catching it may hurt. The reason is energy. The faster the ball moves, the more energy it contains.

When an object that is moving quickly collides with another object, more energy moves from one object to the other. The palm of your hand hurts when you catch a faster ball because more energy moves into it. Some body parts allow us to absorb extra energy. But even they cannot protect us from too much energy.

Engineers work on developing ways to prevent people from being injured by too much energy.

People can get hurt when their bodies absorb too much energy. For example, when two cars collide, energy is exchanged. The faster the cars are moving, the more energy there is to exchange. Some of that energy can transfer to the people in the cars and hurt them. People can be hurt when they absorb too much of other kinds of energy, too.

Differentiate Which type of injury is caused by heat energy?

a. cuts

c. frostbite

b. bruises

d. burns

Identify Which of the following can cause an electrical injury?

a. strong winds

c. a speeding car

b. a damaged lamp cord

d. a hot stove

Relate Draw a line from each form of energy to the injury it can cause.

Energy form	Possible injury
chemical energy	shock from an electrical outlet
sound energy	damaged eardrum
electricity	sunburn
light energy	skin irritation from household cleaner

 EVIDENCE NOTEBOOK You have learned about different types of energy and the problems they can cause. Think of other ways in which engineers are trying to protect people from injury. List them in your Evidence Notebook.

 Engineer It!
Motion Protection

Engineers use crash test dummies to test how motion energy affects the human body. They come up with ways for cars to absorb more energy when the cars are in accidents. This helps prevent injury to the people in the cars.

Other objects can also be damaged by motion energy. Safety devices can protect objects from receiving too much energy. **Design** a simple device to protect an egg from motion energy as it falls from a height. Draw your device in your notebook. Once you have designed and built your device, your teacher will help you test it.

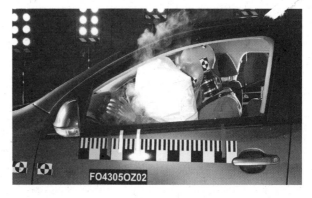

When this egg dropped, it broke. Its shell could not absorb all of the energy.

Explain How does the device you built work?

_____

_____

_____

_____

Apply Where does the energy go when an object in motion is stopped by a solid object? Circle all that apply.

    a. Some of it moves into the solid object.

    b. Some of it vanishes.

    c. Some of it becomes heat.

    d. Some of it becomes sound.

Language SmArts
Cause and Effect

Match each cause with its effect.

Cause	Effect
Two objects collide.	It contains more energy.
An object receives too much energy.	It is damaged.
An object moves fast.	Energy exchanges between them.

Discover More

Check out this path . . . or go online to choose one of these other paths.

People in
Science &
Engineering

- **Vampire Appliances**
- **Potato Power**
- **Careers in Science & Engineering**

People in Science & Engineering

Explore
Online

Mayra Artiles, Car Engineer

Have you ever thought of becoming an automobile engineer? Mayra Artiles did, and now she's an engineer working on hybrid electric vehicles. She enjoys designing, building, and testing cars. She even gets to program software for the cars. She likes the teamwork with other engineers, and she also likes test-driving the cars.

Mayra Artiles pays close attention to transfer of energy. Car design, especially weight, affects battery life. Batteries are also sensitive to outdoor temperatures during a hot summer day or in the cold of winter.

Mayra Artiles driving a hybrid car

Apply What forms of energy do you notice when a car's engine is turned on?

Zena Mitchell, Electrical Engineer

Engineers design how lighting and other electrical systems in buildings work. Zena Mitchell is an electrical engineer who designs electrical systems. She has designed electrical systems in small structures and in large structures, including some found in theme parks. She often uses CAD, or computer-aided design, in order to make sure a design will work in real time.

Zena Mitchell

CAD is often used by engineers and architects because it allows them to test a design before it is built. Since it costs less to test using CAD, costs can be kept low when designing new structures. Zena Mitchell uses CAD to make sure that lighting and other electrical systems will work once a building is constructed.

Design Think of an engineering project. What could you design to protect a battery from hot and cold weather? Remember that the protected battery still has to work. It also has to be able to give off some heat while it's working. Draw a sketch of your design in the space below.

Describe Explain how your design would work.

_____

_____

_____

Lesson Check

Name _____

Can You Explain It?

1. You have learned about energy and how one form can change into another. Think back to the photo of the train. Where do you think the energy came from to make the heavy train speed along the track?

   • When the train stopped, where did the energy go?

   • Describe how energy causes change.

   • Explain how energy changes form.

EVIDENCE NOTEBOOK Use the information you've collected in your Evidence Notebook to help you cover each point above.

_____

_____

_____

_____

_____

_____

_____

_____

Checkpoints

2. Which of the following shows motion energy?
   a. a car that has tires
   b. a car that begins to move
   c. a car parked in a garage
   d. a picture of a new car

3. Which of these is a form of energy?
Circle all correct answers.

  a. heat
  b. oven
  c. electricity
  d. light
  e. lamp
  f. microwave oven
  g. sound
  h. motion
  i. popcorn maker
  j. chemical

4. Which of the following occur when
you push one marble into another?
Circle all that apply.

  a. Energy from your finger moves to the
marble.
  b. Energy remains the same in both
marbles.
  c. Energy moves from one marble into
the other.
  d. Energy does not act on either marble.

5. Why does a person feel pain when
catching a ball that is moving too fast?

  a. Too little energy was absorbed by
the hand.
  b. Too little energy was released from
the hand.
  c. Too much energy was absorbed by
the hand.
  d. Too much energy was released from
the hand.

6. What is the most likely result of a person or object receiving too much energy?

_____

_____

_____

_____

_____

Lesson Roundup

A. Which of these devices does NOT change electrical energy into motion energy? Choose the best answer.
   a. DVD player
   b. clock
   c. clothes dryer
   d. electric light

B. Which form of energy can easily be observed in all of these: a washing machine, a printer, and a radio? Choose the best answer.
   a. sound
   b. motion
   c. chemical
   d. heat

C. Write each word beneath the intended energy form that is present when the object is turned on. Some objects will have more than one form of energy.

blender	toy drone
hair dryer	clothes iron

Sound	Light	Motion	Heat

D. Choose the best answer.
   Think about how a cell phone uses energy to send and receive, run apps, and display information. A cell phone battery will last longest if the phone is mostly used to
   _____.
   a. text
   b. use the Internet
   c. play games
   b. watch movies

What Happens to Energy when Objects Collide?

These bubble balls allow bumping game players to bump, roll, and flip over without getting hurt.

Explore First

What Happens to the Movement when Objects Collide? Using the materials your teacher gives you, gently push the first object. Does it continue to move after colliding? Does the second object move in the same direction? Think of other questions to investigate, and test them. Discuss your findings with the class.

Can You Explain It?

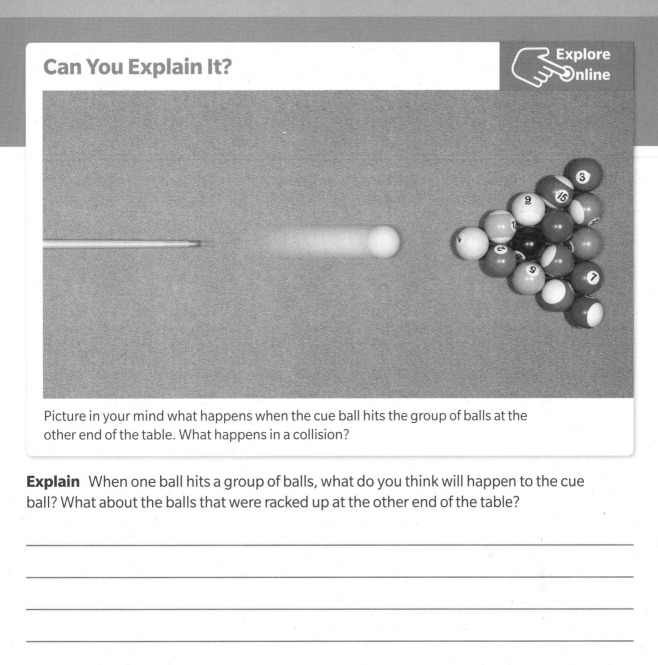

Picture in your mind what happens when the cue ball hits the group of balls at the other end of the table. What happens in a collision?

Explain When one ball hits a group of balls, what do you think will happen to the cue ball? What about the balls that were racked up at the other end of the table?

_____

_____

_____

_____

_____

_____

_____

_____

 EVIDENCE NOTEBOOK Look for this icon to help you gather evidence to answer the questions above.

Things that Move Have Energy

Energy and Things that Move!

Imagine riding on a huge roller coaster with lots of drops and turns. Are you excited? Are you nervous? Think about inching slowly up the hills—and plunging to the valleys below! But what does this all have to do with energy? Think about the roller coaster and energy in this photo.

Explore Online

The coaster is still as the passengers buckle their seat belts, but it's getting ready to move. As the coaster climbs the hill, it slows down. At the top, it slows. As the coaster starts to pass over the top of the hill, it moves faster. The riders can feel the whoosh of air on their faces as the coaster drops. The coaster's speed changes as it climbs and drops.

Decide Does this roller coaster have energy? When does it have energy? How do you know?

_____

_____

What do a moving car, a stretched rubber band being released, and a rolling ball have in common? They all have motion energy! Anything that is moving has motion energy. Objects can also have stored energy, such as the roller coaster on the hill, because of their position. That energy becomes motion when it races down!

There might be a dish on the edge of a shelf, ready to fall. Even before the dish falls, it has energy because of its position up on the shelf.

When you swing on a swing set, you have motion energy. At the top of each swing, you stop moving but have stored energy to move again.

When an archer pulls back on the string to shoot an arrow, energy is being stored. What will happen when the archer lets go of the string?

A rolling soccer ball has motion energy. Kicking it adds to that energy, making it move even faster, scoring a goal!

Identify Choose the best phrase to complete the sentences.

have motion energy	become motion energy	speed up

The objects that are moving _____. The objects that are about

to move have energy that can _____.

Swifter and Stronger!

Do you think the speed of an object affects its energy?

Is the ball swung slowly or quickly? How does the gong react?

Is the ball swung slowly or quickly? How does the gong react this time?

A slow-moving ball and a fast-moving ball strike a gong. The more energy a ball applies to the gong, the more the gong moves and the louder the sound it produces.

HANDS-ON Apply What You Know

Bang a Gong

Gather materials to experiment with what you have seen in the pictures. Set up the materials and test. Tell how your setup was the same and how it was different. What does this show you about the relationship between speed and energy?

_____

_____

Identify Choose the best words to complete the sentences about objects of the same weight.

all	faster	slower	can	cannotnever

_____ objects have more energy that can move to the objects they hit.

_____ objects have less energy that can move to the objects they hit.

The speed of an object _____ show(s) the amount of energy the object has.

The Faster They Are Hit, the Harder They Fall

A game of bowling is a lot like a pool game. You roll the bowl toward the pins, trying to knock down as many as you can. How does energy change your bowling score? Let's find out!

Slide a bowling ball slowly toward the pins.

When the ball hits the pins, how many pins fall down? Do they topple over or fly from the other pins?

Now move the ball more quickly. How many pins fall?

What else do you notice about the pins when a ball thrown quickly hits them?

You noticed on the previous page that the faster you swung the ball, the more energy it had. The increased energy made the gong move more. Was the same true for the bowling balls? Now think back to the pool game. If the cue ball moved slowly toward the group of balls at the end, what would happen? What if the cue ball were moving very fast?

Explain Use the slow and fast bowling ball example to explain the relationship between speed and energy.

_____

_____

_____

_____

_____

Motion Energy and Size: It's a Big Deal!

You know that an object's speed affects energy. But what about size and weight? Which would knock down heavy bowling pins, a bowling ball or a tennis ball? Think about which ball is bigger and heavier.

Look at the two vehicles. Imagine that they are both moving at 80 km/hr (about 50 mph). Which do you think has more energy? If the speed is the same, how does one have more energy than the other?

How do size and weight affect energy? Think about this demonstration to decide.

Notice the table tennis ball above the pan of flour. What happens when the ball hits the flour? Only a little of the flour moves. The ball didn't have much energy to release into the flour.

This baseball is dropped from the same height but is heavier than the table tennis ball. It also falls at the same speed. The crater left by the baseball is larger than the crater left by the table tennis ball. That's because the heavier ball had more energy to release.

Flour Power

Try the activity with the flour and two different balls. Change one thing from the way the activity was done. Record your results. How were the results in the picture and your results the same? How were they different? What does this show you about the relationships among speed, weight, and energy?

_____

_____

Language SmArts

Cause and Effect

Summarize Explain how weight can affect collisions.

_____

_____

 EVIDENCE NOTEBOOK Explain what would happen to the flour if the balls you used were heavier. Explain what would happen if the balls were lighter.

Putting It Together

Think about how weight and speed affect energy. If the ship and sailboat in the pictures collided, what would happen? Draw your answer in the space below.

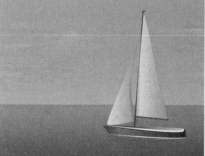

Test It! Stored Energy in a Rubber Band

Objective

Collaborate to compare amounts of stored energy. You know that energy is stored in a rubber band—but how much energy?

Form a question: What question will you investigate to meet this objective?

_____

_____

Materials
- safety goggles
- giant rubber band
- chair
- tape
- ruler
- toy car or truck
- meterstick

Procedure

STEP 1 CAUTION: Wear safety goggles. Cut a giant rubber band in half, and tie the ends around the legs of a chair. Place two metersticks in front of the chair. They should be 20 cm apart and in parallel lines to serve as a track for the toy.

What role does the rubber band play in this investigation?

_____

_____

STEP 2 Tape an index card to the floor behind the rubber band. Mark lines on the card that are 2 cm and 4 cm behind the rubber band. Choose a third distance, and mark it on the card.

What do the marks represent?

_____

_____

_____

104

STEP 3 Place a toy car or truck against the rubber band. Pull the toy back to the 2 cm mark, and release it. Measure the distance the toy travels. Record the data. Repeat this step two more times.

Why do you repeat this step at the 2 cm mark?

_____

_____

_____

Distance Toy Travels					
Rubber band stretched 2 cm		**Rubber band stretched 4 cm**		**Rubber band stretched ___ cm**	
Trial	Distance (cm)	Trial	Distance (cm)	Trial	Distance (cm)
1		1		1	
2		2		2	
3		3		3	

STEP 4 Repeat Step 3 using the 4 cm mark and the third distance you selected. Record your data.

How might your result change if the 4 cm mark had been measured incorrectly and it was actually 6 cm?

_____

_____

_____

Use the data you collected to answer these questions. Write your answers in the table.

Were your results similar for all the trials with the rubber band stretched back 2 cm? What about 4 cm and the distance you chose?	
If your results were inconsistent across the trials, what do you think caused those differences?	
With which of the stretching distances did the toy travel the longest distance?	
Compare your data with the data of another group. Are the other data the same? If not, why do you think they are different?	

Make a **claim** about how much stored energy exists in a rubber band based on your experiment. Cite **evidence** to support your **reasoning.**

_____

_____

_____

Compare the third distance you selected with the other groups in your class. What conclusions can you draw about the distances selected?

_____

_____

_____

What is one question you have about stored energy?

_____

_____

_____

Wonderful Springs

Ready to GO!

As you've seen, anything that is moving has energy. A ball on top of a hill has the potential to move. When it does, it has energy of motion. You know that if you pull a rubber band back farther and farther, you can let it go—and it will go far! Energy is stored in the stretched rubber band.

Explore Online

Springtime!

Circle the picture that has no stored energy.

At the bottom of the jump, the spring is fully compressed. All the energy is stored in the spring.

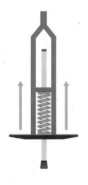

As the pogo stick goes up, the energy in the spring is released and becomes motion energy.

At the top of the jump, the spring has changed all the energy that was stored in it to motion energy.

As the pogo stick compresses, some energy is being stored in the spring. The spring has the potential to push up and become motion.

The Bigger, the Better

You saw that the farther you pulled back the rubber band, the more energy you released to move the car. But what if you replaced the small car with a larger car or one made of heavier steel? How far would the car travel then?

Mass and Energy

Take a look at these spring setups. Consider the relative weights of the balls and the relative amounts of stored energy in the springs. Then predict which balls will travel the least distance, the middle distance, and the greatest distance.

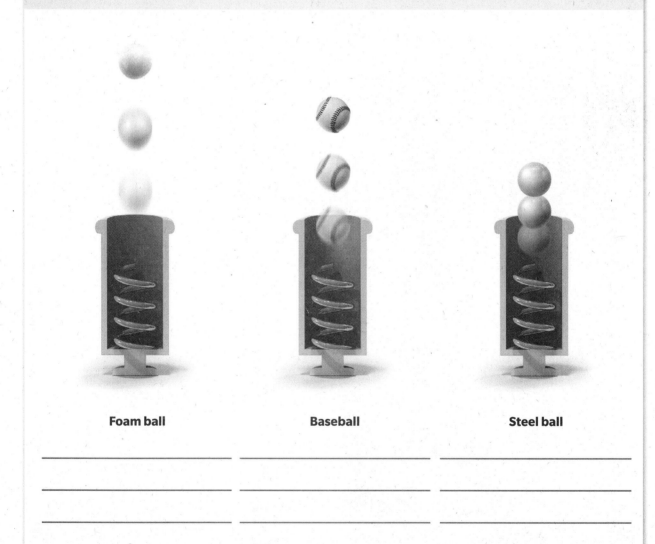

Foam ball	Baseball	Steel ball

 EVIDENCE NOTEBOOK In your Evidence Notebook, explain where the energy is going when the pogo stick is compressing.

Engineer It!
Shocking

When a bumpy road causes a truck to bounce, the truck experiences a collision every time it hits the ground. The motion energy from those collisions jolts the truck and the riders inside. This presents a **design problem**.

Cars and trucks are designed with springs near the tires. When a spring is compressed, it absorbs and stores energy. The springs in an off-road truck are big and store a lot of energy. That reduces the amount of energy transferred to the riders every time the truck hits the ground after bouncing into the air.

Evaluate Design Solutions Explore your school or home looking for designs that use springs. Furniture and doors are good places to look. Choose an example, and explain how the spring functions in the design. What criteria do you think springs help the design meet?

_____

_____

Identify Choose the best word or phrase to complete each sentence in the paragraph.

more	less	lighter	heavier

An object will travel farther when the compression energy launching it is compressed

_____. If two objects are launched by a rubber band with the same

amount of compression, the object that is _____ will travel farther.

Language SmArts
Key Ideas and Details

Considering the examples presented, identify another object that is able to absorb and store energy that is useful.

_____

_____

_____

Collisions

Scatter!

What is a collision? A **collision** happens when two objects bump into each other.

Explore Online

Think about a game of pool. When the cue ball hits the other balls, there are collisions. When these happen, energy is transferred. The total energy of all the balls is the same, but energy transfers to make the balls move in different directions. When a cue ball hits one of the balls, its motion slows. It transfers energy to the other balls and then moves in a different direction.

Language SmArts
Cause and Effect

Explain Describe what happens to the other balls that are racked up when the cue ball hits them. Explain the transfer of energy.

_____

_____

_____

If you were going to collide with something, would you rather collide with something moving quickly or slowly? A slow-moving object has less energy, so the collision has less of an impact. A fast-moving object has more energy—so the object it collides with moves fast, too! You can see this in sports. If you want a soccer ball to go fast, you kick it hard!

 EVIDENCE NOTEBOOK You see collisions every day. List some examples in your Evidence Notebook.

Crashing Dummies

Using dummies gives us a lot of information about what can happen in a collision without hurting anyone. These tests allow engineers to evaluate vehicle safety.

This crash test dummy, is built to the size and weight of a human.

Inside each dummy are sensors. They record how energy from the motion of the cars changes and affects the body.

Energy from a slow-moving collision is absorbed by the car and body. Some of it is transferred to sound.

In a high speed collision, there is more damage to the crash test dummies.

Analyze Identify which car would have more damage after crashing into the wall. Explain why there is typically more damage in a high-speed collision than a slow-speed collision.

15 KPH

45 KPH

_____

_____

_____

_____

_____

Too Hot to Handle!

Have you ever hit a nail with a hammer? That collision makes a lot of noise! What else did you notice about the nail? If you had touched the nail, it would have been warm. The hammer would be warm, too! What causes the nail and hammer to heat up?

When energy moves between objects, it can be transformed into heat, sound, motion, or other forms of energy.

When a screw and wood collide, energy moves. Thermal imaging shows a difference in temperature. As the drill pushes the screw, it causes motion and heat energy!

Do the Math
What Happens to Energy in a Drop

Different objects bounce differently on different surfaces. With a partner, test the bounce of at least two types of balls, such as a tennis ball and baseball.

Hold a meterstick perpendicular to the ground. Drop one ball from the top of the meterstick. Observe it as it bounces. Record the height of the bounce. Repeat the test several times. Calculate the average height of the bounce.

Test another type of ball in the same way.

Calculate Make a bar graph of your results for each ball. Calculate the difference between the average heights.

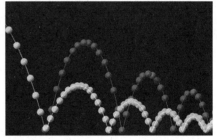

A tennis ball bounces back high, but not as high as from where it was dropped. Why?

Putting It Together

What conclusion can you draw about how energy changes based on what you observed with the balls?

_____

_____

© Houghton Mifflin Harcourt Publishing Company • Image Credits: (t) ©Joseph Giacomin/ Culture/Getty Images; (b) ©Marco/Getty Images

Discover More

Check out this path . . . or go online to choose one of these other paths.

People in Science & Engineering

- **Bump!**
- **Collision Game!**
- **Careers in Science & Engineering**

People in Science & Engineering

Amanda Steffy

When we drive on roads, we think about the interaction of the tires with the ground. How do we design tires that don't heat up too much? How do we handle roads that aren't perfectly flat?

Now imagine that you design tires for a vehicle on Mars. That's what Amanda Steffy does! She is an engineer for NASA's Jet Propulsion Laboratory (JPL). Her team tests the wheels and tires of the Mars rovers in different conditions. To do this, Steffy and her team had to recreate the surface of Mars in California.

Explore Online

Amanda Steffy works for NASA's Jet Propulsion Laboratory.

The tires of the Mars rover were designed for rough terrain.

113

The surface of Mars is different than what scientists believed it to be. Some of the rocks are sharp and can cut the tires. Some rocks are held tightly to the ground, while other rocks are very loose.

When a rover tire hits a loose rock, the tire spins faster, but if it hits a sharp rock held tightly to the ground, the sharp rock can damage the tire. Amanda tests tires until they fail in order to find those designs that will last longest on the rough surface of Mars. Understanding these collisions on Earth helps scientists guide the rover on Mars.

Rovers are tested on rough terrain similar to that of Mars.

Explain What factors do Amanda Steffy and other scientists who work on vehicles such as the Mars rovers need to consider about the energy of motion as they work?

_____

_____

_____

Describe How is Amanda Steffy's work related to collisions? Write a few ideas below.

_____

_____

_____

Lesson Check

Name _____

Can You Explain It?

1. What will happen when the cue ball hits the group of balls? Write a few sentences below to explain what happens to all the balls on the pool table. Be sure to do the following:

   • Describe the motion and collisions.

   • Identify energy movement.

   • Mention heat or sound.

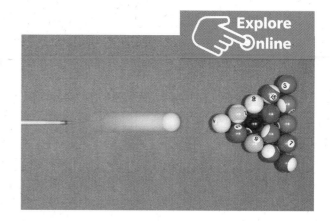

> **EVIDENCE NOTEBOOK** Use the information you've collected in your Evidence Notebook to help you cover each point above.

_____

_____

_____

_____

_____

_____

_____

Checkpoints

2. A soccer ball sits in the grass. A girl pulls her leg back to kick the soccer ball. She kicks! What happens next? Circle all the correct answers.
   a. The ball travels in one direction while the leg continues to travel.

   b. The ball travels in one direction while the leg stops.

   c. The collision of the leg and ball makes the ball travel quickly.

   d. The collision of the leg and ball produces a noise.

   e. The ball travels in one direction while the leg moves backward.

3. A child plays hopscotch. When she jumps on the ground, which of the following things happen? Circle all the correct answers.
   a. The ground absorbs some of the energy.
   b. The collision produces light energy.
   c. The collision produces heat energy.
   d. The collision produces sound energy.
   e. The girl continues to bounce, going higher each time.

4. In a collision, what happens to the motion energy? Circle all the correct answers.
   a. It becomes sunlight.
   b. It becomes sound.
   c. It becomes heat.
   d. It becomes weight.
   e. It becomes motion in other objects.

5. A roller coaster moves to the top of a hill, where it stops. What happens to the energy when the coaster stops?
   a. The energy becomes motion energy.
   b. The energy is stored energy.
   c. The energy converts to heat energy.
   d. The weight of the roller coaster causes it to collide with another car.

6. An archer is shooting an arrow with a bow. He pulls the string far back, lets the arrow go, and watches it fly far. On his second try, he uses a lighter arrow while pulling the string on the bow back a distance equal to his first try. Tell what happens next. How do you know?

_____

_____

_____

_____

Lesson Roundup

A. You and a friend are sitting on the ground a few meters apart. You each have a basketball that you roll toward each other. The ball that your friend rolls is moving faster. Write a few sentences to tell what happens next.

_____

_____

_____

B. Which of these types of energy changes occur in a collision? Circle all that are correct.

   a. heat   **d.** stored

   b. sound   **e.** electrical

   c. motion

C. Match each effect of a collision with the transfer of energy.

the noise of of a ball hitting a bat		motion energy changing to heat energy
a volleyball going over the net		motion energy becoming different motion energy
the warmth of a nail after it has been pounded into wood		motion energy changing to sound energy

D. Choose the phrase that makes the sentence correct.

| **tennis ball**   **bowling ball**   **table tennis ball** |

If a spring is compressed at the same compression and is used to launch a table tennis ball, a tennis ball, and a bowling ball on the same

flat surface, the _____ will go the farthest distance.

117

Colliding Objects

The publisher you work for is putting together a book called *Energy Collides*. Your team has been assigned to write a section about how objects can be set in motion by collisions. To do that, you'll need to set up some experiments, run them, and collect and analyze the data. Then you'll create a multimedia presentation that reports on your procedures, results, and conclusions.

How will you know if your project is successful? Before beginning, review the checklist at the end of this Unit Performance Task. Keep those items in mind as you proceed.

Use different materials to determine how objects are set in motion by collisions.

DEFINE YOUR TASK: What form will your completed project take?

_____

_____

RESEARCH: Use online or library resources to learn more about collisions and motion. Find out about the kinds of experiments that have been performed to show how motion can be caused by collisions. Cite your sources.

_____

_____

_____

EXAMINE DATA: Examine the experiments you have found for ideas your team can use to investigate collisions further. Focus on simple activities using marbles, model cars, or other objects that can collide. Which approaches seem best to you, and why?

_____

_____

_____

_____

PLAN YOUR PROCEDURE: Consider the questions below as you plan your procedure and presentation. Write a few sentences below to briefly summarize your plan.

1. What materials will you need, and how will you use them?

2. How will your experiment be set up?

3. What will the basic steps of your procedure be?

4. What variables (such as size and number of objects or speed or movement through the collision) will you introduce into your procedure? How?

5. How will you record, compare, and chart your results?

6. What will be the content, approach, and organization of your multimedia presentation?

_____

_____

_____

_____

_____

PLAN AND RECORD: Execute your procedures as planned, and record and analyze your results.

COMMUNICATE: Prepare and give a multimedia presentation that describes your team's research, procedures, results, and conclusions.

☑ Checklist

Review your project and check off each completed item.

_____ includes a clear statement of your task

_____ includes a list of cited sources

_____ includes a description of your procedure and the materials used in conducting it

_____ includes results and analysis of those results

_____ includes a multimedia report about your team's research, procedures, results, and conclusions

Unit Review

1. Which part of the picture is an example of motion energy?

    a. picnic basket on the ground

    b. blanket unfolded on the grass

    c. a child dropping a drink

    d. tree standing tall

2. Which of these descriptions include examples of energy?

    a. heat cooking food in an oven

    b. a battery running a computer

    c. a bike parked in a bike rack

    d. a doorbell ringing

3. In your own words, define energy. Then name some examples of energy that you experience every day.

_____

_____

_____

4. Sort each example as requiring energy or not requiring energy.

    | flying a kite | empty shell in the sand | kicking a soccer ball |
    | pencil on the ground | heating up food | |

    Requires energy: _____

    Does not require energy: _____

5. A gymnast jumps onto a trampoline. Number these statements so that their order explains the role of a spring's stored energy to released energy.

    _____ The trampoline springs stretch.

    _____ The gymnast gains energy of motion.

    _____ Energy transfers to the trampoline.

    _____ Energy releases.

120

6. Which kind of energy is being demonstrated in this image?

  a. motion

  b. spring

  c. wind

  d. heat

7. What happens to a cue ball when it collides with another ball? Circle all that apply.

  a. It changes direction.

  b. It gains stored energy.

  c. It gains energy of motion.

  d. It loses some of its energy.

8. When a ball is dropped on the ground, it _____ energy with each bounce and eventually becomes _____.

9. Which of these objects has stored energy? Circle all that apply.

    a. a stretched rubber band

    b. a battery in a radio

    c. a skateboard on a flat surface

    d. a compressed spring

10. What can you tell about energy from this picture?

    a. The ball that bounced higher has more energy at the top.

    b. The red ball is sharing energy with the yellow ball.

    c. Neither ball has energy.

    d. The yellow ball has more stored energy.

UNIT 3
Renewable Energy

Explore Online

You Solve It: Developing Renewable Energy Guidelines You will be working with an engineer and a project manager to make environmentally friendly decisions for your town and its residents.

Heat energy is continuously produced inside Earth. People use this heat as steam, as hot water to heat buildings, or even to generate electricity.

At a Glance

UNIT PROJECT

Natural Resources Report Card

We depend on resources, such as renewable and nonrenewable resources, more than ever. We need these resources to fuel our cars and to provide electricity to our homes. However, there are pros and cons to each of these resources.

Suppose you are a teacher who is working on report cards, but instead of giving grades to your students, you were chosen to give grades to 3 nonrenewable resources and 3 renewable resources. You will make a claim on how well you expect a resource to do in the areas of: cost, damage to the environment, effectiveness, and ease of use. Support your claim with evidence and reasoning. Present to your classmates.

Ask Your Question Think about the renewable resources and nonrenewable resources you use on a daily basis. Write a question that you will investigate as you write the Natural Resources Report Card and develop a presentation for your class.

_____

_____

Materials Think about how you will put your research, presentation, and visual aids together. What materials will you need?

_____

_____

Think about how you will organize the information about the resources before grading or scoring each resource. Develop points you wish to discuss. Then, come up with visual aids to support your arguments with examples.

_____

_____

Research and Plan Make a plan for the research you will be doing about the cost, damage to the environment, effectiveness, and ease of use of each resource. As you write your report cards, think about the following:

- Can your claims be supported by facts and data?

- Can you show those facts and data graphically?

- How will you justify the grades given to each resource?

- What will be the content, approach, and organization of your presentation?

_____

_____

_____

_____

_____

_____

_____

_____

Rehearse your presentation. Describe any modifications you would make and why.

_____

_____

_____

_____

_____

Analyze Your Results Analyze your presentation. Focus on how many of your claims are supported by reasoning.

_____

_____

_____

_____

_____

Restate Your Question Write the question you investigated.

_____

_____

_____

Claims, Evidence, and Reasoning Make a claim that answers your question.

_____

_____

_____

_____

Review your plan. What evidence from your plan supports your claim?

_____

_____

_____

Discuss your reasoning with a partner.

Language Development

Use the lessons in this unit to complete the network and expand understanding of the science concepts.

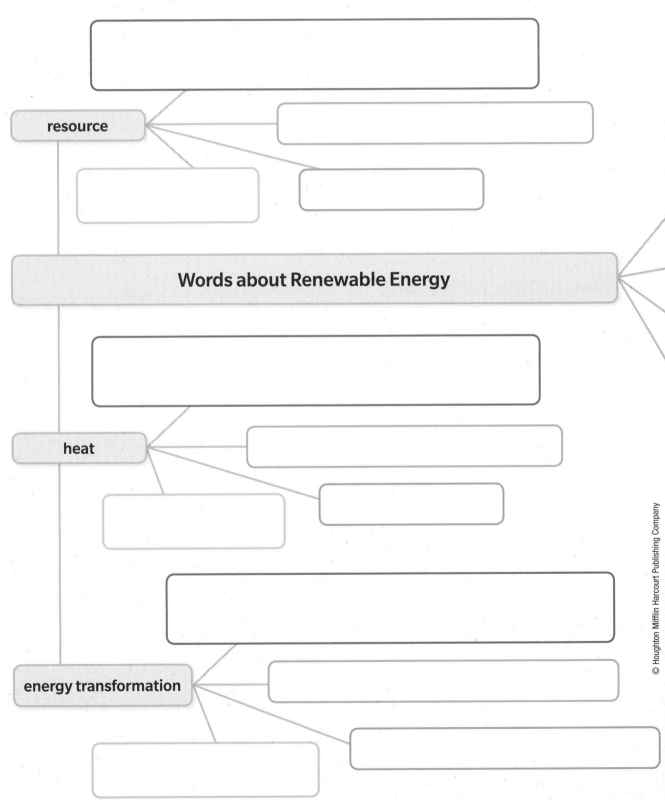

resource

Words about Renewable Energy

heat

energy transformation

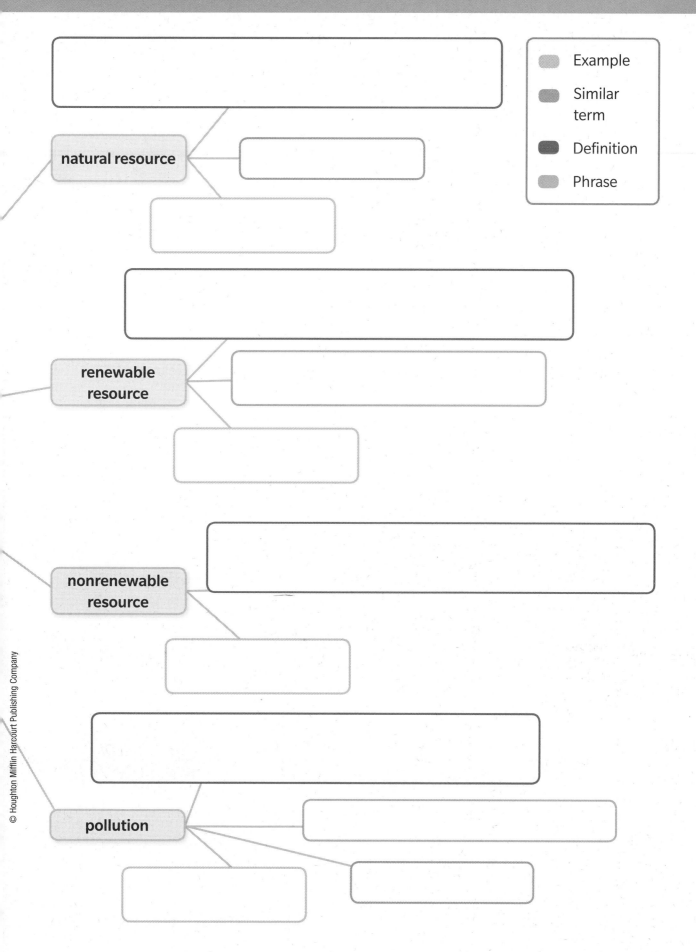

natural resource

renewable resource

nonrenewable resource

pollution

Example

Similar term

Definition

Phrase

How Is Energy Transferred?

A band produces sound energy that is transformed in different ways. Motion energy in an electric guitar, for example, is transformed into electric current by wire coils. This electric energy is transformed into sound energy by speakers. The sound is transferred through air to reach your ears.

Explore First

Transfer Energy Work with a partner. Put a piece of waxed paper over the top of a plastic cup. Use a rubber band to hold it tightly in place. Then place a small object on top. How many ways can you transfer energy to the object without touching it?

Can You Explain It?

Explore Online

Some people like their bread warm and toasted. Do you? Think about where the toaster gets its energy. Then think about where the energy goes once the toaster is turned on.

People can use their tablet devices for work or for play. Where does the tablet get its energy? Where does the energy go to make the screen dim and the low battery message appear?

Explain We use energy every day. Using the toaster as an example, explain how energy can transfer from place to place. Then explain how energy can be transformed.

_____

_____

_____

_____

_____

_____

 EVIDENCE NOTEBOOK Look for this icon to help you gather evidence to answer the questions above.

Energy Transfer

Transfer to Transform

We observe energy changes every day. It takes energy to turn on the lights. Think about where the energy comes from and where the energy goes. Explore the images to discover how energy works with items we use in our daily lives.

A battery stores chemical energy. With the help of a flashlight, chemical energy is *transformed* into electrical energy. This energy is *transferred* to the light bulb, which *transforms* it into light energy.

Electrical energy *transfers* into the cell phone. The electrical energy is *transformed* into sound energy by the phone, which allows you to have a conversation. Does it transform into another type of energy?

Chemical energy inside the battery is *transformed* into electrical energy by the drone. This electrical energy is *transferred* to the drone's propellers. Then, the electrical energy *transforms* into motion and sound energy when it flies.

Energy from the sun *transfers* to the solar panels. The solar energy is *transformed* into electrical energy in the solar panels. The electrical energy is *transformed* into heat energy by a water heater.

You walk into a dark room, flip a switch, and a lamp turns on. What kind of energy from the lamp allows you to see? How did energy change from one form to another?

The switch allows electrical energy to flow through the lamp cord and into the lamp. This is an *energy transfer*, a movement of energy from place to place or from object to object.

Inside the lamp, electrical energy is transferred to the light bulb. The bulb transforms the electrical energy into light energy. **Energy transformation** is a change in energy from one form to another. Which other type of energy does the light bulb transform electricity into?

 Language SmArts Interpret Think about the energy transformation that occurs when you listen to the radio. Explain what happens to electrical energy when you turn on the switch. Base your answer on information in the text.

_____

_____

_____

_____

Analyze Electrical energy can be transformed into which of these energy forms? Circle all that apply.

   a. light   **c.** sound

   b. heat   **d.** motion

 EVIDENCE NOTEBOOK Look back at the photos of the drone device. What evidence in the second photo proves that energy has been transferred?

Many from One

When you turn on a television, electrical energy *transfers* through the electrical cord into the television. Inside the television, the electrical energy *transforms* into light, sound, and heat energy.

Explore Online

Energy Transformations

Look at the systems in each photo. What forms of energy does the electrical energy transform into after it transfers into each device? Write *sound*, *heat*, or *motion* on the lines below.

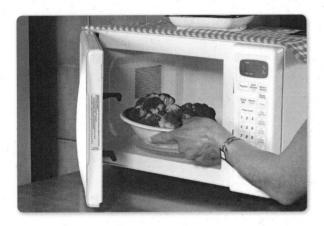

a. When this microwave is running, you hear sounds and see lights and movement. When the broccoli comes out of the microwave what kind of energy can you feel?

_____

b. The drone is moving. In addition to energy of motion, what form of energy do you hear?

_____

c. The electrical energy transferring into this blender changes into several different types of energy. Which type is seen when the blade is spinning?

_____

d. A hair dryer produces sound and other forms of energy. What kind of energy helps dry your hair? More than one answer is possible.

_____

A vacuum cleaner transforms electrical energy into motion, sound, and some heat energy. When electrical energy transfers into a device, it usually transforms into more than one form of energy.

Classify Write the name of each object below the energy form that is produced when the object is turned on. Each object will have at least two forms of energy. Then come up with your own example, and write it in the table below.

| blender | toy drone | lamp | hair dryer | television | microwave |

Sound	Light	Motion	Heat

Explain Look back at the photos on the previous page. Where did the energy for the microwave come from? What about the blender?

_____

_____

 Language SmArts Research How can electrical energy be transformed? Plan and carry out a short research project to investigate objects that use electrical energy to produce motion. Identify one that has not been discussed in this lesson. Then present your findings in a short oral presentation.

_____

_____

Change Forms of Energy

Have you ever used a laptop computer and had the battery "die"? Why do laptop batteries need to be recharged so often?

Right after being plugged in and recharged, the battery indicator shows a full charge. After the laptop has been used a lot, the energy stored in the battery is nearly gone.

When a laptop is active, its stored energy is being used. You need to recharge the battery after all its stored energy is used. Typing a document uses energy. Watching videos uses more energy. Playing games can use a great deal of energy. Where does the battery's energy come from? How did it change?

Apply Think of an example from your life of a battery running out of energy. What do you do to conserve battery energy?

_____

_____

Stored chemical energy in the laptop battery is transformed into electrical energy. This electrical energy can then be transformed into light, sound, and heat energy by the laptop.

When you see an example of energy such as a warm bowl of soup, you know the energy was transferred from somewhere else. You also know that the energy will eventually transfer or change form. The soup will cool off, warming the air around it. Energy moves and changes, but it does not disappear.

Explain Give an example of a battery-operated device that you use at home. How does energy transform in that device?

_____

_____

Putting It Together

Energy can be transferred from place to place. Make an observation about an energy transfer that you can see right now. Identify the type of energy, and describe its transfer or transformation.

_____

Full of Energy!

Energy is all around us. Different processes can move energy from one place to another.

Objective

Collaborate to conduct a series of investigations. You will observe, model, and explore different systems where energy is transferred from one object to another, transferred from place to place, or transformed from one form of energy to another in a system.

Materials

- safety goggles
- bouncy balls
- popper or pop-up plastic toys
- heat lamp
- thermometer
- hand warmer
- pinwheel
- wind-up cars
- tuning forks (different sizes)
- small light bulbs

- light bulb holders
- wires with alligator clips
- bulb holder
- battery
- battery holder
- erasable pen with eraser on cap
- paper
- animals to observe: classroom pets, insects, or mealworms

Form a Question

What questions will you investigate to meet this objective?

_____

Procedure

STEP 1 With your group, discuss where you observed energy today, from the moment you woke up to the moment you got to school. Make a list of your observations.

_____

_____

_____

STEP 2 You will be exploring different systems while rotating through stations. Your teacher will explain the materials in each station. In the table on the next page, make a **claim** about the types of energy you will observe in each station. Record the **evidence** you based your claim on.

Station	Claims of energy observed	What is your evidence?
station 1		
station 2		
station 3		
station 4		
station 5		
station 6		
station 7		
station 8		
station 9		
station 10		

STEP 3 Your teacher will assign your group to a station where you will observe a system. As a class, you and your classmates will come up with a list of the forms of energy observed in each system.

What system did you explore with your group? What forms of energy did you observe?

_____

_____

STEP 4 You will rotate through each station. You will be recording the forms of energy observed, the changes observed in the interactions, the transfers of energy (from one object to another or from place to place), and the transformations of energy for each station below.

	Forms of energy observed	Transfers of energy from one place to another	Transformations of energy
A moving ball colliding into another ball			
Popper or pop-up toys			

Heat lamp on a surface			
Hand warmer			
Blowing on a pinwheel			
Wind-up car			
Vibrating tuning forks			
Electric circuit with battery			
Writing with an erasable pen and erasing what you wrote			
Observing a living animal			

Make a **claim** about the relationship between the battery, its stored energy, and the light energy it is able to produce based on your investigation. Cite **evidence,** and explain your **reasoning.**

_____

_____

_____

_____

Compare your results with other groups in your class. What conclusions can you draw from the investigation?

_____

_____

What is one question you have about energy transfers or transformations?

_____

_____

Heat

Hot or Not?

How do we know if something is cold or hot? Sometimes, we can see clues. Other times, we can feel whether something is hot or cold. The terms hot and cold are ways to describe temperature. These photos show evidence of energy transfer as heat.

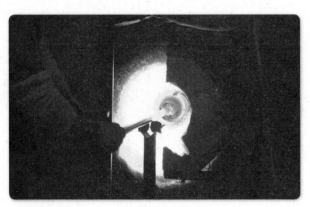

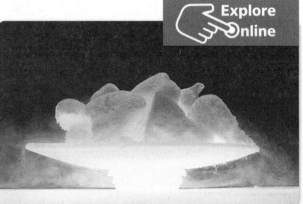

Glassblowing involves high temperatures. Glass is heated to the point that it becomes molten. It can then be shaped. This involves using a blowpipe to insert air into the glass.

Dry ice is a solid form of carbon dioxide. Freezing carbon dioxide takes a much colder temperature than that needed to freeze water. Because dry ice is so cold, it is dangerous to touch.

Heat is energy that transfers, or moves, between objects with different temperatures. Think about where you have observed heat energy today.

Compare and Contrast   Look at the two pictures. How would you describe the differences? What details in each picture gave you clues?

_____

_____

We use words such as *hot*, *cold*, *warmer*, and *cooler* to describe temperature without being exact. To get an exact measurement of temperature, we use a tool called a *thermometer*. Temperature can be measured using degrees. The thermometer on the next page has two scales, Celsius (°C) and Fahrenheit (°F).

Is it hot or cold in your city today? Use a thermometer to find out the temperature. Mark the temperature on the thermometer on the next page.

 EVIDENCE NOTEBOOK   Heat is a form of energy. What evidence have you gathered so far to help you explain how heat energy is transferred?

Differences in Degrees

This thermometer shows measurements in Celsius (°C) and Fahrenheit (°F). The symbol that looks like a little "o" stands for "degrees." Write a letter in each circle to identify the temperatures shown in the pictures.

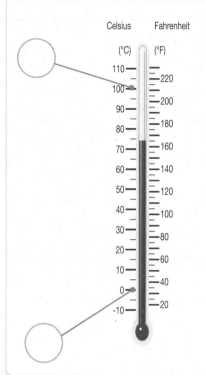

The girl's clothes trap heat near her body. Her jacket slows down energy transfer to the cold air. The girl stays warm while playing in the snow in temperatures as low as 0 °C (32 °F) or below.

Heat transfers from the stove to a tea kettle, then from the kettle to the water, and finally from the water vapor to the air. Water boils at 100 °C (212 °F).

 Engineer It!

Thermal Imaging

Thermal imaging devices can "see" how hot or cold air moves into and out of a house. By knowing how energy is being transferred, people can insulate areas of the house to help themselves stay warmer or cooler.

Thermal imaging devices are also used by fire departments. Because firefighters cannot see through the smoke, they cannot see if anyone is trapped in a house. To **solve this problem,** firefighters use a thermal imaging device to help them see the cooler bodies in all the hot smoke.

Thermal imaging of buildings can help save energy.

Analyze Two objects on a thermal image are different colors. What must be true of these objects? How could you test your theory?

_____

_____

_____

Hot by Contact

Remember that heat is energy that transfers between objects with different temperatures. Heat energy sometimes transfers easily between objects that are touching. When objects of two different temperatures touch, heat energy moves from the warmer object to the cooler object.

Energy is transferred as heat moves from a stove burner to a skillet.

Explore Online

Energy is also transferred as heat moves from the hot skillet to the colder pancake batter.

How does this energy transfer work when cooking a pancake? A pancake skillet starts out at room temperature. When the stove burner is hot, it transfers heat to the bottom of the skillet. The heat spreads through the whole skillet. The heat energy in the hot skillet then transfers to the cooler pancake batter. As the batter warms, the pancake cooks.

Define Select the best words to complete each sentence.

batter	burner	cooler	energy
faster	skillet	slower	warmer

Heat is _____ that moves from a _____

object to a _____ object. A pancake cooks when energy

transfers from the _____ to the _____

to the _____. The last pancake in the batch cooks

_____ than the first pancake because the skillet is hotter.

Distant Heat

Pancakes cook because objects are in contact. The transfer of energy as heat can also occur between objects that are not touching each other.

Determine the heat source in each system below—where you think the heat is coming from. Then locate the objects the heat is transferring to.

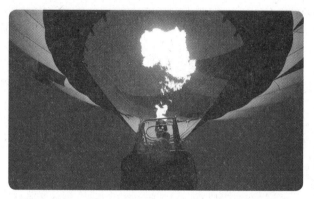

The flame of a gas burner heats the air above the burner. The hot air is buoyed up and fills the balloon. Heat transfers into the balloon. Soon the whole balloon is full of hot air.

The space heater transfers heat to the air around it. This makes the air in the room gain heat energy and become warmer. Soon, the room is nice and warm.

 Language SmArts Cause and Effect Complete the chart by writing the cause and effect from each example.

Heat Transfer without Touch		
Example	Heat source	What heat finally transfers to
marshmallows roasting over a campfire		marshmallows
heat lamp incubating hatching chicks		
snow melting on a sidewalk on a sunny day		

Gather Evidence What energy transformations take place when a candle burns and when a glow stick lights up? Do research to find out. Explain how stored energy is transformed in these examples. Write your findings in your notebook. Then share and compare with a partner.

A Family of Waves

Light from the sun is a form of energy that we can see. Light travels as waves. These waves travel outward in all directions from the sun and spread out as they move. Other kinds of waves are not visible but also carry energy as they travel and spread out. These other types of energy waves include radio waves, microwaves, and x-rays. Read below to explore the different energy waves.

Each type of wave has a certain level of energy. The five types of energy waves discussed here are arranged in order of lowest energy (radio waves) to highest energy (x-rays).

Energy rays

Have you used a microwave oven to heat food? **Microwaves** are higher in energy than radio waves. They have less energy than visible light waves. Weather radar images are also often made using microwaves.

Lowest energy

Radio waves spread out and travel from a broadcast tower to radio receivers such as car radios. Radio waves have low energy compared to other waves.

Visible light includes all the colors that we see. A rainbow shows a range of colors from red to violet. What we see as red light has the lowest energy. Violet has the highest energy.

Ultraviolet light is higher in energy than the range of light humans can see. Some insects, however, can see UV light! The Hubble Space Telescope senses UV light. Images from the telescope show us the UV light given off by many different objects in space.

X-rays have much more energy when compared to visible light and radio waves. X-rays pass through the body and are processed to make images of bones and tissues.

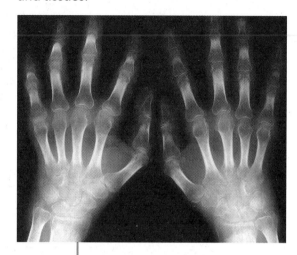

Highest energy

Explain Choose the best answer to complete the sentences below.

less	microwaves	more	visible light	ultraviolet light	x-rays

Visible light waves have _____ energy than radio waves and _____ energy than x-rays. One type of energy wave that people cannot see but some insects can is _____. _____ can be used to make weather maps. _____ can be used to study bones and tissues.

Language SmArts **Recall Relevant Information** Which of the energy waves shown on these pages have you experienced? What evidence do you have of each type of energy?

_____

_____

_____

_____

145

Lighting Up Life

The sun is a star that gives off light and heat. These forms of energy are important to Earth and the things that live on it.

Analyze What else do you know about energy from the sun? Brainstorm a list of ways in which the sun's energy affects Earth and living things.

_____

_____

_____

All life on Earth depends on light and heat from the sun. Sunlight makes it possible for plants to grow and provide the oxygen that we breathe. Plants also provide us with some of our food. The sun's heating of Earth's atmosphere sets the water cycle in motion. Energy from the sun causes wind and weather patterns, too.

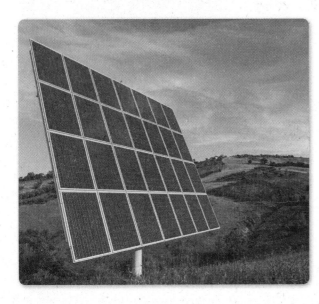

Solar panels such as these transform light energy into electrical energy that can be used to heat buildings. Solar panels can also change light energy into energy that heats the water used in buildings.

Evaluate Solar panels are evidence for which of these statements?

a. Light can be transformed into other energy forms.

b. Heat energy moves toward warmer objects.

c. Sound transfers heat energy.

d. Life on Earth depends on sunlight.

Putting It Together

Summarize ways that energy can travel from place to place. Include an example, and use the words _heat, warmer, cooler, light, waves, touching,_ and _not touching_ in your summary.

_____

_____

_____

_____

_____

© Houghton Mifflin Harcourt Publishing Company • Image Credits: (l) ©Thuy Mai/NASA;

Energy of Sound

Sound All Around

Sounds are all around you. But what is sound?

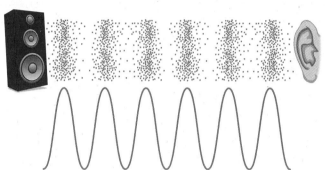

You can't see sound waves. But the small particles that make up all kinds of matter vibrate as sound waves strike objects.

Sound is energy that travels in vibrations. To vibrate means "to move back and forth." Sound vibrations come from an object or organism that starts the vibration. Then the vibration travels through the air or surrounding objects. When a sound vibration reaches your ear, you sense the sound. Soft sounds have smaller waves than louder sounds.

 EVIDENCE NOTEBOOK How does sound move from place to place? Give an example of how sound moves. How is this like the transfer of heat energy in a toaster? How is it different?

When you pluck a string guitar, it vibrates. If you pluck it hard, you transfer a lot of energy to the string. The sound is loud. If you pluck it softly, you transfer less energy. The sound is soft.

Telephones, televisions, radios, and computers all have speakers. Speakers transform electrical energy into vibrations. A speaker vibrates and transfers sound energy through air to your ear.

Model Gently place your fingers on your throat and say "la la la." Compare what you feel to what happens when a guitar and a speaker produce sound. Write how they are similar.

Loud and Soft, High and Low

Sounds are everywhere. Some sounds, such as whispers, are soft. Other sounds, such as fireworks and thunder, are very loud.

Explore Online

Sound Off!

Look at the photos. Decide if each sound is soft or loud. Then decide if each has low energy or high energy. Circle your answers.

A plane's engines roar as the plane takes off and touches down.

The airplane makes a (soft, loud) sound,

which has (high, low) energy.

A mouse is a small animal that makes squeaky sounds.

A mouse makes a (soft, loud) sound

when it squeaks, which has

(high, low) energy.

Model Select another object or organism that makes sound. Draw the object or organism in your Evidence Notebook. Describe the sound as soft or loud and whether it has high or low energy.

Why do sounds differ? It's the energy transfer. If a lot of energy is transferred from or to an object, the sound is loud. If less energy is transferred from or to an object, the sound is softer. Loud sounds have more energy than softer sounds.

Loud sounds cause particles to vibrate vigorously with much energy. Soft sounds cause them to vibrate with less energy.

Energy on the Move

Sound vibrations can travel through any substance. As you can see in the models below, sound travels faster through solid materials than through liquids or gases. This is because the particles in solids are usually closer together than the particles in liquids or gases.

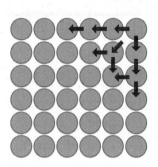 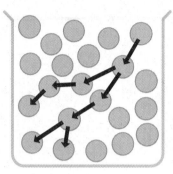 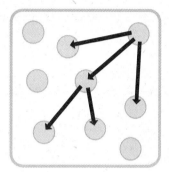

Describe   Notice in the models above how sound moves in a solid (left), a liquid (middle), and a gas (right). What effect does the distance between particles have?

_____

_____

Do the Math
Compare the Speed of Sound

Analyze the data in the table. Order the speeds from fastest to slowest. Then draw a conclusion about the data.

Speed of Sound in Different Materials

Order	Material at 0 °C	Speed of sound (m/s)
	air	331
	copper	4,600
	fresh water	1,433
	rubber	60
	silver	3,650
	steel	4,970

_____

_____

Tuned In!

A tuning fork is a tool that is used to tune musical instruments. When struck, the fork vibrates. The sound does not travel very far in the air. The sound travels much farther through a solid because the particles are closer together.

The tuning fork is vibrating in the air.

The fork is vibrating against a metal railing.

HANDS-ON Apply What You Know

Tune In

Plan and carry out an investigation on how sound travels through different materials. If you don't have a tuning fork, use something else to make a sound along a metal railing or in the air. On a sheet of paper, list the materials you will use. Explain the steps you will take to carry out the investigation. Submit your results to your teacher.

Distinguish Which of these is true? Circle the answer.

a. Sound vibrations travel faster through air than through metal.

b. Sound vibrations travel faster through water than through wood.

c. Sound vibrations travel faster through solids than through gases.

d. Sound vibrations travel through wood, metal, and air at the same speed.

Putting It Together

| materials energy loud vibrations soft transferred |

Sound moves from place to place in the form of _____. Sound can move

through any _____, including solids, liquids, and gases. How loud or

soft a sound is depends on how much _____ is _____.

_____ sounds are produced from a lot of energy. Less energy makes

_____ sounds.

Discover More

Check out this path . . . or go online to choose one of these other paths.

People in Science & Engineering

- **Keep It Cold**
- **The Paynes and Fast-Traveling Whale Songs**

Geisha Williams

Geisha Williams works in the energy industry. Williams believes in finding ways to use energy efficiently and effectively. She has been involved with many impressive contributions to the energy industry. One such contribution was overseeing the integration of new smart grid technologies.

A common electrical grid supplies electricity from electricity-generating stations to users through a one-way network of electrical lines. On the other hand, a smart grid is a more efficient electrical grid. It uses technology to send data about energy use from users back to the energy supplier. The advanced technology systems for measuring and conducting energy make the system more efficient and reliable. For example, too much electric demand in one area can lead to a blackout, or failure. A smart grid can supply more energy at times of high demand. Often it includes renewable energy sources. Technology on a smart grid can also help utility companies make repairs faster.

Williams is finding better ways to provide clean energy solutions to power people's homes and businesses. She believes in the use of renewable energy sources. She is also working to ensure that cities in California are equipped to support the use of more electric vehicles in the future.

Geisha Williams has been ranked as one of the most powerful women in business.

Obtain and combine information about smart grids. What are some of the benefits of using smart grid technology?

_____

_____

_____

Although Geisha Williams used to design technology when she worked as an engineer, she is now responsible for other types of things, like coming up with the vision and plans for how to get more renewable energy sources out to the public. What else do you think she is responsible for?

Choose all that apply.

  a. drawing the engineering plans for new technology

  b. developing goals for the company

  c. working together with companies that build solar panels

  d. educating people about the need for cleaner energy

Investigate What types of energy are considered renewable, or free of greenhouse gases?

_____

_____

_____

_____

Circle the statements that are true about solar energy.

  a. Solar energy is not a clean source of energy.

  b. The sun's energy will not run out.

  c. Solar energy is hard to find.

  d. Solar energy is clean energy.

© Houghton Mifflin Harcourt Publishing Company • Image Credits: (t) ©Paul Morigi/

Lesson Check

Name _____

Can You Explain It?

1. You have learned about energy and how one form can be changed into another. Think back to the photos of the toaster. Where did the energy for the toaster come from, and where did it go?

• Define *energy transfer*.

• Explain the evidence from the photos that shows that energy transferred and caused change.

• Describe the path the energy took as it moved from place to place.

EVIDENCE NOTEBOOK Use the information you've collected in your Evidence Notebook to help you cover each point above.

_____

_____

_____

_____

_____

_____

_____

_____

Checkpoints

2. Number these sentences in the order in which they occur.

a. Electric energy transforms to light energy. _____

b. Electric energy transfers through the cord. _____

c. Electric energy transfers into a lamp. _____

d. You turn on a light switch. _____

3. Select the words that correctly complete the sentences in the paragraph.

| heat | thermometer | warmer | cooler | increasing | decreasing |

Energy that transfers between objects with different temperatures is called

_____. Temperature measures how hot an object is. You can

use a _____ to measure it. When temperature rises, it is evidence that heat

energy is _____. When temperature falls, heat energy is _____.

4. Which of the following are evidence of energy transfer involving sound? Circle all that apply.

a. a burning candle

b. an airplane taking off

c. water dripping

d. orchestra playing music

e. using a solar cooker

f. plucking of a guitar string

g. kids whispering

h. water heating on a stove

5. You have a new toy that requires batteries. You insert the batteries and turn it on. Which of the following are evidence that the batteries have transferred energy to the toy? Circle all of the answers that apply.

a. The toy makes noise.

b. The toy breaks.

c. The toy stays still.

d. The toy lights up.

e. The toy moves.

6. Read each example. Write the word *heat, light, sound,* or *motion* to tell what kind of energy is present. Some examples may use more than one kind of energy.

a. a rolling soccer ball _____

b. cooking soup _____

c. using a microwave _____

d. a burning candle _____

e. turning on a faucet _____

Lesson Roundup

A. Decide which kinds of energy transfer are involved in each example below. Sort each example into the correct column in the table. Some examples might fall into more than one category.

orchestra	teakettle	solar panels	fireworks	toaster

Sound	Light	Heat	Electric current

B. Choose the words that make the sentences correct.

cooler	warmer	high	low

When a warmer object touches a cooler object, heat

transfers from the _____ object to the

_____ object. The sound of a jackhammer

transfers _____ energy, while a whisper

transfers _____ energy.

Celsius   Fahrenheit

(°C)   (°F)

C. Which of these devices does NOT change electrical energy into heat energy? Choose the best answer.
  a. microwave
  b. clock
  c. clothes dryer
  d. electric stove

What Nonrenewable Resources Are Used for Energy?

Oil is buried deep within Earth's surface. In order to remove it, big drills have to dig down into the ground—or even into the ocean floor. Gasoline and diesel fuel for cars is made from oil. Look at the image to learn more.

Explore First

Finding Resources Explore your classroom, and collect the different beans your teacher has placed. These beans represent different resources found in nature. Which resource did you find the most of? How do you think this compares to actual resources in nature?

Can You Explain It?

You discovered that it only takes a push to move a toy car. But how do you move a big car, such as the one pictured above?

Explain Look at the car in the photo above. Where is this car getting the energy from motion to move? Where does it come from?

_____

_____

_____

_____

_____

_____

_____

_____

_____

_____

 EVIDENCE NOTEBOOK Look for this icon to help you gather evidence to answer the questions above.

Modeling Energy Resources Use

Objective

Collaborate as a team to develop and model matter and energy flows related to nonrenewable energy sources.

Materials
- small paper cups
- counting chips
- posterboard
- drawing and writing tools
- other objects you need to complete your plan

Procedure

STEP 1 There are costs and benefits of getting and using nonrenewable energy. What questions come to mind when you think about that sentence? Write down as many questions as you can on a separate sheet of paper. Be ready to share your questions.

STEP 2 With your class, select the most important questions about nonrenewable energy resources. Write down the questions your class thinks are the most important.

Questions We Think Are Most Important

_____

_____

_____

_____

_____

STEP 3 How can you use a model to investigate the questions your class picked as most important? Think about the materials your teacher shows you and what else you might need. Write your investigation plan on a separate sheet. Show it to your teacher to see if you can get the other things that you need. If you use things other than those your teacher shows you, be sure to write them down in the plan.

_____

_____

_____

_____

_____

STEP 4 Carry out your plan, and record your results. Present your data in a way that everyone can see what you did and what happened. You may wish to use a table or graph as a presentation tool. Or you might choose to make a poster with photographs.

_____

_____

_____

_____

_____

Make a **claim** that answers the question or questions your class decided to explore. You may need to have a claim for each question. Support your claims with **evidence** from your investigation **and reasoning** to show how the evidence supports your claim. Record your claims, evidence, and reasoning below or on a separate sheet of paper.

_____

_____

_____

_____

_____

Take It Further

What new questions do you have about nonrenewable energy use after your investigation? You can start your questions with "What happens if . . ." or "Is this always . . ."

_____

_____

_____

_____

_____

Materials We Use

Resources around You

Explore below to find out more about resources that are used on a day-to-day basis.

Identify Match the text to the picture above by writing the correct letter in each circle.

a. The water you drink comes from a river, a lake, or an underground well.

b. The part of the pencil that writes is made of graphite, a substance called a mineral.

c. Most paper is made from the mashed-up wood of trees.

d. Metals are found in Earth's rocky layers.

e. Cotton is often used to make curtains. Cotton comes from a plant.

f. Plastic is made from petroleum. Petroleum is also known as crude oil, a fossil fuel.

A **resource** is anything that you use to live. Your house is a resource because it gives you shelter. The clothes you wear are a resource because they keep you warm and protect you. A **natural resource** is a material from nature that people can use. Water, air, trees, wind, fossil fuels, minerals, and sunlight are examples of natural resources.

Explain how three different items you see in your classroom are made from materials found in nature. Choose different examples from the ones above.

_____

_____

_____

Limited Supply

Explore the images to explore more about nonrenewable resources.

Crude oil formed mainly from the remains of tiny living things that lived in the sea and were buried under mud. It is used for heat and to fuel vehicles; it is also an ingredient of many products, such as plastics and paints.

Coal formed from the buried remains of plants that died millions of years ago. In some places, coal is used for heat and for cooking.

Natural gas also formed from the remains of tiny living things. It is used for heat and as a fuel source for buses and other vehicles.

Uranium is a natural element. It is not the remains of living things, but is found in rocks formed billions of years ago. Uranium is used to produce nuclear energy that is used to generate electricity.

Summarize How do these nonrenewable resources help people in their daily lives?

_____

_____

A **nonrenewable resource** is a resource that, once used, cannot be replaced in a reasonable amount of time. Fossil fuels, such as crude oil, coal, and natural gas, are nonrenewable resources. These fossil fuels are burned to release energy and generate electricity. They are nonrenewable because they take thousands to millions of years to form.

Language SmArts
Compare and Contrast

How are crude oil, coal, and natural gas different from uranium?

_____

Collecting and Processing

Renewable resources are first removed from Earth's crust. Then they can be used by electricity-generating stations to provide electricity to homes and businesses. Explore the systems below to discover more about how these resources are collected and processed.

Gasoline used as fuel in vehicles comes from crude oil. Crude oil is pumped from underground wells, including wells that are underwater. It is also burned to generate electricity.

Coal is mined from deposits in layers of rocks. It is taken to electricity-generating stations to be burned and converted to electrical energy.

Natural gas is extracted from rocks deep underground. It is then transported by pipeline and burned for electricity generation.

Uranium is mined from rocks and is used to produce large amounts of energy. The energy is then provided to homes and businesses for heat and electricity. Uranium is a fuel source for nuclear energy stations.

 EVIDENCE NOTEBOOK Are there vehicles that do not run on fossil fuels? List your ideas in your Evidence Notebook.

Apply What You Know

The School's Energy

Obtain and combine information to find out about the energy station that supplies electricity to your school. How does it generate electricity? Make a poster about your findings. Compare your findings with those of your classmates.

What Do They Use?

163

Draw lines to connect the nonrenewable resources with the facilities that use them.

Nonrenewable resources cannot replenish themselves. Efforts have been made to conserve fossil fuels to make sure people have enough energy for future needs. The harmful effects of carbon dioxide are another reason why these efforts have been made.

Do the Math

Calculate Energy Units

Energy use can be measured in amounts called Btu. *Btu* stands for "British thermal unit." Burning 1 gallon of gasoline, made from petroleum, a form of crude oil, to power a car produces about 120,000 Btu.

The United States uses many quadrillions of Btu from different energy sources each year. A quadrillion is a huge number! It is 1 followed by 15 zeros. Energy usage in the United States has changed over time. Use this timeline to find out how.

1990

U.S. population = 249 million
Petroleum use = 34 quadrillion Btu
Natural gas use = 20 quadrillion Btu
Coal use = 19 quadrillion Btu
Nuclear energy use = 6 quadrillion Btu
Renewable energy use =
1 quadrillion Btu

1995

U.S. population = 263 million
Petroleum use = 34 quadrillion Btu
Natural gas use = 23 quadrillion Btu
Coal use = 20 quadrillion Btu
Nuclear energy use = 7 quadrillion Btu
Renewable energy use =
2 quadrillion Btu

2000

U.S. population = 281 million
Petroleum use = 38 quadrillion Btu
Natural gas use = 24 quadrillion Btu
Coal use = 23 quadrillion Btu
Nuclear energy use = 8 quadrillion Btu
Renewable energy use =
2 quadrillion Btu

2005

U.S. population = 296 million
Petroleum use = 40 quadrillion Btu
Natural gas use = 23 quadrillion Btu
Coal use = 23 quadrillion Btu
Nuclear energy use = 8 quadrillion Btu
Renewable energy use =
2 quadrillion Btu

2010

U.S. population = 309 million
Petroleum use = 36 quadrillion Btu
Natural gas use = 25 quadrillion Btu
Coal use = 21 quadrillion Btu
Nuclear energy use = 8 quadrillion Btu
Renewable energy use =
4 quadrillion Btu

Identify Choose one of the resources from the timeline. Graph in your notebook how the use of that resource has changed over time.

Determine Do the data in the timeline support the statements below?
If they do, circle *true*. If it they don't, circle *false*. Coal use in the United States decreased about 2 quadrilllon Btu between 2005 and 2010.

true   false

Renewable energy use increased between 1990 and 2010.

true   false

Explain What is one way you can think of to decrease people's use of petroleum?

_____

_____

_____

Evaluate Between the years 2005 and 2010, petroleum use went down. Which of these is the most likely explanation for the decreased petroleum use?

a. The population went up, so more people were driving cars.

b. The population went down, so fewer people were driving cars.

c. The population went up, but more of the cars must have been electric or hybrids.

d. The population went down, and most people stopped driving.

Putting It Together

Write the word or phrase that correctly completes each sentence. Terms may be used more than once.

| petroleum | fossil fuels | resources | renewable | nonrenewable |
| disappear | increase | nature | technology | |

Some natural resources are _____ because they cannot be replaced in

a reasonable amount of time. Examples include _____ such as coal and

crude oil, or petroleum. People can develop new _____ to use fewer

_____ resources.

Search and Find

Digging a Little Deeper

It can take thousands to millions of years for nonrenewable resources to form. We are using them much more quickly than they can be replaced. Why could this be a problem? The demand for coal and crude oil remains high. Today, drills dig deep into Earth's rock layers to remove crude oil and natural gas, which are used as fuel sources to generate electricity. See the models below to discover more.

Natural Gas and Oil Formation

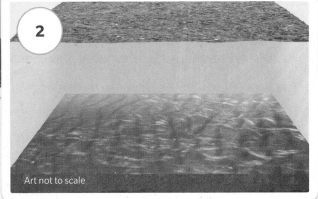

1. When tiny living things that live in the ocean die, they settle to the bottom.

2. Layers of sediment slowly bury the once-living things. Over millions of years, these layers pile up and become rock.

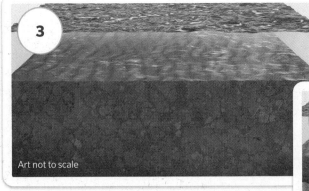

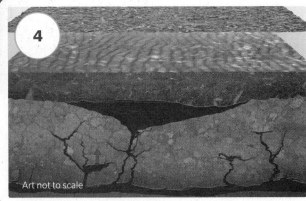

3. Pressure from these layers produces heat. The pressure and heat slowly turn the remains of the once-living things into oil and natural gas.

4. Oil and natural gas flow through rocks with pores. There they become trapped and are concentrated into pockets called reservoirs.

Coal Formation

Coal is reached when people dig deep into the earth or strip away its surface. Digging for coal is called mining. There is underground mining and surface mining. Once mined, the coal is burned to provide heat and electricity.

Art not to scale

1. Decaying, once-living plants sink into a swamp and change into a material called peat.

2. Sediment buries the peat. As more sediment is deposited, growing temperature and pressure change peat into the first stage of coal, which is brown.

Art not to scale

3. As more sediment is deposited, increased temperature and pressure cause the formation of the second stage of coal. This coal is dull, black, and burns hotter than the brown coal.

4. More layers of sediment are deposited. Temperature and pressure rise, transforming the dull black coal into the third and final stage of coal. This coal is black and shiny and burns the hottest.

Art not to scale

Uranium

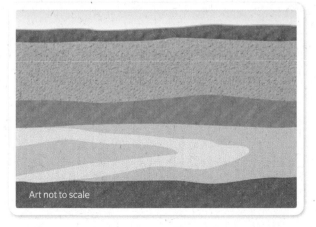

Art not to scale

Uranium is a material found in certain rocks and rock layers. It is removed by surface mining or by deep underground mining.

It can also be removed from rocks by leaching. Leaching is using water and chemicals to release it from rock.

How to Get It

Using the models you just explored, identify how each resource is mined. Write the letters on the lines. Some will contain more than one letter.

a. underground mines

b. surface mines

c. drilling

d. leaching

_____

_____

_____

_____

Before the 20th century, people relied mainly on wood and coal for heating and cooking. Burning coal started the industrial age with the development of steam engines that drove trains and electricity-generating stations. Cars and other engines increased the use of crude oil as a source of energy. As technology improved, people found ways to mine and use natural gas and uranium.

Language SmArts

Summarize

What do the methods of extracting these fuels all have in common?

_____

_____

 EVIDENCE NOTEBOOK Where do we get the fuel to run cars? What are some pros and cons of cars that run on gasoline?

Where Are They Found?

Scientists and engineers use special nonrenewable resource technology to locate, remove, and process coal, crude oil, natural gas, and uranium. Each of these methods has certain benefits and risks. Some cause **pollution**, or waste products that damage an ecosystem.

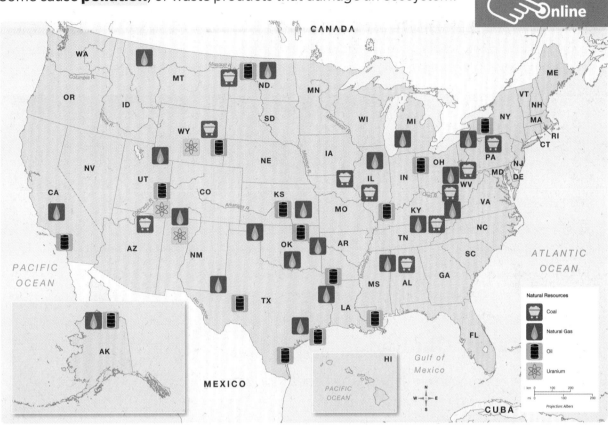

 In the United States, crude oil is found mostly in the Midwest, South, Southwest, Alaska, and around Pennsylvania.

 The Midwest, Montana, Wyoming, and Pennsylvania are the main sources of coal in the United States.

 Natural gas is found mostly in Alaska, Texas, Oklahoma, New Mexico, Wyoming, and Louisiana. Some can also be found in the Midwest.

 The United States was once the leader in uranium mining. Today, however, uranium is mined in only a few places, including New Mexico, Utah, and Wyoming.

Identify Choose the word or phrase that correctly completes each sentence.

crude oil	coal	natural gas	uranium	Wyoming	Pennsylvania

Natural gas, _____, and coal can be found in the Midwest. Natural gas

and uranium can be found in New Mexico and _____. Oklahoma has

both _____ and crude oil. Pennsylvania is one of the main sources of

_____ in the United States.

What Does It Use?

Write *u* for uranium, *o* for oil, *c* for coal, or *g* for gas to identify the nonrenewable resource shown in each picture below.

Many kitchen stoves cook food with an open flame. A fossil fuel is piped into the stove, where it ignites and heats up the food.	Early trains had steam engines. A fire heated up water, which turned to steam. The steam then helped the trains to move.	Paint is a product of fossil fuels. The same product that is used in paint is also used in plastic, rubber, and soap.

Kitchen stove

Train

Paint

HANDS-ON Apply What You Know

Energy Challenge

Model using nonrenewable energy. The beads represent nonrenewable energy sources such as gas and coal. The sunflower seeds represent renewable energy.

> **Materials**
> - 15 beads
> - sunflower seeds

On a sheet of paper, make a table with these five columns: Home Heat, Electricity, Water Heat, Car Trip 1, and Car Trip 2.

You have 20 beads of energy. Divide the beads as follows, and place them in the columns on your chart. Your house uses 5 beads for heat, 5 beads for electricity, and 1 bead to heat the water. Your car uses 6 beads per trip.

Explain What problem do you face?

_____

Analyze How can you solve this problem? (Think about what the sunflower seeds represent.)

_____

_____

_____

Pros and Cons

The pros and cons of something are similar to its benefits and risks. The pros are the positive things about it and the cons are the negative things, or *drawbacks.* Using fossil fuels has some pros and some cons. A *pro* is that they give us affordable fuel. A *con* is that using them often causes pollution, harms ecosystems, or produces harmful substances when mixed with water, air, or soil.

Humans have used coal for energy for thousands of years. Some forms of strip-mining for coal harm ecosystems.

Many vehicles run on gasoline. Hazardous oil spills have occurred when transporting crude oil.

Airplanes use fossil fuel to run their engines. This fuel is expensive and also adds pollution to the air.

Burning fossil fuels in cars and at electricity-generating stations generates energy, but it also causes pollution and harmful gases in Earth's atmosphere.

Burning natural gas or using nuclear energy produces less pollution than coal and oil, but transporting uranium is dangerous.

Assess Write the letter of the sentence that completes the chart.

Cause	Effect
	Pollution and harmful gases are added to the air.
New nuclear stations are built.	
	Habitats and farmland are lost.
Crude oil is transported.	

a. Uranium must be moved long distances.
b. Fossil fuels are burned.
c. Oil spills pollute water and destroy wildlife.
d. Resources are surface mined.

Engineer It!
Hybrid Cars

As you learned, cars need energy to move. Most of it comes from oil. Oil is the main source of gasoline. Hybrid cars, however, are **designed** to use two or more different methods to generate energy. Some hybrid cars can run on both gasoline and electricity. The model below shows a standard hybrid.

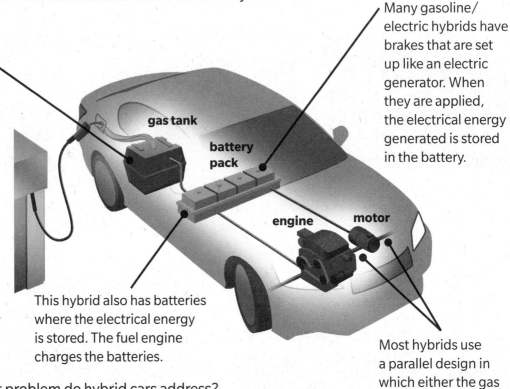

This hybrid uses gasoline as one energy source. A small number of hybrids use biofuels instead of gas. Biofuels are renewable resources made from plant material or animal waste.

Many gasoline/electric hybrids have brakes that are set up like an electric generator. When they are applied, the electrical energy generated is stored in the battery.

This hybrid also has batteries where the electrical energy is stored. The fuel engine charges the batteries.

Most hybrids use a parallel design in which either the gas engine or the electric motor alone can drive the wheels, or they can work at the same time.

Analyze What problem do hybrid cars address?

_____

_____

Summarize How does a hybrid car such as the one in the diagram help protect the environment?

_____

Language SmArts
Write a Paper

Write a paper with at least three paragraphs about cars of the future.

- Explain how these cars will be different from most cars used today.
- What will be their energy sources?
- How will they help solve the problem of pollution?

Use both the library and the Internet, and include images in your paper. Share your findings with the class.

Discover More

Check out this path . . . or go online to choose one of these other paths.

Careers in
Science &
Engineering

- **What's around You?**
- **On a Mining Mission**
- **People in Science & Engineering**

Types of "-ISTs"

As we use up nonrenewable fossil fuel supplies, the need for alternative energy resources increases. Different scientists do work related to fossil fuels.

A petroleum geologist locates and discovers places where new fossil fuel deposits can be found. George V. Chilingarian is a petroleum geologist and professor. His greatest involvement in the petroleum industry was finding a method of identifying oil-rich rock. His method was used in discovering one of the largest oil fields in Iran.

Ahmed Hassan Zewail was a chemist, who was awarded a Nobel Prize in Chemistry. He developed methods for studying chemical reactions in detail. Chemists take on many responsibilities. Some perform research, while others may investigate how chemicals found in fossil fuels can be used as fuel and to make products.

Evaluate Decide if each description is a discovery or an invention. Match each to the scientist who was most likely responsible for it.

a. located deposits of crude oil in North Dakota

b. used technology to inform other experts where to drill

petroleum geologist

c. developed new types of sunglasses

chemist

d. invented new instant glue

e. stopped underwater oil spill

Climatologists study weather patterns and processes that cause them. They also study long-term changes in climate. These changes are related to use of fossil fuels. Roberto J. Mera is a climatologist and a Climate Change Program Coordinator at North Carolina State University. He has also worked on analyzing specific carbon emissions to determine how they are affecting global temperatures and extreme heat events.

Marine biologists study marine animals in their natural habitats. They evaluate the effects of environment and industry on such animals. They can also describe the effects of fossil fuel pollution on the plants and animals living in the ocean. Mariana Fuentes is a marine biologist. Her main research is on conservation planning, natural resource management, and climate change impacts on marine animals.

Describe Describe a similarity and difference among the four different types of scientists.

_____

_____

_____

Explain Pick your favorite type of scientist from the ones described here. Research interesting facts about that type of scientist's job. Which type of scientist did you choose, and why?

_____

_____

Summarize Describe where that type of scientist does most of his or her work.

_____

_____

Compare and Contrast Compare your research with that of a classmate who researched a different type of scientist's job. Which job would you rather have? Why?

_____

_____

Lesson Check

Name _____

Can You Explain It?

1. Think back to the car from the beginning of the lesson. Now that you've learned about nonrenewable resources, explain how car designs need to change to better conserve resources and protect the environment. Be sure to do the following:
   - Identify the types of fuel sources to be used and whether they are renewable or nonrenewable.
   - Identify technologies that engineers build into things in order to replace fossil fuels.
   - Identify the benefits and drawbacks of each fuel source used.

EVIDENCE NOTEBOOK Use the information you've collected in your Evidence Notebook to help you cover each point above.

_____

_____

_____

_____

_____

_____

_____

_____

Checkpoints

2. Which of the following is a nonrenewable resource that is not a fossil fuel?
   - **a.** natural gas
   - **c.** uranium
   - **b.** oil
   - **d.** coal

3. Write the letter that identifies each nonrenewable energy resource.

   a. natural gas
   b. coal
   c. uranium
   d. crude oil

4. Write the words or phrases that make each sentence correct.

inexpensive	decreasing quickly	increasing quickly
increasing slowly	hundreds	hundreds of millions

Fossil fuels were once easy to find and _____ to use because there was so much of each available. But today, we are using so much that supplies are _____. It took _____ of years for fossil fuels to form, so there will be no more when our current supply is gone.

5. Which of the following results from using fossil fuels? Circle all that apply.
   a. Air is polluted with harmful gases.
   b. Nonrenewable resources are conserved.
   c. Ecosystems can be harmed.
   d. Renewable resources are all used up.

6. Write *renewable* or *nonrenewable* to complete the sentence.

Hybrid cars reduce the use of fossil fuels by also using resources that are _____.

© Houghton Mifflin Harcourt Publishing Company • Image Credits: (bl) ©Getty Images; (tr) ©Lakeview Images/Shutterstock; (tl) ©Harry Taylor/Dorling Kindersley/Getty Images;

Lesson Roundup

A. The box contains descriptions labeled with letters. Write these letters beneath the images to correctly describe each nonrenewable resource.

| a. solid | b. nonrenewable | c. used to generate electricity | d. fossil fuel |

_____ _____ _____ _____

B. Which of the following is needed for nonrenewable resources to form?

a. days to weeks

b. weeks to months

c. weeks to a few years

d. thousands to millions of years

C. What could explain why an oil rig is no longer able to get crude oil from an area?

a. The oil has become solid.   **c.** The drill needs to be replaced.

b. All the oil has been removed.   **d.** The oil has moved to a different area.

D. Which of the following are ways to reduce the use of fossil fuels and decrease pollution? Circle all that apply.

a. Drive hybrid vehicles.

b. Use natural gas.

c. Drive standard vehicles.

d. Use less plastic.

E. Circle the sources of energy that are the remains of once-living organisms.

a. uranium   **c.** natural gas

b. coal   **d.** crude oil

What Renewable Resources Are Used for Energy?

A wind farm is a place where several turbines are installed to convert wind to electrical energy.

Explore First

Catching the Wind What's the best way to transfer energy from a balloon to a wind turbine? What evidence do you need to convince others? Use a balloon and pinwheel to find out.

Can You Explain It?

Explore Online

Look carefully at this house. Even though it's not close to any town, it still has electricity. When you look at most houses, you see wires connected to them. Wires bring electricity to the house so that the refrigerator, lights, TV, heating and cooling system, and other electrical appliances work. Some houses have underground wires, while others get their electricity from other sources.

Explain This home has plenty of electricity during both day and night. How does it get most of its electricity?

_____

_____

_____

_____

_____

_____

_____

_____

 EVIDENCE NOTEBOOK Look for this icon to help you gather evidence to answer the question above.

Exploring Renewable Resources

Use It Again

Identify Explore below to find out more about renewable energy sources. Then match by writing the letter that best describes each source next to the picture that shows it.

a. Using wind as an energy source does not produce pollution. Because wind will not run out, it is a renewable resource.

b. Geothermal stations use the heat below Earth's surface to produce electricity. Earth's heat is a renewable resource.

c. The energy of water flowing through a dam is called hydroelectricity. Hydroelectric dams use water, which is a renewable resource.

d. Solar energy is clean, renewable energy from the sun. When solar panels capture energy from the sun and change it to electricity, no pollution is given off.

e. Biomass is fuel that comes from dead organisms. The most common type is wood. Other types include cornstalks and animal waste. When burned, biomass is used to generate electricity.

Compare and Contrast What is the difference between a renewable and a nonrenewable resource?

How Does That Work?

Decide Draw a line to match the electricity-producing device to the natural resource.

You've already discovered that nonrenewable resources cannot be replenished in a reasonable amount of time. However, **renewable resources** are resources that can be replenished within a reasonable amount of time. Before the 20th century, renewable resources were the main forms of energy used. They are now used to generate electricity.

 EVIDENCE NOTEBOOK Could any of these renewable resource uses provide electricity for the house at the start of the lesson? Record your observations and reasoning in your Evidence Notebook.

 Language SmArts
Making Connections

Describe two renewable and two nonrenewable resource uses where you live. What are the natural resources and the electricity-producing devices?

_____

_____

_____

Energy Stations

Explore the images to discover more about different forms of renewable energy.

Wind energy does not pollute the air. Wind spins the blades of huge turbines. The spinning blades turn a device called a generator inside the turbine. The generator spins to produce electricity.

Hydroelectric energy is fueled by water, a clean energy source. Hydroelectric stations are dams with machinery inside. Water flows through the dam, turning the blades of a turbine. The turbine then spins a generator, producing electricity.

Geothermal energy is heat from Earth. Geothermal stations use steam from underground to spin the blades of a turbine. The turbine spins a generator that makes an electric current. Once the steam is used, it condenses and is pumped back into the ground as water.

Solar energy is considered to be clean energy. Each solar panel contains several dozen solar cells. These are devices that turn the sun's energy into electricity.

Identify Choose two energy sources from the ones you explored. How are the processes to produce energy alike? How are they different?

_____

_____

_____

Engineer It!
Tidal Energy

Scientists and engineers are working on tapping into tidal energy as another source of renewable energy.

Gravity helps produce tides—the predictable rise-and-fall action of the ocean. Huge amounts of seawater flow over the ocean floor in between tides. By anchoring turbines in areas of the ocean floor where tidal flow is strong, electricity can be produced.

AK-1000 is the world's largest tidal turbine. Its rotors have a diameter of 18 m (60 ft) and will harness enough tidal energy to generate electricity for more than 1,000 homes.

Define What are two **criteria** and two **constraints** that define the problem of building a tidal turbine?

_____

_____

_____

_____

 EVIDENCE NOTEBOOK Have you identified any sources of energy that could provide electricity to the house without being visible from the outside? Record your findings in your Evidence Notebook.

Putting It Together

Apply Test your knowledge of renewable resources by completing the questions below.

replaced	solar	dams	generators	water	wind

Choose the correct words that complete each sentence.

Renewable energy sources are those that can be _____ in a reasonable amount of time. Energy from the sun is called _____ energy.

_____ spins the blades of giant turbines to capture wind energy.

Hydroelectricity uses moving _____ to produce electricity.

Renewable Natural Resources

Cloudy Days, No Wind, Little Water

While sources of renewable energy won't run out, they can be affected by different factors. Explore the conditions below to learn more.

Explore Online

Solar, Wind, and Water Energy

a. Electricity from solar energy can come from large fields of solar panels and through an electricity-generating station. But solar panels can also be installed directly onto houses.

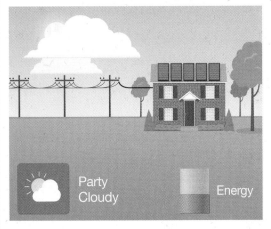
Party Cloudy — Energy

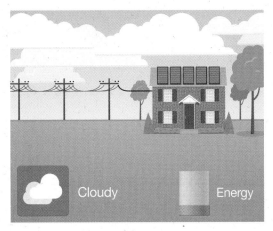
Cloudy — Energy

Summarize What can you conclude from the pictures of solar panels?

_____

_____

b. Wind farms are built in very windy areas because wind is needed to spin the turbines. Most wind farms have many wind turbines that are used together to capture energy.

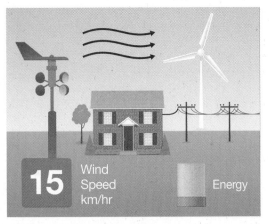
15 Wind Speed km/hr — Energy

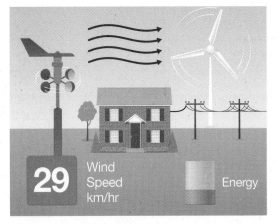
29 Wind Speed km/hr — Energy

What can you conclude from the images of this wind turbine?

_____

c. Hydroelectric dams are not set up at individual houses. Instead, the electricity is captured at the hydroelectric dam and sent to homes.

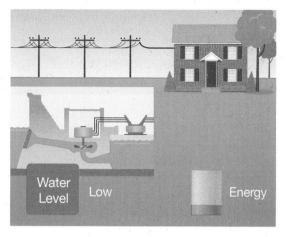
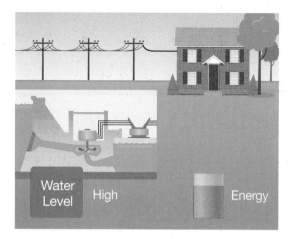

Identify Which of the following best describe the relationship between water and energy in a hydroelectric dam? Circle all that apply.

a. More water moving through the dam means less energy.

b. More water moving through the dam means more energy.

c. Less water moving through the dam means more energy.

d. Less water moving through the dam means less energy.

Analyze Based on the pictures you see here and on the previous page, what do you think are the benefits and drawbacks of using renewable energy sources?

_____

_____

Evaluate One of the drawbacks of many renewable energy sources is that there are times that they cannot be used to collect energy. For example, solar energy cannot be collected at night. How do you think scientists and engineers get around this problem?

_____

_____

When the renewable resources are not available, the house will get its electricity from another source, such as a power grid. Energy generated by using renewable technologies can be stored in batteries for later use.

 EVIDENCE NOTEBOOK Do you think that renewable sources of energy can generate electricity for a house by themselves, or are other sources of energy needed? Record evidence in your Evidence Notebook.

Do the Math
Bright Savings

Think about the light bulbs in your home. Chances are that you'll see a variety of types. It used to be that the most common light bulbs were incandescent light bulbs. Newer types, such as compact fluorescent bulbs, are far more efficient and use less energy.

Explore the chart to discover more.

	High-efficiency incandescent, 43-watt bulb	Compact fluorescent, 15-watt bulb
Average number of hours it lasts	2,000	10,000
Typical yearly cost	$3.50	$1.20
Benefits	• uses less electricity than regular incandescent bulbs • less air and water pollution from fossil fuel stations that supply most electricity • last longer than regular incandescent bulbs, so less use of resources to make them	• uses less electricity than high-efficiency incandescent bulbs, which means less use of fossil fuels that produce most electricity • less air and water pollution from electricity-generating stations
Drawbacks	• burns hotter than regular incandescent bulbs	• contains a small amount of poisonous mercury that can be released when broken or thrown out in regular garbage

Explain Have you seen high-efficiency, incandescent, or compact fluorescent bulbs in your home? Which would you choose to use, and why?

_____

_____

_____

Compare the cost of a high-efficiency incandescent bulb and a compact fluorescent bulb. Use the space below to solve the problem, and then select the best answer.

a. The high-efficiency incandescent bulb costs 2 times as much as the compact fluorescent bulb.

b. The high-efficiency incandescent bulb costs about 3 times as much as the compact fluorescent bulb.

c. The high-efficiency incandescent bulb costs almost 5 times as much as the compact fluorescent bulb.

d. The high-efficiency incandescent bulb costs 6 times as much as the compact fluorescent bulb.

Analyze How many hours longer will the compact fluorescent bulb last compared to the high-efficiency incandescent bulb? Use the space below to solve the problem, and then select the best answer.

a. The compact fluorescent bulb will last 2,000 hours longer.

b. The compact fluorescent bulb will last 4,000 hours longer.

c. The compact fluorescent bulb will last 8,000 hours longer.

d. The compact fluorescent bulb will last 10,000 hours longer.

Benefits and Drawbacks

Renewable energy resources have benefits. The table below shows the benefits and drawbacks of several. Fill in the source for each type of energy.

| hydroelectric dam   solar panels   wind turbines   geothermal station   biomass station |

Source	Benefits	Drawbacks
	• will never be used up • reduces waste that goes in landfills	• can pollute air
	• clean energy source • will never be used up	• habitat loss • can harm wildlife • floods valuable land • expensive to build or set up
	• clean energy source • will never be used up	• can harm wildlife • can be noisy and unattractive • only works well on windy days
	• clean energy source • will never be used up	• expensive to build or set up • works better on sunny days
	• will never be used up	• can be used in a limited number of places • releases chemicals that can pollute air • expensive to build or set up

Identify Which benefits do all renewable sources of energy share? Select all that apply.

a. Their waste is easy to clean up.

b. They are cleaner than nonrenewable resources.

c. They will never be used up.

d. They work well in all environments.

Solar panels, hydroelectric dams, and geothermal stations can be expensive to build or set up. Both wind turbines and hydroelectric dams can harm wildlife. Biomass and geothermal stations may also pollute the air. Hydroelectric dams can cause habitat loss and even flood valuable land. However, they still cause less pollution to the air than nonrenewable resources, and they will never run out.

Explain Match each cause with its effect.

Cause

People think that these can be unattractive and make too much noise.

At times, these can flood valuable land and harm wildlife.

Effect

A community meeting is being held to stop the construction of a hydroelectric dam.

Some people prefer not to install wind turbines.

Going Green Debate

Choosing energy efficiency means to use products or technologies that perform the same function but consume less energy. As you have discovered, a compact fluorescent bulb is more energy-efficient than a traditional incandescent bulb. It uses much less electrical energy to produce the same amount of light.

How do you think renewable and nonrenewable resources compare? Which one do you think is more energy efficient? Consider both types of energy resources, then fill out the table below.

- Under *Claim*, fill in either "renewable" or "nonrenewable" to complete the sentence.

- Then under *Evidence*, give three facts that support your claim.

- Use facts from this lesson and the previous one. Research any other facts you need to use as evidence.

Claim
I think that _____ energy is the most efficient type of energy.
Evidence
a. _____
b. _____
c. _____

Language SmArts

Making Connections

Describe Discuss your answer with a classmate. Do you agree or disagree with his or her claim? Explain why or why not.

_____

_____

Conclude Solar panels can power homes. Why don't all homes have solar panels?

_____

_____

Plastics from Plants

Typical plastics are made from petroleum (oil), a fossil fuel. But did you know that we now have ways to make plastics from plants?

Procedure

a. Place 1 tbsp of cornstarch in a plastic bag. To the cornstarch, add 1 tbsp of water, 2 drops of corn oil, and 2 drops of food coloring.

b. Seal the bag until it is nearly closed. Tilt the bag so that all of the contents settle in a corner, then squish them together to mix.

c. Your teacher will place the contents of the bag in a microwave-safe container. Then, your teacher will put the container in the microwave for 20 seconds.

d. Allow the container to cool before removing the contents.

e. Shape the "plastic" you've made with your fingers. Once you've worked with the plastic for a few minutes, dip it in water.

Materials

- zip-top plastic bag
- measuring spoons
- 2 drops of food coloring
- 2 drops of corn oil
- 1 tbsp of cornstarch
- 1 tbsp of water
- microwave oven
- microwave-safe container
- safety goggles

Plastic water bottles, such as this one, are often made from petroleum.

Some plastic water bottles are made of plant-based materials.

Analyze Think about how simple it was to take a few different corn-based ingredients and turn them into a substance you could work into different shapes. Think also about what happened when you dipped the corn plastic into water. How do you think corn plastic compares to petroleum-based plastics in terms of environmental impact?

_____

_____

_____

Solar Energy!

Solar energy has many different uses. Write what solar energy is being used for on the line below each picture.

_____

_____

_____

_____

_____

_____

_____

_____

Language SmArts

Cause and Effect

Identify Choose the best words to complete each sentence.

> microwaves pollution electricity generator turbine fan

Most renewable energy sources do not cause _____.

Rooftop solar panels turn sunlight into _____. Wind spins

the blades of a _____ to make electricity.

Running on Sunshine

Objective

Suppose you are going on a camping trip in a remote spot. You don't have a battery-powered stove. The park has banned campfires. You decide to build a solar water heater to bring on the trip. You need the heater to heat to the maximum possible heat in 20 minutes. You have a budget of $10.

Collaborate to design a solar water heater.

Materials	Budgeted materials
• water container	• cardboard box—$5
• scissors	• black paint—$3
• tape	• black construction paper—$2
• thermometers (2)	• plastic wrap—$1
• timer or watch	• packing peanuts—$2
• measuring cup	• newspaper—$1
• 2 separate cups (same size)	• cotton balls—$1
	• aluminum foil—$3
	• wax paper—$2
	• paper plates—$1
	• plastic shopping bags—$1
	• paper towels—$1

Find a problem: What problem will you solve to meet this objective?

_____

Procedure

STEP 1 Research with your group to find more information about which materials you can use that will help you capture solar energy. Think about the color and texture.

STEP2 Define the problem.

What are your criteria?

_____

_____

What are your constraints?

_____

STEP3 Brainstorm solutions for your device. Then, **evaluate** your solutions and **choose the best.**

_____

STEP 4 Develop and test a model. On a separate sheet of paper, draw your device with your group. Label its parts. On the lines below write how you will test it. Get your teacher's approval before you follow your plan.

_____

_____

_____

_____

Build and test your device. You will be recording your results in your data table.

Test your solar water heater outside. Fill 2 separate cups with equal amounts of water. Use the thermometers to record the starting temperature of the waters. Record the temperatures in the table under 0. Place the heater in bright sunlight. Place one cup of water in the heater. Place the other in the sun nearby. Record the temperature of the water in both cups every 5 minutes for 20 minutes.

How will you know whether your results are correct? What steps can you take to ensure your measurements are correct?

_____

_____

_____

What was the highest water temperature you recorded? What was the difference between that temperature and your starting temperature?

_____

_____

_____

STEP 5 **Evaluate** your test. Use the data from your test.

Compare the water inside the heater and the water outside the heater. Did your materials help your heater work? If not, could you improve your design with a larger budget? How?

_____

_____

_____

_____

STEP 6 **Develop and test a new model:** Develop a new model. Take the improved heater outside and retest. Record the temperature in the table every 5 minutes for 20 minutes. What improvement did you make to your design?

How well did your improved design meet the criteria and constraints? Explain.

_____

_____

STEP 7 **Communicate** to compare your results to those of the other groups in your class. Did their solar water heaters work better than yours? Why or why not?

_____

_____

Make a **claim** based on your investigation. Cite **evidence** from your design and other designs to support your claim. Explain your **reasoning**.

_____

_____

_____

_____

_____

Think of other problems you would like to solve related to solar water heaters.

_____

_____

Discover More

Check out this path . . . or go online to choose one of these other paths.

People in Science & Engineering

- **Sort It Out**
- **The Hoover Dam**
- **Careers in Science & Engineering**

Elon Musk

Elon Musk is a successful businessman and physicist who has founded several companies. In 2004, one of his companies began work on producing electric cars. The cars run on lithium ion batteries and go about 275 miles before needing to be recharged.

In 2013, Musk announced a new transportation idea in which people ride in pods through interconnected tubes. The pods would run on solar energy and move at speeds of 700 miles per hour.

He also developed a rechargeable lithium-ion battery made for home use. It stores electricity and can provide backup electricity in case of an outage. It can also save up to 20% on a home's electric bill.

Elon Musk

An electric car

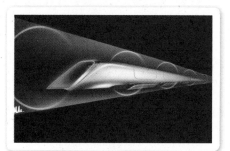

Transportation pod

Rechargeable lithium-ion battery for home use

Analyze Suppose you live in an area where you normally use renewable resources. What would happen if one day those resources were not readily available to you? Think about environmentally-friendly technologies that you can use instead to meet your energy needs.

The History of Cars and Batteries

Most cars today run on fossil fuels such as gasoline and diesel fuel. It is possible, however, for cars to run on electricity alone. Electric cars are not common, but they are becoming more popular.

This timeline shows some important events in the development of electric cars and the batteries that help them run.

Development of Electric Car Batteries and Cars

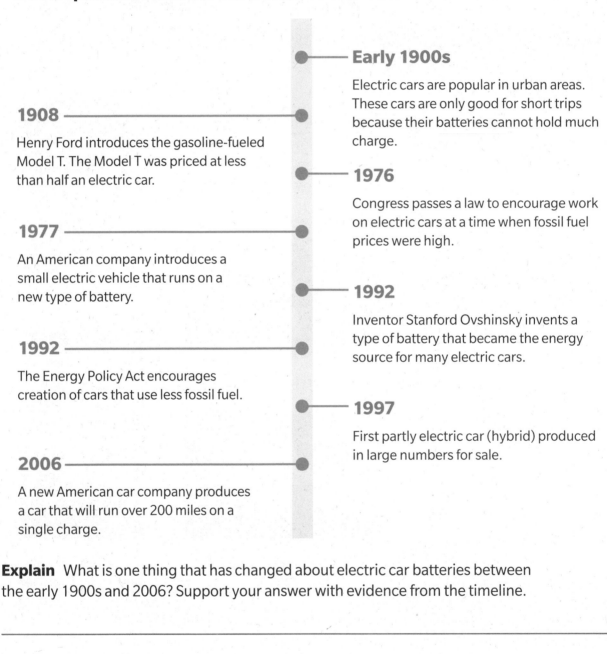

Early 1900s

Electric cars are popular in urban areas. These cars are only good for short trips because their batteries cannot hold much charge.

1908

Henry Ford introduces the gasoline-fueled Model T. The Model T was priced at less than half an electric car.

1976

Congress passes a law to encourage work on electric cars at a time when fossil fuel prices were high.

1977

An American company introduces a small electric vehicle that runs on a new type of battery.

1992

Inventor Stanford Ovshinsky invents a type of battery that became the energy source for many electric cars.

1992

The Energy Policy Act encourages creation of cars that use less fossil fuel.

1997

First partly electric car (hybrid) produced in large numbers for sale.

2006

A new American car company produces a car that will run over 200 miles on a single charge.

Explain What is one thing that has changed about electric car batteries between the early 1900s and 2006? Support your answer with evidence from the timeline.

_____

_____

_____

_____

Lesson Check

Name _____

Can You Explain It?

1. Remember the house you saw at the start of the lesson? Most houses have wires connected to them that bring electricity for people to use day and night. How does this house get its electricity? Consider the following:

   • evidence of how the house is getting energy in the form of electricity

   • wires and other things that are necessary to send electricity to a house from an electricity-generating station

   • potential downsides to how this house gets its electricity

EVIDENCE NOTEBOOK Use the information you've collected in your Evidence Notebook to help you cover each point above.

_____

_____

_____

_____

_____

_____

_____

_____

Checkpoints

Choose the correct answer.

2. A family wants to use a renewable energy resource to help provide electricity to their house. Which of these energy resources should they use?

   a. oil   **b.** solar   **c.** coal   **d.** natural gas

3. A new electricity-generating station wants to avoid using any nonrenewable energy resources to produce electricity. Which energy resource should the station not use?

   a. solar

   b. geothermal

   c. hydroelectric

   d. natural gas

4. Read the sentence below. Choose the best phrase to complete the sentence.

> **it is available everywhere**
> **it never harms wildlife**
> **it will never run out**
> **it produces little or no pollution**

There are many benefits to using

renewable energy sources. One of the benefits of using a renewable energy

source is that _____. Another benefit is that

_____.

5. Match each cause with its correct effect.

Cause	Effect
Large spinning blades of turbines turn.	Geothermal stations can cause pollution.
Dams are built.	Birds can be harmed.
Some processes release water that contains chemicals.	Valuable land can be flooded.

6. Choose the correct answer. An electricity-generating station doesn't want to use biomass to produce electricity due to its drawbacks. Which of these is a drawback of using biomass to produce electricity?

   a. It is nonrenewable.

   b. It is very costly to use.

   c. It can be used in few places.

   d. It can produce air pollution.

Lesson Roundup

A. Choose the correct words to complete each sentence.

coal	pollution	natural gas	biomass
oil	severe weather	radiation	

One example of a renewable energy resource is _____. One drawback

of nonrenewable energy resources is that they can produce _____.

B. Fill in the term of the renewable resource to the row that features the benefits and drawbacks.

hydroelectric	solar	biomass	wind	geothermal

Renewable resource	Benefits	Drawbacks
	• renewable • clean energy	• Panels need sunshine to work. • Equipment is expensive.
	• renewable • clean energy	• Long, spinning blades can hurt birds. • Turbines are loud. • A large area of land is needed.
	• renewable • clean energy	• Dams are expensive. • Reservoirs flood valuable land. • Dams can harm fish by changing the depth and temperature of rivers. • Reservoirs take away wildlife habitats.
	• renewable • low pollution	• It is only available in certain areas. • Some processes release water containing chemicals that can pollute the air.
	• renewable • less pollution than fossil fuels	• Burning the material can produce air pollution.

C. What other information did you find out about the benefits or drawbacks of using renewable resources for energy?

_____

_____

Adding Renewable Energy

You are a small-town mayor in the western United States. Your local public utility company depends on fossil fuels. The city council has decided that the city must diversify its energy sources. You have chosen to focus on adding a solar energy station to the mix.

DEFINE YOUR TASK: How will you know if your project is successful? Before beginning, review the checklist at the end of this Unit Performance Task. Keep those items in mind as you proceed.

_____

_____

_____

RESEARCH: Use online or library resources to learn about solar energy stations. Find out how other cities or regions have successfully added renewable energy stations. Note which methods seem most efficient. Cite your sources.

_____

_____

_____

_____

_____

BRAINSTORM: Brainstorm solar energy station benefits and issues. Use what you have learned about renewable energy impacts to identify what your strategy must achieve to be effective and safe.

_____

_____

_____

_____

PLAN YOUR PROCEDURE: Consider the questions below as your group plans its energy strategy. Be sure to address the resources you will need and your overall goals and limits. Write a few sentences below to briefly summarize your strategy.

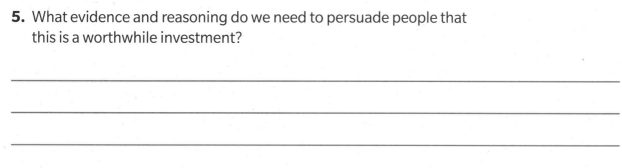

1. What kind of solar energy stations should we build, and where should we build them?

2. What environmental costs do we need to consider?

3. How can we educate the community about our plans?

4. What possible objections from the community do we need to plan for?

5. What evidence and reasoning do we need to persuade people that this is a worthwhile investment?

_____

_____

_____

_____

REPORT: Make a document that details your energy strategy. Describe any concerns and how they will be addressed. List steps to complete the development. Be specific and complete.

COMMUNICATE: Present your plan to your class orally and with multimedia. Explain the reasoning behind your plan, and discuss possible ways to revise and improve it.

☑ Checklist

Review your project, and check off each completed item.

_____ includes a statement defining your group's task

_____ includes research into and consideration of various solar energy strategies with sources cited

_____ includes a list of solar energy concerns to be addressed

_____ includes a description of solar energy stations and locations

_____ includes a plan of action, including educating the community

_____ includes an explanation of how the solar energy station will be paid for

_____ includes an oral presentation with multimedia support

Unit Review

1. Which fuel source is made entirely of once-living plants? Circle the correct choice.

   a. oil

   b. coal

   c. uranium

   d. natural gas

2. Which of the following is true of the product sold here? Circle all that apply.

   a. It is a natural resource.

   b. Its use causes pollution.

   c. It is a renewable resource.

   d. It is a nonrenewable resource.

3. Use the word bank to complete the sentences.

Oil	Uranium	Coal	Natural gas

   _____ and oil are the remains of once-living things

   that died in the ocean millions of years ago.

   _____ does not come from once-living material.

4. Which statement best describes the energy transformation shown here? Circle the correct choice.

   a. electrical energy into light and heat

   b. sound and motion into light and heat

   c. light and heat into sound and motion

   d. electrical energy into sound and motion

5. Use the word bank to complete the sentence.

| stored | created | reduced | increased |

Energy from this source can be _____ for times when it
is not being produced.

6. The methods used to generate electricity from both wind and water
are similar. Explain how they are alike.

_____

_____

_____

_____

_____

_____

_____

7. Which choices describe the temperature in
the pot of water? Circle all that apply.

a. 0 °C

b. 32 °F

c. 100 °C

d. 212 °F

8. This energy station uses gravity-driven water flows in the ocean. What best describes it?

Circle all that apply.

a. nonrenewable energy station

b. renewable energy station

c. geothermal energy station

d. tidal energy station

9. Use the word bank to complete the sentences.

renewable energy	nonrenewable energy	solar	wind	fossil fuel

A _____ is a useful, concentrated source of energy,

but is _____. Tidal, _____, and

_____ energy are _____. They can be

replaced naturally in a reasonable time.

10. Suppose you wanted to move into a wilderness cabin and use only renewable energy sources. What would you need to know about the location? Why?

_____

_____

_____

_____

Shaping Landforms

Explore Online

You Solve It: Evidence of Change You can apply ways to shape Earth's surface. Then, you collect observations to explore the effects of weathering and erosion that surround you.

Lake Tahoe was formed by active fault lines.

At a Glance

UNIT PROJECT
Nearby Weathering

Have you ever left something out in the rain or sunshine for a long time and noticed that it changed how that object looked? For this project, you will investigate forms of weathering that happen at or near your school and decide what you can do to help prevent more weathering in the future.

Work with a partner to develop a question about the forces of weathering you want to answer.

Ask Your Question Think about the last time you saw something that was weathered. What were the causes of weathering that you identified? Write a question that you will investigate as you perform your analysis of nearby weathering.

_____

_____

_____

Materials Think about how you will need to perform this investigation. What materials will you need?

_____

_____

To carry out this investigation, go around your school with your team and teacher to locate evidence of weathering. Take pictures or draw your observations. What kinds of things will you be looking for?

_____

_____

_____

_____

Research and Plan Make a plan for how you will carry out this investigation and how you will be able to make changes so that weathering is reduced. As you make your plan, consider the following:

- What force(s) could have caused the weathering?

- Can that force(s) be prevented? How can further weathering be avoided?

- How will you make a plan to affect weathering?

_____

_____

_____

_____

_____

_____

_____

Develop your plan, and share your ideas with your team. As a group, vote on the plan that your group wants to present to the rest of the class. It's possible that you might want to take parts of different plans to make one master plan. Think about ways to improve your plan by looking for opportunities where your plan might not work. Can your plan be improved?

_____

_____

_____

_____

_____

Analyze Your Results Look for evidence of cause and effect in the data you found. Using your investigation, make a conclusive observation about weathering at or near your school.

_____

_____

_____

_____

Restate Your Question Write the question you investigated.

_____

_____

_____

Claims, Evidence, and Reasoning Use **evidence** to make a **claim** that answers your question. Explain your **reasoning.**

_____

_____

_____

_____

_____

Review your investigation. What evidence from your investigation supports your claim?

_____

_____

_____

_____

_____

Discuss your reasoning with a partner.

Language Development

Use the lessons in this unit to complete the network and expand understanding of the science concepts.

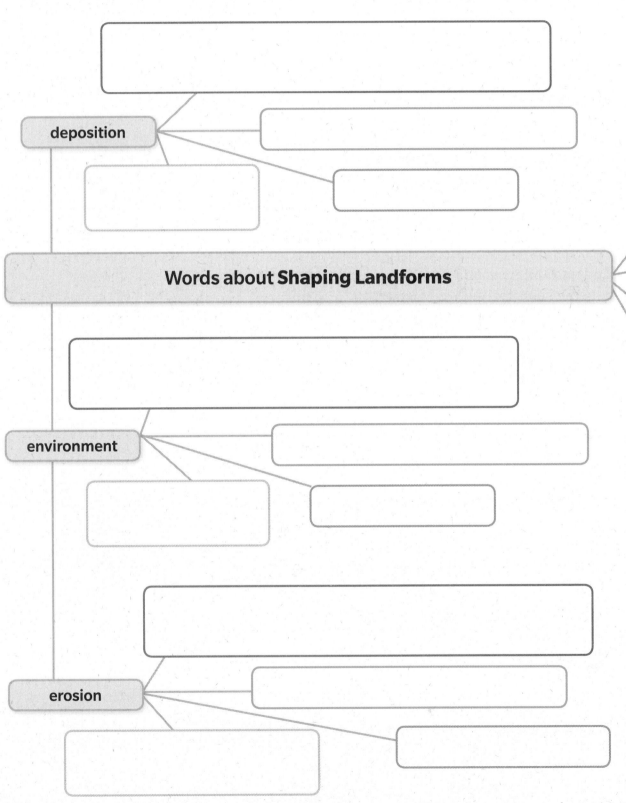

deposition

Words about **Shaping Landforms**

environment

erosion

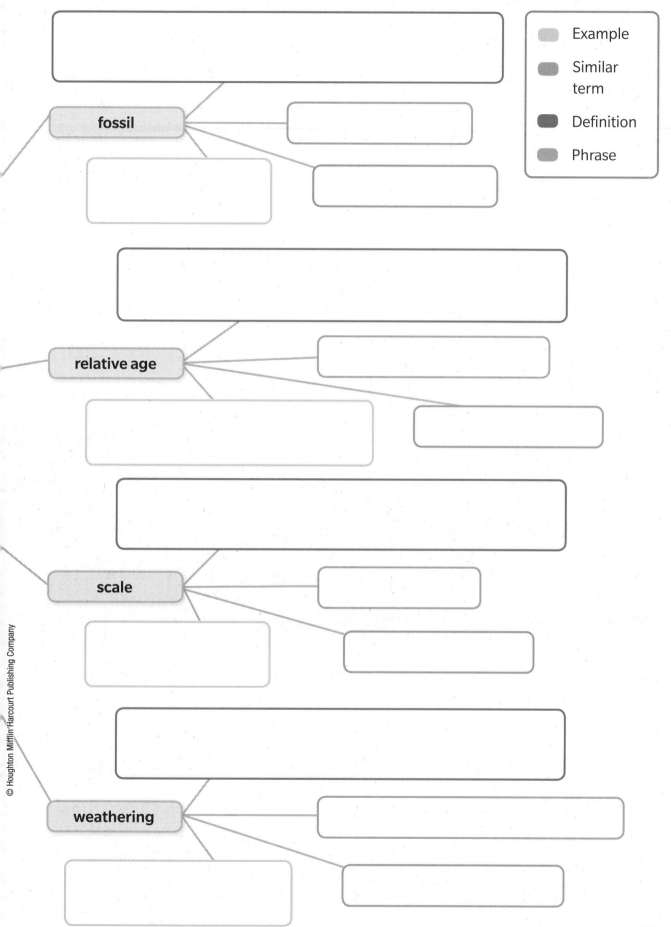

fossil

relative age

scale

weathering

Example

Similar term

Definition

Phrase

What Factors Shape Earth's Surface?

The Grand Canyon is a landform, or a natural land feature. People from around the world come to visit the Grand Canyon. Look at the photo above. What are some features of the landscape that you notice?

Explore First

A Sweet Test Have you ever wondered why mountains grow and shrink? Or how a beach changes size and shape? Use a small, lidded container, sugar cube, and water to model Earth's surface changes. Shake the sugar cube inside the closed container dry, then with a few drops of water. What happens? Sand, rocks, and other landforms can respond in a similar way to wind and water.

Can You Explain It?

Explore Online

A river flows through the bottom of this canyon. Imagine walking through the bottom of the canyon, near the river. What would you see and hear? Think about how the canyon may have formed.

How do you think this canyon formed? What could have reshaped the rock?

_____

_____

_____

_____

_____

_____

 EVIDENCE NOTEBOOK Look for this icon to help you gather evidence to answer the questions above.

Modeling How Far Sediment Travels

Objective

Collaborate as a team to develop a model and test the factors that affect how far sediments travel.

Materials

- fan
- butcher paper, 1.5 m per team
- masking tape
- 200 mL beaker of silt
- sand
- gravel
- meterstick
- stopwatch
- safety goggles

Procedure

STEP 1 There are many factors that affect how landforms change. Wind can change the way landforms look. Wind moves sediments from place to place. What questions come to mind when you think about that sentence? Write down as many questions as you can. Be ready to share them with the class.

_____

_____

_____

_____

_____

STEP 2 With your class, select the most important questions about wind moving sediments and changing landscapes. Write down the questions that your class thinks are the most important.

_____

_____

_____

_____

_____

STEP 3 How can you use a model to investigate the questions that your class picked as most important? Think about the materials your teacher shows you and what else you might need. Write your investigation plan on a separate sheet. Show it to your teacher to see if you can get the other things you need. If you use other things than those your teacher shows you, be sure to write them down in the plan.

_____

_____

_____

STEP 4 Carry out your plan, and record your results. Observe evidence of change. Present your data in a way that everyone can see what you did and what happened. You may wish to use a table or graph as a presentation tool. Or you might choose to make a poster.

STEP 5 Make a **claim** that answers the question or questions your class decided to explore. You may need to have a **claim** for each question. Support your **claims** with **evidence** from your investigation and **reasoning** to show how the **evidence** supports your **claim**. Record your **claims, evidence,** and **reasoning** below:

_____

_____

Take It Further

After your investigation, what new questions do you have about wind moving sediments from place to place? You can start your questions with "What happens if . . ." or "Is this always . . ."

_____

_____

Earth's Surface

Changes You Can See

Forces on Earth's surface constantly change, sculpt, and reshape rocks. Small changes might happen near you. Big ones might occur, too.

Have you ever noticed that sediment and debris get washed onto the sidewalk after it rains? This is an example of a local, or small-scale, change caused by Earth's surface processes.

Some processes that changed the way the sidewalk looks after it rains also changed the Sierra Nevada Mountains. Ice, wind, and running water have shaped these mountains.

Identify Using the pictures above, identify factors that shape Earth's surface.

_____

Apply The Sierra Nevada Mountain range had its wettest season with record-breaking rainfall. What kinds of changes do you think the water caused to the landscape, such as the rocks, soil, and debris? Explain your answer.

_____

_____

Do the Math
Calculating Changes

The Sierra Nevada Mountain range is growing! Some peaks are growing 1 mm every year. How many years will it take those peaks to grow 5 mm?

_____

_____

Earth's Changing Surface

There are many processes that constantly change Earth's surface.

Weathering is the breaking down of rocks on Earth's surface into smaller pieces. Weathering may occur in rivers when the current causes rocks to bump against one another and break apart.

Erosion is the process of moving weathered rock and soil from one place to another. This happens when rivers move rock and soil downstream. Factors such as wind and gravity can also cause erosion.

Deposition occurs when water slows downs and drops the rocks and sediment it carries. This occurs at the mouth of rivers and anywhere water stops moving. Sand dunes are also a result of wind deposition.

Analyze Water breaks down rock into smaller pieces during

    a. deposition.   **b.** erosion.   **c.** landslide.   **d.** weathering.

Describe Gold was discovered in California long ago. It was found in material that was worn away from the Sierra Nevada Mountains. People found the gold in Central Valley. Which natural process would have moved the gold from high in the mountains to the valley?

    a. weathering   **b.** erosion   **c.** deposition   **d.** landslides

Water Weathering

    Water is the main cause of weathering and erosion. In most parts of California, flowing water is the most important process that breaks apart rocks and moves them. Rainfall helps shape the land and affects the types of living things found in a region.

Explore Online

Rainfall shapes the land. When a lot of rain falls, it flows in many directions, washing away loose materials and moving soil to different places.

The strong currents of rivers, such as Kern River, can damage landforms by crashing into rocks and other structures.

The waters in Colca Canyon in Peru weathered and eroded parts of the land, carving Earth's surface.

Compare How are the processes of weathering in the examples above alike?

Moving Water!

Moving water, such as rain, rivers, and ocean, can change Earth's surface by wearing it away. It carries away soil and small pieces of rock known as *sediment*. Over millions of years, rivers can carve mile-deep canyons by weathering rock and eroding sediment downstream. Moving water can also change the path of a river.

Language SmArts

Close Reading

Moving water can reshape Earth's surface. But how can seemingly still water change a landform? What are some other ways water erodes landforms?

_____

_____

_____

Identify Choose the word to complete each sentence.

| erosion | weathering | deposition |

When water breaks off part of a cliff, _____ occurs. When part of the cliff falls

and water carries the rocks away, _____ occurs. Finally, the rock settles on a new

shoreline. This is called _____ .

EVIDENCE NOTEBOOK Think back to the beginning of the lesson when you shook the film canisters with sugar cubes and water. How does this resemble what you know about weathering and erosion?

Apply Sandy beaches form when waves break pebbles into smaller pieces. Ocean waves also weather rock and can move sand from one beach to another. Observe the images below. Circle where the evidence of change is taking place.

© Houghton Mifflin Harcourt Publishing Company

Water Levels

Water is a force that can cause weathering and erosion in both its liquid and solid forms.

Procedure

a. With a partner, fill a clear plastic cup halfway with water.

b. Use a permanent marker to make a line on the inside of the cup at the top of the water line.

c. Place the cup in the freezer overnight.

d. The next day, take the cup out of the freezer.

e. Observe the top of the water.

f. Write a claim about your findings related to water and weathering.

Materials
- clear plastic cup
- water
- permanent marker
- freezer

_____

_____

_____

_____

g. What data do you have to support your claim?

_____

_____

_____

h. Write or draw in your Evidence Notebook as you gather your evidence.

Language SmArts
Summarizing Landforms

Landforms change over time. Even the slightest changes to Earth's processes can cause landforms to grow bigger, break apart, or smooth over. Research one of California's most famous landforms, such as San Francisco Bay, Yosemite Half Dome, Lake Tahoe, or Death Valley. Work in groups to describe how the landform formed and explain the processes that have changed that landform over time in a multimedia presentation.

Death Valley is one of the hottest places on Earth and is known for its rocky environment and canyons.

Away It Goes!

As you've seen, water can cause weathering, erosion, and deposition. Gravity can, too! California Highway 1 in Big Sur was damaged during a landslide. During a landslide, soil, mud, and rocks move quickly down a slope because of gravity. Landslides can happen suddenly, especially after heavy rains or earthquakes.

Changes to Earth's surface can be seen from space. This satellite image shows California Highway 1 in Big Sur before the landslide.

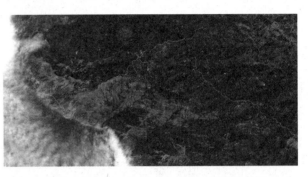

This satellite image shows California Highway 1 in Big Sur after the landslide. Look at both images and compare the changes.

Engineer It!

To Save or Not to Save ... That Is the Question

The Big Sur section of California Highway 1 has had more than 60 landslides! Engineers have cleaned and rebuilt the route in the past. Now, many wonder if this stretch is worth saving. Work with a group to develop arguments for rebuilding or not rebuilding the route. **Argue** Which do you agree with, and why? Compare and refine arguments based on evidence.

Highway 1 is a popular driving route in California. Without it, many people would need to find alternate roads to take to get where they need to go.

_____

_____

_____

Analyze Think about the considerations that engineers have to make when building a bridge on a highway. What are the limitations that they have? What are some of the **criteria,** or needs, for building the bridge?

_____

_____

_____

Cold as Ice

Liquid water becomes ice when its temperature drops to 0 °C or below. Then it becomes liquid again when the ice thaws or unfreezes. This cycle of freezing and thawing happens constantly. Can this pattern cause weathering and erosion? Examine the images to see how ice affects rocks.

1 There are small cracks in the surface of this rock.

2 Precipitation fills cracks in the rock with water. This usually happens after rain falls or snow melts.

3 If the temperature falls below 0 °C, water in the cracks freezes. The liquid water becomes solid ice.

4 When the temperature rises above 0 °C, the ice melts. Compare the crack now to the original one.

5 The crack is now wider. After this pattern repeats many times, pieces may break off, weather, and be carried away or erode.

Predict In the space below, draw and label what would happen next to the rock and ice. Write your own caption.

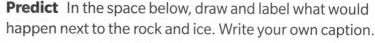

Explain What is the cause-and-effect relationship of ice and rocks?

_____

_____

Windy Forces

Wind may also cause weathering, erosion, and deposition. Over time, sand weathers rock by breaking it into smaller pieces. The weathered pieces of rock are carried by the wind. When the wind slows down, the pieces fall to the ground.

Winds can change the way landforms look. The Jacumba Wind Caves were weathered by winds over a long period of time.

Sand dunes are the result of deposition caused by wind. The wind leaves small piles of sand that grow as more sand is blown into a pile. Slowly, they become sand dunes.

Paria Canyon also shows off neat patterns that were carved by the wind over time.

Find an example of weathering by wind in your state. Draw a picture of your example and write a caption for it inside the box.

Identify Which of the following is an example of erosion?

a. water sitting at the bottom of a lake
b. rain breaking down a rock
c. the sunlight shining on a mountain
d. wind blowing away sediment

Putting It Together

Use the words below to complete the sentence.

| erosion | weathering | deposition |

Rock being worn away over time is an example of _____. _____ happens when sand moved by water settles at the bottom of a bank. An example of _____ is when wind moves loose sediment.

How Do Other Factors Shape Earth's Surface?

Water World

Water can change Earth's surface in direct ways, such as the sea eroding a sandy beach or a river carving a canyon into the land. But water can also allow living things to live, grow, and thrive in their environment. An **environment** is all the living and nonliving things that surround and affect an organism.

Deserts get less than 26 cm of precipitation per year. Because living things need water to survive and grow, this limits the number of living things that can live here.

Rain forests get 203 cm or more of rain in a year. This allows a lot of different living things to survive here. Think about how a single tree in the rain forest could itself be an environment for other living things.

Analyze What differences do you notice between the rain forest and the desert? Why do you think the amount of water is such an important factor in determining the number of living things in these environments?

_____

_____

_____

_____

_____

_____

223

Bactrian camels live in deserts. When water is scarce, the camel converts the stores of fat in its two humps to water and energy. This lets them live without water for months. When water is found, they can drink 135 L in just half an hour!

The sambar deer is a large animal that lives in parts of South and Southeast Asia. It lives in a variety of forests, from tropical dry forests to tropical rain forests. Sambars prefer to be near water, where they can find many plants to eat.

Infer How do you think the behaviors these animals have allowed them to survive in the environment?

Living Things Change Their Environments

Just like water, animals, plants, vegetation, and other living things, or *organisms*, can change the physical features of Earth's surface. Observe the images to see how organisms affect their environment.

As the roots of plants grow, they widen the cracks of the rock, sometimes making rocks split or fall away. This is a form of weathering.

Meerkats live in burrows. Digging a burrow creates a hole in the ground and moves dirt to the surface. This dirt may be eroded by wind or rainwater, or it may be mixed with the dirt at the surface.

© Houghton Mifflin Harcourt Publishing Company • Image Credits: (tl) ©Philippe Michel/

Ivy is a type of plant that grows up and around other objects. As ivy climbs, it sends out small roots that change their shape to cling to the surface the ivy is climbing. These roots can push into cracks in rock.

Evaluate Circle which processes are described in each example.

an animal chipping its way through rock to use as a home

a. weathering   **b.** erosion   **c.** deposition

when a tree's roots grow in a crack of a boulder and the boulder breaks into two pieces

a. weathering   **b.** erosion   **c.** deposition

Organism Cause and Effect

Look at the images to learn how some living things change their environment. Then write the effects caused by these changes.

Beavers are dam builders. By toppling trees across streams, they cause the level of water behind the dam to rise.

This type of termite builds large mounds out of soil. When the mound erodes due to wind or rain, the termites deposit fresh soil to replace what was lost.

_____

_____

_____

_____

_____

_____

Prairie grasses cover the landscape in the Great Plains. When a river floods its banks, the grasses' roots help keep the wet soil in place.

 EVIDENCE NOTEBOOK What evidence is there that plants and animals play a role in how landforms change?

 Language SmArts

Understand Cause and Effect

Think about the photos and information in this section. Fill in the chart below with the missing cause or effect.

Cause	Effect
The amount of water in an environment goes up.	
	Ivy roots can cause weathering when they grow into rock.
Beavers build dams.	

Discover More

Check out this path . . . or go online to choose one of these other paths.

People in
Science &
Engineering

• **Deposition Rate**
• **The Last Ice Age**
• **Careers in Science & Engineering**

Anjali Fernandes

Anjali Fernandes researches to learn how Earth's surface changes over different time periods. She studies how sediment is transported and where it is deposited in both land and water environments.

Fernandes specializes in the formation and changes of channels. A channel is a landform caused by water cutting into Earth. Channels can form over long periods of time by slow-moving water, or quickly by fast-moving floods.

One method Fernandes uses in her studies is field research. This means that she goes to where channels exist and studies them. She also uses laboratory experiments to learn about the movement of sediments and how sediments are deposited in channels.

Anjali Fernandes studies Earth's changing surface.

Identify Think of a question you would like to ask Fernandes about her work.

_____

_____

_____

_____

Opinion Fernandes does both fieldwork and laboratory experiments. If you were a scientist, do you think you would enjoy fieldwork or laboratory work more? Why?

_____

_____

_____

Determine What kinds of changes in Earth's surface would you most like to study?

_____

_____

_____

Do the Math

Measuring Erosion

Each year, water erodes the cliff beneath Horseshoe Falls, Canada. Horseshoe Falls is part of the larger Niagara Falls. Between the years 1842 and 1905, erosion was constant at about 1.16 meters per year.

During the 63 years between 1842 and 1905, how much did Horseshoe Falls erode in meters? in feet?

Lesson Check

Name _____

Can You Explain It?

1. Now that you've learned about factors that shape Earth's surface, explain how you think this canyon formed. Be sure to do the following:

- Explain how the river changed the canyon.

- Describe how weathering and erosion changed the canyon.

- Describe how plants, animals, and other organisms could have helped change parts of the canyon.

EVIDENCE NOTEBOOK Use the information you've collected in your Evidence Notebook to help you cover each point above.

_____

_____

_____

_____

_____

Checkpoints

Answer the questions about how weathering, erosion, and deposition change Earth's surface. Choose the best answers to the questions.

2. Which statement describes the shapes of and dunes?

   a. They are the result of wind deposition.

   b. They were built from water currents.

   c. They are a factor of water erosion.

   d. They are a result of water weathering.

3. Write the word in each blank that makes the sentences correct.

| erosion | deposition | weathering |

When a meerkat wants to find a new home, it must dig into the sand,

making a hole in the ground and moving dirt to the surface. Moving dirt is an

example of _____ . Once the dirt settles, this is an example of

_____ .

4. Which of these would cause erosion? Choose all that apply.
   a. wind
   b. plant roots
   c. downhill stream
   d. broken rock

5. Write the word in each blank that makes the sentence correct.

| ice | weathering | sand dunes | gravity |

_____ can occur when _____ forms inside the cracks in rocks.

6. Which description is an example of erosion?
   a. Ocean waves move sand from one beach to another.
   b. Plant roots break rock beneath the surface of Earth.
   c. Tree roots break parts of a sidewalk.
   d. Heavy blocks of ice crack rocks to form caves.

Lesson Roundup

A. Write the word or phrase in each blank that makes the sentences correct.

melt	reshape	break apart
join together	loose materials	solid rocks

Moving water can _____ Earth's

surfaces. Rivers, for example, can make rocks

_____ and carry them to other parts

of the environment. Heavy rains can wash away

_____ and deposit them in new places.

B. Describe what water, ice, wind, and plants have in common.

_____

_____

_____

_____

C. How can you observe the phenomenon of erosion?
   a. Measure the height of a mountain and monitor the height over time.
   b. Study the temperatures at which water freezes into ice.
   c. Predict how large plant roots will grow.
   d. Follow the weather patterns to see when it will be dry and hot.

D. Which statement about wind is correct?
   a. It can cause rocks to freeze and break.
   b. It can erode loose pieces of sand.
   c. It can make immediate changes to rock.
   d. It can change the direction water flows to avoid erosion.

What Affects How Quickly Earth's Surface Changes?

Landslides are natural hazards that change the shape of the land.

Explore First

Earth Relay Work in groups of three, and assign each person on your team to play the role of weathering, erosion, or deposition. The "weathering" student breaks apart a piece of paper by ripping it, then passes it to the "erosion" student. The "erosion student" carries it to the "deposition" student, who makes a new landform with all the pieces of paper. Speed up and slow down these processes to reenact how the processes happen in real life.

Can You Explain It?

Explore Online

Earth's surface is changing constantly as forces reshape rocks. Sometimes these forces act quickly, while other times they cause more gradual or slow changes. You feel the wind every day. It blows right by you, but did you ever stop to think of how it changes Earth? Do the changes happen gradually or suddenly? Landslides are less common than wind. They can cause rock, soil, and other structures to change. At what rate do these changes occur?

Explain Do you think the changes to Earth's surface caused by wind and landslides happen quickly, or do you think they take time?

_____

_____

_____

_____

_____

_____

 EVIDENCE NOTEBOOK Look for this icon to help you gather evidence to answer the question above.

The Rate of Change

Objective

Collaborate with a partner to investigate, observe, and measure the effect of slope on erosion.

Form a Question What question will you investigate to meet this objective?

_____

_____

_____

Materials

- paper cup
- sharpened pencil
- plastic drinking straw
- scissors
- small piece of modeling clay
- piece of cardboard 31 cm square
- soil
- ruler
- large bottle filled with water (approx. 2 L)

Procedure

STEP 1 Working with a partner, carefully punch a hole near the bottom of the cup with the pencil. Use the scissors to cut a couple of inches from the straw. Push the straw into the hole. Press the clay around the straw to seal any openings around it.

Why is it important to seal the hole with clay?

_____

_____

STEP 2 Place the piece of cardboard on the ground. Shape some dirt into a mound under one end of the cardboard to raise it about 2 in. off the ground so that the cardboard has a slight slope.

How would you describe the slope of the cardboard?

_____

_____

STEP 3 Spread a thin layer of soil over the cardboard. Place the cup on the raised end of the cardboard, with the straw pointing downslope. Block the end of the straw with your finger while your partner fills the cup with water.

What does the water in the cup model?

_____

_____

_____

STEP 4 Take your finger off the straw, and allow the water to flow out onto the top of the soil. Observe how fast the water flows as well as the shape of the stream. Record your results in the box below.

Observations:	

How does the flow of the water affect the soil on the cardboard?

_____

_____

_____

STEP 5 Now use a stable prop to raise the high end of the cardboard to about 6 in. so that it has a steeper slope than before. Repeat step 4 for this second trial. Record your results.

Observations:	

What does this set of steps model?

_____

_____

_____

Did water flowing over a steeper slope or a lower slope produce more erosion?

_____

_____

_____

Compare your results to the results of other groups. Describe any similarities or differences you notice.

_____

_____

_____

State a **claim** that is related to your question at the beginning of this activity.

_____

_____

_____

Cite **evidence,** and explain your **reasoning** to support your claim.

_____

_____

_____

_____

What is one new question you have about the ways in which scientists study erosion?

_____

_____

_____

Fast Changes

It Can Happen in an Instant

The surface of Earth is constantly changing. New mountains, rivers, and lakes are formed, and old ones disappear. A lot of these changes happen slowly. However, there are also many forces that cause landforms to change quickly.

Landslides occur when part of the land breaks apart and falls. Mudslides occur when the land becomes soaked with water and the muddy earth and debris falls down.

Volcanic eruptions can cause fast or slow changes to Earth. When volcanoes erupt, lava and other debris can destroy parts of the land very quickly. Volcanic eruptions make slow changes when they create new islands.

Earthquakes come on suddenly and the changes they make to the Earth can happen very quickly. The force of an earthquake can break rocks and crack the ground.

Identify What are some other factors that can cause fast changes on Earth's surface?

_____

_____

_____

_____

_____

Hurricanes are tropical storms that bring heavy winds and rains. They occur quickly and can cause structural damage and pull out trees.

Floods are overflows of water. They are strong and can move quickly over or through whatever is in their paths. Floods can destroy natural and human structures such as river banks and bridges.

Analyze Which of the following is an example of a fast change to Earth's surface?

    a. a volcano creating a new island in the ocean

    b. an earthquake that breaks apart the ground

    c. a river that flows through a canyon

    d. a windy day that makes small trees shake

Speeding Things Up

Certain events in history have had major impacts on Earth's surface in just a short amount of time.

Northern California has an active volcano! It erupted in 1915, creating a crater, causing flooding, and producing mudslides.

The Landers earthquake took place in 1992 near Landers, California. With a magnitude of 7.6, the Landers earthquake buckled roads and caused rockslides in the mountains in just a matter of minutes.

Major landslides occurred in La Conchita, California, in 1995 and 2005 when a lot of rainfall loosened the earth. The landslides caused land to fall on top of homes.

In 1997, floods devastated parts of Northern California. After a lot of snowfall in the Sierra Nevada Mountain range, warm rains melted the snow, causing flooding. The floods weathered and eroded the land.

Apply What are fast changes to Earth's surface that have occurred in your area? What were the causes of those changes?

_____

_____

Evaluate What kind of fast-changing effects can rainfall have on the earth?

    a. It can flood Earth's surface and cause an earthquake.

    b. It can lead to heavy winds that cause trees to fall down.

    c. It can cause soil to loosen and break apart, causing a landslide or mudslide.

    d. It can make lava harden into mountains.

EVIDENCE NOTEBOOK Think of the landslide at the start of the lesson. How do landslides cause weathering, erosion, and deposition? Record your observations and reasoning in your Evidence Notebook.

Landslides and mudslides both cause fast changes to the shape of the land. Landslides occur after earthquakes, volcanic eruptions, or heavy rains. Mudslides occur because of water-soaked ground. Gravity causes rocks and debris to fall downward during both landslides and mudslides.

Infer Which pictures could likely have loose rocks rolling and cause a landslide?

a.   b.   c.   d.

Engineer It!
Preventing Future Landslides

In 2017, parts of Northern California experienced extreme flooding that caused roads to close due to mudslides. Engineers worry about hills and mountains that have angles greater than 35 degrees. These have a higher chance of rocks tumbling down them. What **criteria** and **constraints** do engineers need when preventing future mud- and landslides?

_____

_____

_____

Language SmArts
Summarizing

Write a summary about fast changes to Earth's surface. Include the factors that can be involved and how they affect weathering, erosion, and deposition.

_____

_____

_____

_____

Slow Changes

Slow and Steady

Some events cause fast changes to Earth's surface. There are also events that cause slow changes. Different factors affect the speed of change or the rate of erosion—the time it takes materials to move from place to place.

Explore Online

Plants can squeeze their way through the soil and slowly wedge pieces apart. These pieces are not moved very far. The amount of rainfall is a factor that can affect how fast plant roots grow.

Sand dunes form when wind blows sand particles into mounds. It takes time and a lot of wind for them to form. Climate wind patterns can affect how fast or slowly sand dunes form.

The Yosemite Half Dome is a giant rock formation in Yosemite National Park. It formed when a slow-moving glacier was strong enough to slice off part of the mountain, leaving the half dome that you see today.

A slow-moving river can weather land structures and cause erosion and deposition. A slow-moving river takes longer to make structural changes because it does not have as much force. Both fast and slow-moving rivers still take years to change the landscape.

Identify Name another factor that can affect the speed at which Earth's surface changes. Explain how that factor causes certain processes to speed up or slow down.

_____

_____

_____

Apply Which factor is involved in plant roots squeezing through soil and rock to break apart parts of Earth?

a. wind   **b.** rainfall   **c.** glaciers   **d.** eruptions

Pushing Through

A glacier is a river of ice moving downhill, often very slowly. Glaciers are found in the cold polar zones or cold, high mountain valleys. Glaciers weather rock beneath them. They scrape and cut rock they slide over. Glaciers also cause erosion by pushing the broken pieces of rock under them and on top of them as they move. Deposition occurs when glaciers melt and leave the rock they carried behind.

Explore Online

As this glacier moves, it pushes rocks along with it.

Glaciers change the land they flow through.

As the ice melts, glaciers also leave sediment behind.

Compare When the temperature rises above 0 °C, ice thaws and becomes liquid again. Freezing and thawing or melting happens constantly in nature. It causes change to Earth's surface. The movement of glaciers does, too. Do these changes happen quickly, or slowly? Compare and contrast the two processes.

	Glacier	Freezing and thawing
Speed		
Effect		

Argue Use the evidence in your completed table to explain which process has a greater effect on the land: glaciers or freezing and thawing.

_____

_____

_____

_____

EVIDENCE NOTEBOOK Wind can take time to cause changes to Earth's surface. What is the relationship between the speed of the wind and how much Earth's surface can change? Record your reasoning in your Evidence Notebook.

Water Processes

Weathering, erosion, and deposition happen at different speeds. Among other forces, the speed of change can be affected by the amount of water, the angle of a slope, and rate of the deposition.

Explore Online

Changing the Shape of Land

Look at the images, and label them with letters for the correct descriptions shown below.

a. Heavy rain can cause mudslides. When the ground is steep, water and mud can slide down faster due to the force of gravity. This causes more erosion.

b. Waves cause weathering and erosion on rocky beaches. The force of the pounding waves splits and chips rock. Then the water carries the pieces away.

c. A swiftly flowing stream carries sediment and rocks downstream, causing erosion.

d. Falling water caused by gravity weathers the stone under the falls. Erosion causes pieces of rock to drop away. Then deposition piles the rocks up under the falling water.

Compare and Contrast Describe the relationship among weathering, erosion, and deposition. When weathering happens quickly or slowly, what effect does this have on erosion and deposition?

_____

_____

Language SmArts
Categorizing Information

Complete the table with these possible causes and effects:
waves, swift current, or mudslide.

Cause	Effect
Heavy rain pours down a steep slope of bare soil.	
	Weathering splits and breaks the rock of a cliff.
	Erosion occurs as rocks move downstream.

Do the Math
A Waterfall over Time

It took one year for 2 cm of rock to erode under a waterfall. Look at the table to see the effect of the waterfall over time. Fill in the table for the unknown amount of erosion.

2 years	50 years	100 years	1,000 years	10,000 years
4 cm	100 cm			

HANDS ON Apply What You Know
Steady Streams

Processes on Earth's surface have factors that influence the speed at which they change landscapes. Plan and carry out an investigation to examine the effect of water on the rate of erosion by making a physical model of a river. Choose one of the categories to model how water affects the rate of erosion: different types of materials on a slope, rate of water flow, and vegetation.

How did a change you made in your experimental system cause a change in the speed of weathering, erosion, and deposition?

_____

_____

Blast Off!

Sandblasting is a technique that is designed for removing paint, rust, or other coatings from things such as cars, steel beams, pipes, and other objects. Sandblasting can smooth a rough surface or roughen a smooth surface. Compressed air is used to spray sand at an object at high speed. The friction from the sand hitting the object physically blasts particles off the object's surface.

This is a sandblaster in use. What natural process do you think inspired the invention of the first sandblaster?

Compare and Contrast How do you think the sandblaster compares to weathering and erosion? What is the difference between a rock that is sandblasted and one that is not?

_____

_____

_____

Moving wind or water has energy. The faster the wind or water moves, the more energy it has. Fast water or winds, with a lot of energy, can erode more sediment than slow moving water or wind.

HANDS-ON Apply What You Know

A Slower Process

With guidance from your teacher, use a piece of sandpaper to remove paint from a piece of wood. Keep track of how much time you spend actively sanding the material and how much debris ends up on the sandpaper or the table. Compare the results with the sandblaster photo. Explain the factors that account for the differences between sandblasting and sanding by hand.

In places that receive very little precipitation, there isn't much erosion, weathering, or deposition that's caused by water or organisms. But rock and sediment in these places can still be eroded and weathered in other ways.

Sand and Time

The images that follow show how wind makes slow changes to landforms over time. Think about how climate can affect how fast or slow wind weathers, erodes, and deposits parts of the land.

Explore Online

Changes over Time

Study the pictures closely. Choose the factor that is involved in each example.

a. Wind transports sand across the landscape. Some of this sand comes into contact with parts of a large boulder. Over time, the boulder is worn away.

Before

After

- **a.** wind depositing the boulder
- **b.** windblown sand weathering the lower part of the boulder
- **c.** moving water eroding the lower part of the boulder

b. Wind can transport sand and other types of sediment from the base of a hill.

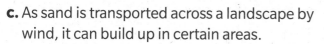

Before

After

- **a.** wind erosion on the lower part of the slope
- **b.** deposition of sand at the top of the slope
- **c.** moving water eroding the base of the hill

c. As sand is transported across a landscape by wind, it can build up in certain areas.

- **a.** deposition of sand
- **b.** weathering of sand
- **c.** moving water deposits sand and erodes dunes

Before

After

The different processes you've learned about change Earth's surface all around the world. The rate at which changes occur depends on many different factors.

Evidence of Change

Explore Online

Observe and record the changes that have occurred and are occurring above. Include the force that caused the change.

Image	What's happening
a. plant roots	
b. waterfall	
c. rocks at base of slope	
d. digging animal	

Putting It Together

Choose the correct words to complete the sentences.

| gravity | time | climate | temperature |

The weathering caused by waterfalls is related to _____. _____ is a factor that affects how fast winds blow or whether an area gets rainfall.

Finding Change

Objective

Collaborate with your team to model processes that produce change on Earth's surface, and determine what kinds of evidence those processes leave behind.

Form a question What question will you investigate to meet this objective?

_____

_____

Materials
• 4 cookie sheets with raised edges
• sand
• fan
• ice cubes
• modeling clay
• wooden stirring sticks
• beaker or small jug of water
• ruler
• safety goggles

Procedure

STEP 1 Go to the station your teacher assigns you to. Make observations of the model at your station. Record your observations. Then rotate through the other stations and record your initial observations. When done, return to your original station.

Why do you think there are four different stations?

STEP 2 Find your station below, and complete step 2 for that station.

• **Hillside model:** Use a small stack of thin books to slowly elevate the height of the sandy end of the cookie sheet. Watch the sand. When it begins to slide downhill, record the height of the higher end of the cookie sheet. Leave the cookie sheet in that position so that other groups can observe the same results.

• **Sand dune model:** Turn on the lowest speed of the fan at one end of the cookie sheet, and observe what happens. Record your observations in the data table. Turn off the fan and leave the model so that other groups can record their observations.

• **Glacier model:** Use a book to gently prop up the end of the cookie sheet nearest the ice cube. Firmly press the ice against the clay, and slowly slide the ice down the slope. Record your observations in the data table. Leave the model alone so that other groups can record their observations.

• **Beaver dam model:** Use the wooden stirrer or alternate materials to build a beaver dam across the middle of the river. Be sure that the dam is relatively watertight. Slowly add water to the river on just one side of the dam, and observe what happens. Record your observations. Leave the model alone so that other groups can record their observations.

STEP 3 Rotate through the stations again, recording your observations. Compare your observations and experiences with the models as a class, and revise your data table, if needed.

List your comparisons below. How were your observations similar and different?

_____

_____

_____

_____

Model	Initial observations	Observations after change
hillside		
sand dunes		
glacier		
beaver dam		

Describe the changes to Earth's surface you modeled in this activity. Include the forces that caused these changes in your descriptions. Use the terms *weathering, erosion,* or *deposition* as well as other terms if they fit your results.

_____

_____

_____

_____

_____

_____

_____

How could you modify one of the setups in this activity to model how earthquakes can trigger erosion? Suggest one modification of materials and one modification of how you physically handle the model.

_____

_____

_____

Make a **claim** about factors that change Earth's surface.

_____

_____

_____

Cite **evidence,** and explain your **reasoning** from the models to support your claim.

_____

_____

What is one new question you would like to ask about factors that change Earth's surface?

_____

_____

_____

Effects of Earth's Changes

People and Earth's Changing Surface

Natural processes change Earth's surface. There are some things people can do to limit damage and still protect the environment. For example, planting more trees and other vegetation keeps soil and earth from becoming too loose and wet, which can lead to mudslides and landslides. If there are more trees and vegetation when rains fall, then more roots can soak up the water from the ground.

River erosion in California means that sand and sediment are being moved to other parts of the state or out at sea.

The All-American Canal is a waterway made by people. It flows through one of the driest regions of California. The canal's water allows people to grow crops in an area where they normally would not be able to.

Planting trees along riverbanks can help slow down river erosion.

Because fast-flowing water can erode land quickly, most rivers erode on their banks and cause the river to move and flow in new directions. Rivers define many property boundaries, even the southeastern edge of the state of California at the Colorado River. If a river bank erodes, people's properties can get smaller. If river water reaches buildings, the foundations can be worn away and the buildings will fall down. If people build protection for their home, they must consider the possible damage to the neighbors' properties and the possible damage to the natural river system.

 EVIDENCE NOTEBOOK Now that you've learned some more about the rate of change to Earth's surface, do you think there are ways to prevent landslides? Record your response in your Evidence Notebook.

Analyze Think of an erosion problem, or possible problem, that you have in your area. What measures do you think people could take to slow down the erosion? How would those measures affect the natural environment?

Beach Erosion

Worldwide, beach erosion changes Earth's surface. Erosion can speed up depending on the force of the ocean's waves.

These pictures show a seaside town in England, named Birling Gap. The town is near cliffs by the sea. The cliffs are made of a very soft rock called chalk. Strong waves pound the cliffs, especially during storms.

1905: This picture shows several houses at Birling Gap. They are a short distance from a cliff that drops into the sea.

1930s: Compare this photo to the one from 1905. You can see that some of the cliff has fallen away.

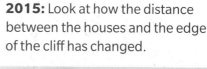

1970s: In this photo from the 1970s, more of the cliff has disappeared.

2015: Look at how the distance between the houses and the edge of the cliff has changed.

What are some engineering solutions that you can think of for beach erosion?

_____

_____

Language SmArts What happened to the distance between the houses and the cliff from 1905 to 2015? What caused this change?

_____

_____

_____

Engineer It!
Wind Barriers

Wind is one of Earth's processes, but too much of it can cause weathering and erosion. Strong winds or too much wind can also destroy crops and affect agriculture by blowing away soil.

Natural wind barriers, such as trees or shrubs, help slow down the wind and can prevent wind erosion and weathering. Human-made wind barriers, such as silt barriers, keep soil where it should be. This protects landscapes and agricultural properties.

How can this silt barrier be used to reduce erosion?

Fences like this are designed to protect properties from blowing sand and snow.

Evaluate solutions In your Evidence Notebook, develop a prototype of a wind barrier solution. Describe the technology and its connection with science and natural processes.

_____

_____

Communicate If your solution is used, do you think it would affect the rate and speed at which wind causes erosion? Explain how. Present your solution to your class.

_____

_____

Putting It Together

Evaluate Can people prevent natural processes that cause weathering, erosion, and deposition?

_____

_____

_____

Discover More

Check out this path . . . or go online to choose one of these other paths.

People in Science & Engineering

- **Extremes!**
- **The Science of Slopes**
- **Careers in Science & Engineering**

Kerry Sieh

Kerry Sieh is a well-known geologist and seismologist. A geologist studies the earth, and a seismologist studies energy waves such as those caused by earthquakes.

In Sieh's early career, much of his time was spent studying the San Andreas fault in California. By studying the fault, Sieh made an important discovery. He learned how often the San Andreas fault produced large earthquakes in California.

Sieh discovered that very slow processes have been causing small changes along the fault line for the past 40 years and that these small changes could add up to one big change if a large earthquake were to occur.

Kerry Sieh is an American born scientist who studied and worked in California.

Sieh studied the Sunda megathrust, which is a great fault line under the sea. His studies allowed him to predict earthquakes and tsunamis in Asia.

Explain How has Sieh's work helped people to understand seismic activity?

_____

_____

_____

Aaron Velasco

When people ask Aaron Velasco, "What's shaking?" he knows the answer. When Velasco became interested in learning more about Earth's processes, he decided to become a seismologist. Velasco made an important discovery when he found that drilling for oil and gas can cause earthquakes to happen. He has also studied tsunamis and worked with other scientists to make a system to warn people when a tsunami is coming.

By studying patterns of the past, landforms, and other geological and seismic data, seismologists can form predictions about future events that would cause very fast and devastating structural changes to Earth's surface. Having this information can help save lives and environments.

As a geologist and seismologist, Aaron Velasco works all over the world to research energy and activity that occurs inside Earth.

The San Andreas fault in California is an active fault that causes small, slow changes and rarely large, fast changes to Earth's surface.

Explain How could digging for oil or gas cause changes in the Earth?

_____

_____

Evaluate What factors do geologists and seismologists who work with structural damages to Earth's surface need to consider about weathering, erosion, and deposition as they work?

_____

_____

_____

Lesson Check

Name _____

Can You Explain It?

1. Now that you've learned more about other factors that shape Earth's surface, explain how this rock formed. Be sure to do the following:

   • Describe what the rock probably looked like before it changed.

   • Explain what forces shaped the rock.

   • Explain whether the changes to the rock probably happened slowly or quickly.

   • Predict what might happen to the rock in the future, based on patterns that you see.

   • Use the terms erosion, weathering, and deposition in your answer.

> **EVIDENCE NOTEBOOK** Use the information you've collected in your Evidence Notebook to help answer these questions.

_____

_____

_____

_____

_____

_____

_____

_____

Checkpoints

2. What effect does gravity have on structural changes to Earth's surface?
   a. Plant roots are pushed up and out of the soil.
   b. Cracks along the ground are made over long periods of time.
   c. Rocks, water, and mud fall from higher points to lower points.
   d. Digging animals are prevented from burrowing too far into the earth.

3. Choose the correct words to complete the sentences.

bigger	quickly
slowly	smaller

Fast flowing water erodes _____. As banks erode away, people's

properties can get _____.

4. Which force likely caused the changes
shown in the picture?
   a. wind
   b. rainfall
   c. glacier
   d. vegetation

5. Which process is best depicted in this image?
   a. Sand was deposited by wind.
   b. Glaciers carried sand to this new location.
   c. Gravity forces the piles up higher.
   d. Sand is being weathered by water.

6. Choose the correct word or phrase to complete each sentence.

is	is not	can	cannot

In places that have very little precipitation, there _____ a lot of

erosion, weathering, or deposition caused by water or organisms. Rock

and sediment in these places _____ be eroded and weathered

by other causes.

Lesson Roundup

A. Which was responsible for creating the landform shown in the picture?

   a. flood

   b. landslide

   c. glacier

   d. waves

B. Which can cause structural changes on Earth?
Choose all that apply.

   a. vegetation   **c.** clouds

   b. glaciers   **d.** floods

C. Choose the correct words to complete the sentences.

fast	slow

Floods, hurricanes, landslides, mudslides, and earthquakes are examples of

things that cause _____ changes to Earth's surface. Glaciers, trickling

streams, and wind are examples of things that cause _____ changes to

Earth's surface.

D. Which factor can influence how long it takes for plant roots to weather rocks in the ground?

   a. rainfall   **c.** wind

   b. gravity   **d.** waves

E. Why is it important to know about the patterns of change and how long it takes for changes to happen?

   a. It can tell people whether plants will be able to continue growing in certain areas.

   b. It can serve as a reminder to not make quick changes to landforms.

   c. It can keep people focused on the future and not on the past.

   d. It can help people protect themselves and the environment from future changes.

How Do Rock Layers Record Landform Changes?

Rocks can give clues about things that happened on Earth long ago. They can also provide evidence of how our planet has changed over time. Some of these rocks formed in ancient oceans. Some of them formed on dry land. What else might rock layers tell us about the past?

Explore First

Playing for Patterns With a partner, shuffle a deck of playing cards. Deal ten cards into a stack. Turn the cards face-up in a column, preserving the order in which they were dealt. Using the remaining cards in the deck, line up another card column that displays a similar pattern to the row you first dealt. Describe how the two patterns are alike.

The Cal Orcko is a location in Bolivia where dinosaur footprints are found on a steep wall of rock. The footprints belong to more than 200 different species of dinosaurs. The current rock layer and prints were revealed after a previous layer collapsed.

The rock face where the dinosaur footprints are found is nearly vertical. The depth of the prints suggests that they were left by large animals. How do you think they were able to walk on this rock?

_____

_____

_____

_____

_____

_____

EVIDENCE NOTEBOOK Look for this icon to help you gather evidence to answer the question above.

Layer by Layer

Objective

Collaborate with your group to investigate how to use evidence to determine what an environment was like.

Form a question: What question will you investigate to meet this objective?

_____

_____

Materials
- nature magazines
- colored pencils
- scissors
- circular stencils
- construction paper
- white construction paper for drawing
- tape

Procedure

STEP 1 Your teacher will provide you with magazines or other sources of images of present-day environments. Individually, each person in your group will choose a specific environment, such as a desert, swamp, or underwater habitat. From the materials provided, select an image that best represents your environment. It should show animals and plants that live there.

STEP 2 Use a stencil to cut out two to three round holes in a sheet of construction paper. The round holes will be windows that show some, but not all, of the organisms in your environment. After cutting the holes, place the construction paper over your drawing paper. Trace the cut-out circles on your drawing paper.

What do you think you are modeling by using paper to block portions of the images?

_____

_____

STEP 3 Draw or cut out a picture of the environment and its plants and animals. Be sure one plant or animal is in each circle you drew in step 2.

What do you think the climate is like in the environment you chose?

_____

_____

_____

STEP 4 Place the construction papers on top of your environment. Make sure that you can see plants and animals through the windows. Tape the pages together.

STEP 5 With your group, layer all the environments by stacking them one on top of another.

What are you modeling when you layer the different pictures on top of one another? What does the stack represent?

_____

_____

STEP 6 Trade your layers with another group.

STEP 7 Look at each layer of your new stack. Use the images you can see through the windows of each layer to identify each environment.

STEP 8 Talk with other members of your group about which environment came first and which came later.

List the environments in the chart, layer by layer, from oldest to youngest. Include observations that helped you identify the environments.

Relative age	Observations	Type of environment
1st environment		
2nd environment		
3rd environment		
4th environment		
5th environment		

By covering up most of the picture and leaving only a small window to see what lived in that environment, what do you think you modeled?

_____

_____

_____

Compare your results with those from another group. How are the results similar and different?

_____

_____

_____

_____

Based on where each layer is in the stack, which environment came first in this area? Which is the newest environment?

_____

_____

_____

Make a **claim** about fossils and environments, and cite **evidence** and explain your **reasoning** to support it.

Claim	Evidence

What is one new question you have about fossils and environments?

_____

_____

Layers of Rock

Observing Rock Layers

Have you ever seen layers of rocks along a highway or hillside? Have you ever wondered why they look the way they do? Conduct the activity below to explore these questions.

HANDS-ON Apply What You Know

Layered Landforms

Consider the rock layers you've seen. Different kinds of materials form layers that can become rock. Can you see patterns in rock layers?

Use the materials that your teacher has provided to follow the steps below.

STEP 1 With your group, select one of the materials. This will be the first layer in your jar.

STEP 2 Pour the material you selected into the jar at a steady rate for 4 seconds.

STEP 3 Repeat step 3 three times. Change the material and length of time you pour each time. Pour one time for 7 seconds, another time for 13 seconds, and another time for 10 seconds. However, always pour at the same rate.

Which rock layer in your model is the oldest? Which is the youngest?

_____

_____

How did pouring the material for different amounts of time affect the layers? What can this tell you about rock layers in nature?

_____

_____

Layer upon Layer

These photos show rocks in places from different parts of the world. Study the photos to construct an explanation about patterns in the rocks.

Akaroa Head is in New Zealand, a country near Australia. The ocean has shaped this landform.

The Alps are mountains that stretch across Europe. Ice and water have shaped the Alps.

Cabrillo National Monument is in San Diego, California. Layers of rock have been washed away by ocean waves over a long time.

The rock layers surrounding this waterfall are near Stoney Creek, Ontario. The rock layers show many different colors of rock.

The rock formations shown on this page are located in different parts of Earth. Construct an explanation, based on evidence, to describe patterns in these rock formations.

_____

_____

Telling a Story

If you looked at another team's layered landform, what would you be able to tell about it? Based on your own experience, you would likely be able to correctly describe the relative age of the layers. Scientists can usually tell the relative age of rocks by looking at their order in a sequence. **Relative age** is the age of one thing compared to another. Relative age explains things in terms of older and younger.

Identify Choose the words or phrases that correctly complete each sentence.

at the top	at the bottom	in the middle
older	younger	

In a sequence of rock layers, the oldest layer of rock is _____ of

the sequence. The youngest layer is _____. As the layers form,

_____ rock forms on top of _____ rock.

Engineer It!
Built to Last

The ancient Romans were master builders. They built thousands of kilometers of roads paved with rock. They also used rock materials to construct buildings such as the Roman Coliseum, which is still standing after more than 2,000 years.

Engineers study the **design** and makeup of Roman structures to learn how Roman engineers were able to make their structures last for so long. They look at how the materials were assembled and how they are held together. Research shows that to bind together layers of rock, the Romans used types of cement and concrete made of rock materials that could not be easily dissolved.

Plan Think about the different types of glue that you have used. Design a test for measuring glue strength. Then propose at least one way to improve it. How do you think this is like the work of engineers studying Roman building materials?

_____

_____

_____

Roman structures were built out of cement and concrete that used special combinations of materials to stay strong for so long.

Layers of materials had to be used to give structures their strength.

California Rock Clues

Which is easier to move: a large rock or a small one? The small one, of course! The size, shape, and composition of rock layers can tell us about how and where they formed and how they have been shaped.

A Long, Long Story!

Use a thin highlighter or a pen to trace the tops and bottoms of as many layers as you can in this photo of a rock formation found in Capitol Reef National Park. Then number the layers, marking the oldest layer as *1*.

Infer Where in the image is the oldest layer of rock found?

_____

_____

_____

Explain What can the thickness in the rock layers tell you?

_____

_____

_____

_____

_____

There are patterns in the color of the rocks. What could these patterns mean?

_____

_____

_____

When one rock layer differs from another, it shows that the layers formed in different ways. For example, layers might contain different materials. This would mean that the environment where the rock formed had to change between the time one layer formed and the next. Different thicknesses of layers also suggest differences in conditions when the layers formed. Thicker layers might have formed over longer periods of time when conditions remained steady.

Do the Math
Canyon Clues

You have data about five rock layers labeled *A* through *E*. Use these clues to determine the relative ages of the rocks from youngest to oldest, and complete the table.

- Layer A is 200 million years old, but it is 100 million years younger than Layer C.
- Layer B is the top layer of rock.
- Layer C has more layers above it than below it.
- Layer D is older than Layer B and younger than Layer A.
- Layer E is 480 million years old.

Youngest	
1	Layer _____
2	Layer _____
3	Layer _____
4	Layer _____
5	Layer _____
Oldest	

Language SmArts
Conducting Research

Explain Rocks that form from sediment are called *sedimentary rock*. Use online or print resources to find out more about sedimentary rocks and how they form. Identify a type of sedimentary rock that has similarities to your rock layer model. Describe the similarities.

_____

_____

_____

_____

_____

_____

Rock Layer Clues from Past Living Things

Dinosaur bones are examples of fossils. **Fossils** are the preserved remains or traces of an organism, such as a plant or animal. Fossils provide clues about the age of rocks and changes in the environment.

HANDS-ON Apply What You Know

Fossils in Order

Apply Use the materials your teacher provides to follow the steps below.

1. Your index cards represent rock layers. The shapes represent fossils found in the rock layers.

2. Use this key to sort the cards to represent the order and relative ages of rock layers.
   - The diamond is the youngest fossil.
   - The card on the bottom of the stack contains the square.
   - The star fossil formed in a layer above the layer showing a heart.
   - The star fossil is older than the circle.
   - The only fossil older than the heart is the square.

_____

_____

Which "fossil" in your deck of cards is the oldest? _____

What can you tell about the layer that contains the diamond fossil?

_____

Fossils form in different ways. A mold fossil is the imprint of an organism left in rock that surrounded it. A cast fossil forms when minerals enter into the empty space in a mold fossil and fill it to resemble the shape of the organism. A trace fossil is a footprint, burrow, or some other evidence that an organism was in a place, but not a shape left of the organism itself.

Identify the types of fossils shown below.

| Mold fossil | Trace fossil | Cast fossil |

Fossils and Environments

Your backyard might once have been at the bottom of a sea. Fossils in your area can tell you whether that was the case.

Fossils and Ancient Lands

Read the descriptions of these fossils. Then write whether the organism lived in a land or water environment.

Ammonites were animals that lived in coiled shells. They moved by squirting jets of water from their bodies.

_____

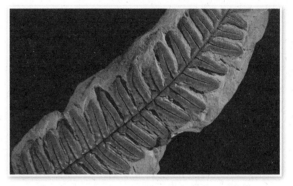

Ferns are plants that live in warm, moist environments such as rain forests. This fossil is an imprint of a fern leaf.

_____

Fish use their fins and tails to move. They often move in large groups, called schools.

_____

Snails these small animals lived within coiled shells. They slid slowly along surfaces with one flat foot made of muscle.

_____

Fossils provide clues about the type of environment in which the organisms lived. Fossils such as fish and ammonites indicate an aquatic environment. Finding fossils of organisms such as ferns and other plants indicates a land or terrestrial environment.

Make a claim about the type of environment an alligator-like fossil would indicate. Support your claim with evidence and reasoning.

Apply Match the environment with the most likely fossil that may be found there.

Scientists can study fossils and get a sense for how old they are. They do this by testing and analyzing the mineral deposits in the fossil. Knowing the age of the fossils helps scientists determine approximately how old rock layers. This data provides clues to how fast or slow the environment has changed over time.

tropical rain forest	bear
desert	seashell
beach	cactus
forest	palm tree

Predict From studying fossils, we learn that aquatic environments can become dry land over time. Study the environment shown in the picture below. In a group, discuss what it could look like millions of years in the future. In the box below, draw a rock formation that has fossils that represent this environment. Write a description of how the rocks would preserve the characteristics of the environment.

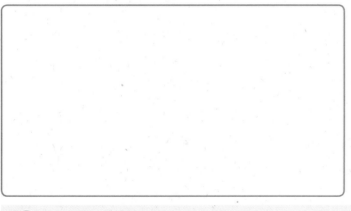

 EVIDENCE NOTEBOOK How can you use what you have learned to describe the fossil footprints found at Cal Orcko? Record your ideas in your Evidence Notebook.

Putting It Together

Explain Suppose you are studying a rock formation composed of multiple layers. Some layers are thicker than others, have different colors, and are made of different particle sizes. Apply what you learned in this section to make a claim supported by evidence about the processes that formed this rock formation.

_____

_____

_____

_____

Evidence of Environments

Seeing History

Many locations around the world are rich with fossils. Some of these places have rock layers where fossils from many types of organisms can be found. The fossils below were all found in one of these locations.

Identify the Fossil

Look at the fossils. Match each description to the correct fossil.

a. This fossil is a snake. You can see its backbone, skull, and ribs.

b. Small fossil shrimp are common in this area. This is one example.

c. The leaf of a plant clearly shows in this fossil. It is the leaf of a willow tree. Plants give scientists important clues to past environments.

d. Some rock layers here are full of fish fossils. Consider the types of environment in which fish were common.

Building the Story

Take a look at the picture. It shows several rock layers.

Analyze Describe the fossils in the rock layers and the types of environments they would have lived in.

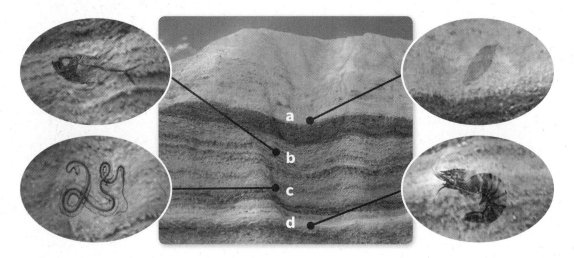

	Type of fossil	Where organism lived
Layer A	leaf	
Layer B	fish	
Layer C	snake	
Layer D	shrimp	

With fossils, you can infer the characteristics of the environment. Scientists look for similar evidence when they look at rock layers.

Identify Which rock layer is the oldest?

a. Layer A   c. Layer C

b. Layer B   d. Layer D

Analyze How do you know the layer you chose is the oldest?

a. The oldest layer is usually on top.

b. The oldest layer usually has land animals.

c. The oldest layer is usually on the bottom.

d. The oldest layer is between layers of limestone.

Infer Use the evidence to identify the oldest type of environment represented in these rock layers.

a. desert   c. forest

b. water   d. mountain

EVIDENCE NOTEBOOK You learned that examining fossils allows you to make inferences about past environments. Go back to the Can You Explain It section and look at the Cal Orcko formation. Make an inference about the conditions at the time the fossils were made.

Evaluate Look at the four environments below, and read their descriptions. Use the rock layers on the previous page as evidence to number the environments in order of age, with 1 being the oldest.

This area was once covered by a freshwater lake. Many fish, turtles, and other aquatic animals lived here at that time. Terrestrial animals also lived on the land around the lake. They used the lake as a drinking source.

Willow trees once grew here. At the time, the climate was much warmer than it is today. It had a temperate to subtropical environment, unlike today. Summers were hot and humid, and winters were mild but sometimes cool. Some trees lost their leaves in the winter.

The area was also once covered by a saltwater sea. Many saltwater animals lived in the water, including clams, shrimp, sharks, and other fish.

At another time, the area was covered by a cypress forest. The ground was moist. Once in a while, organisms might become trapped in the mud in this environment.

Global Stories

The types of fossils found in any given location may also be found in other parts of the world. And the order in which fossils are found in rock layers is often the same at different locations around the globe.

Where Else?

Choose a fossil from this lesson that interests you. Research to find out where else in the world it has been found. List those places on a sheet of paper. Use a world map and colored pencils to mark where similar fossils have been found.

Language SmArts

Summarize You have read descriptions about environments that organisms lived in millions of years ago. How can you tell that environments on Earth's surface have changed over time? Explain.

_____

_____

Putting It Together

Analyze How can fossils serve as evidence of specific events and environments in Earth's history? How can they show patterns in that history?

_____

_____

_____

Choose the correct words to complete the sentences.

| shrimp | aquatic | plants |

The rock layers from the previous pages show change over time. The first animals

there were _____. This shows that the environment at the time was

_____. Over time, most of the water disappeared. A forest formed.

The forest had many types of _____ that are common in warm climates.

The Stories Rocks Tell

Rock Patterns

When you dig deep enough into rock layers, you can discover patterns. These patterns can tell us a lot about the kinds of changes that took place inside Earth over long periods of time.

 Apply What You Know

Disordered Days

You have seen rock layers that lay flat, one on top of another. But some rock layers are not quite so neat.

a. Label five pieces of paper with the days of the week, starting with Monday.

b. Stack the papers one on top of the other in the order of the days, with Monday at the bottom.

c. Before putting Thursday on the pile, remove Wednesday. Then put Thursday on top of Tuesday.

d. Finish by adding Friday.

e. Create a second set of layers by repeating the first two steps. Do not remove the Wednesday layer this time.

Compare and contrast the two sets of layers. Think about what the missing layer could represent if the layers were made of rock. What could cause a layer to be missing? Answer the questions below.

Apply How does the first stack model erosion? Which layers can be eroded? And what do you think would happen if erosion removed the third layer before the fourth layer formed?

_____

_____

_____

_____

_____

Layering Up

Recall that processes such as weathering, erosion, and deposition can add and remove rock layers. Think about how fossils can be used as evidence to identify places where these sort of changes have occurred.

Identify Study the rock formations at locations A and B. Use the fossils and your understanding of how layers form to write the correct numbers in the circles to identify the rock layers present at both locations. Explain your reasoning to a partner.

Breaks, gaps, and other patterns found in layers of rock can indicate past weathering and erosion. Look at the images below. Think about how erosion has revealed the history of the Western United States, resulting in landforms such as the Grand Canyon.

Over a long time, water cut deep through the Colorado plateau to form the Grand Canyon.

Today dozens of rock layers can be seen in the Grand Canyon.

Explain Studying landforms such as canyons, we can learn about the age of rocks and past environments. How does running water shape landscapes such as the Grand Canyon?

    a. Water carves land that is in its path and transports sediment to other places.

    b. Water helps trees and other vegetation grow, so the roots expand and break rock.

    c. Water settles in areas and stays there, so the rest of the environment forms around it.

    d. Water makes fast changes to landforms by constantly crashing down onto rock.

Rock Forms and Forces

Rock formations are like books that contain chapters about Earth's history. They can record changes that were caused by natural forces that were strong enough to bend and break rocks.

Analyze What do you think causes the position and layers of rock to be offset when the rock used to be continuous?

a. erosion   **b.** earthquake   **c.** wind   **d.** flood

Earthquakes are caused by forces that are active in Earth's interior. These forces can change the position of rock over time. Evidence of this motion is recorded in the rock layers.

Rocked and Rolled?

The same forces that cause earthquakes also cause rock layers to bend, break, fold, and tilt. Factors such as rock composition and depth below Earth's surface affect which of these features form.

Explore Online

Deep below Earth's surface, under high heat and pressure, forces can cause rocks to bend and fold.

Near the surface, forces cause faults. These are cracks along which large blocks of rock can move.

Under what conditions do rocks bend and fold?

Interpret Layers

Scientists use patterns in rock layers to read Earth's history. Examine the image, then answer the questions below.

Identify Circle the correct answer.

The oldest fossil is the fossil shrimp.
a. I agree because the shrimp fossil is in the oldest layer.
b. I disagree because the fish is in the oldest layer.

Interpret Circle the correct answer.

The snake lived after the fish but before the shrimp.
a. I agree because the snake fossil is in a younger rock layer than the fish fossil but in an older layer than the shrimp fossil.
b. I disagree because the snake fossil is in an older rock layer than the fish fossil and in a younger layer than the shrimp fossil.

 EVIDENCE NOTEBOOK You learned that rocks tell stories about the past. Go back to the Engage section and look at the Cal Orcko formation and explain whether or not scientists can read these fossils "like a book."

 Language SmArts
Close Reading

Summarize the way or ways that rock layers act as "record keepers" of Earth's history. Be sure to include the term *fossil* in your response.

_____

_____

_____

Discover More

Check out this path . . . or go online to choose one of these other paths.

People in
Science &
Engineering

- Changes in Environments
- Careers in Science & Engineering

Studying Evidence from the Past

Read these profiles of important people in science. The field of paleontology has changed over time.

Edward Cope

Edward Cope was a paleontologist who lived in the 1800s. He discovered the fossils of more than 1,000 species of extinct animals. Many of his discoveries were made during the 1860s. At that time, there was little technology to assist in locating fossils and recovering them.

In the late 1800s many new fossil deposits were being found in the American West. Fossil hunters like Cope competed to find new fossils first, and write about them. Great discoveries were made. However, people also sabotaged each other's reputations and work. And, sometimes fossil deposits were damaged or destroyed.

Analyze Did competition for fossil finds harm or help understanding of ancient life? Why?

_____

_____

_____

Luis Alvarez

In 1980, **Luis Alvarez,** along with his son, **Walter,** proposed a new explanation for the extinction of the dinosaurs. They claimed an asteroid hit Earth 65 million years ago. The result was the extinction of many species, including the non-birdlike (nonavian) dinosaurs.

The Alvarez's and their team had made an extraordinary **claim**. Here is the **evidence** they used to support it:

- A similar layer of clay is found all over the world.
- The layer is in rocks just before the mass die off of dinosaurs.
- The clay contains lots of a metal called iridium [eer•ɪH•dee•uhm].
- Iridium is rare on Earth's surface, but common in asteroids.

They **reasoned** that it would take a big explosion to spread iridium across all of earth so quickly. An asteroid collision would provide the "boom" and the iridium. It would also cause climate changes deadly to dinosaurs.

Identify Choose the correct words to complete the sentences.

species	metal	asteroid
competed	dinosaurs	fossils

Edward Cope discovered many species of extinct animals before technology existed to locate _____. Cope _____ with rivals to find many _____ of extinct life. Luis and Walter Alvarez proposed the idea that many dinosaurs were wiped out by an _____. Part of their evidence was deposits of a rare _____ found all over the world.

Lesson Check

Name _____

Can You Explain It?

1. Remember the image of Cal Orcko from the beginning of the lesson. How do you think these footprints can help scientists understand more about changes to Earth's surface? Be sure to do the following:

- Describe the kind of fossil you see in the picture and why it is important.

- Discuss what is unusual about the orientation of the rock layers.

- Explain what you think the Cal Orcko formation suggests about Earth's history and the relative ages of the rock in this area.

> **EVIDENCE NOTEBOOK** Use the information you've collected in your Evidence Notebook to help you cover each point.

_____

_____

_____

_____

_____

_____

_____

Checkpoints

2. Use the words in the bank to complete the sentences.

cast	mold	trace
environment	relative age	

Dinosaur footprints are an example of

_____ fossils. They can tell a lot about

the past _____ where the rock was found.

Fossils can also help figure out the _____ of rocks.

3. Choose the correct words to complete the sentences.

> youngest   thickest   oldest   thinnest

If there are four rock layers, the layer at the bottom is most

likely the _____. The top layer is most likely

the _____.

4. Which of these features would you expect to find in an aquatic fossil? Choose all that apply.
   a. the outline of seashells
   b. the molding of a bear's claw print
   c. the shape of a fish's fin
   d. the cast of a cat's jaw

5. What is similar about fossils of organisms that lived in the same time period found in different parts of the world?
   a. They are found in similar rock layers.
   b. They are the same shapes and sizes.
   c. They are all cast or mold fossils.
   d. They are found at similar times.

6. Infer why it could be possible to find the same type of dinosaur fossil in the third rock layer from the top layer in Spain and in the fifth rock layer from the top layer in England. Choose all that apply.

   a. It is not possible for one type of fossil to be in different layers.
   b. Some rock layers may have eroded in Spain but not in England.
   c. Dinosaurs are extinct in Spain, but they are not extinct in England.
   d. The environments changed at different rates in both locations.

Lesson Roundup

A. Choose the answer that correctly orders the environments represented by the rock layers to the right in order from oldest to youngest.

a. lake, swamp, grassland, forest
b. lake, grassland, swamp, forest
c. forest, grassland, swamp, lake
d. forest, swamp, lake, grassland

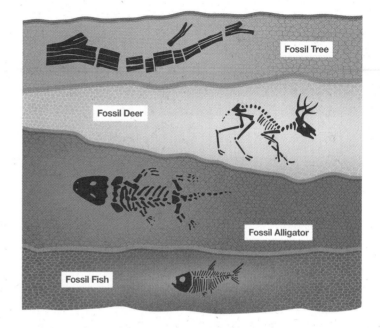

Fossil Tree

Fossil Deer

Fossil Alligator

Fossil Fish

B. What are some limitations of using fossils to learn about past environments? Choose all that apply.

a. Fossils are not common in many places.

b. Fossils might indicate more than one type of environment.

c. Fossils do not show enough detail to identify an environment.

d. There are many different types of fossils.

e. Fossils are often missing pieces.

C. Explain how rock layers form and how their patterns can show signs of changes, such as from an earthquake.

How Can Maps Help Us Learn about Earth's Surface?

Earth has many landforms, such as mountains, valleys, and plains. Maps can model the surface features of Earth. Lines on a map can show the shape of the land. Numbers on the lines tell how high or low the land is.

Explore First

Secret Feature What's the best way to find your way around a new place? A map, of course! Draw a simple map of your classroom. Choose a feature of the classroom, such as a bookshelf or certain person's desk, and mark it with an *X* on your map. Share your classroom map with a classmate. See if he or she can identify the object you meant from your placement of the *X* on your map.

Can You Explain It?

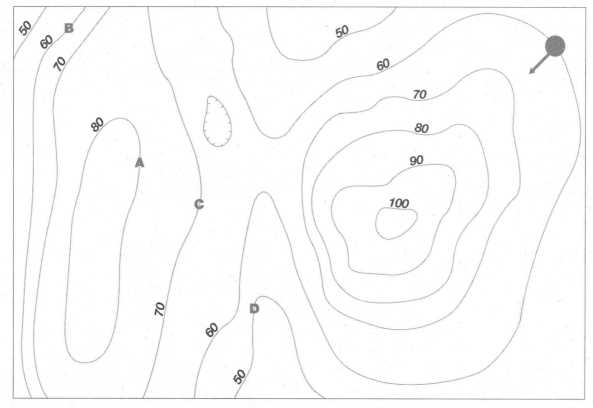

This is a topographic map. The lines and numbers tell the shape of the land.

Explain Imagine standing at the place marked by the red dot. What would you see if you looked in the direction of the arrow? How can you tell?

_____

_____

_____

_____

_____

 EVIDENCE NOTEBOOK Look for this icon to help you gather evidence to answer the questions above.

What Is a Map?

Map It Out

If you wanted to go somewhere you had never been before, how would you know how to get there? You would probably use a map. Maps are visual descriptions that show where things are located. They can give you directions. There are many different kinds of maps.

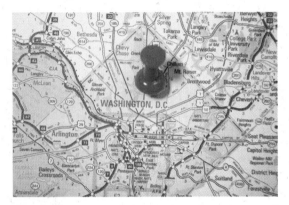

Printed road maps show not only major roads but also less traveled minor roads. Maps are changed and reprinted as new roads are constructed. Before the invention of smartphones or GPS, a family driving across the United States would carry a road map.

Global Positioning System (GPS) technology uses information from satellites. The GPS picks up information from satellites and uses it to determine your position on Earth. Using a map like this shows you exactly where you are while you are traveling.

Identify What is a disadvantage of a printed road map?

  a. Printed road maps cannot be used without a smartphone or GPS.

  b. They only show major roads and aren't very detailed.

  c. Printed road maps can be carried from place to place.

  d. When new roads are constructed or old roads are removed, a new road map needs to be printed.

How Many Maps?

Different maps show different things. You choose a map depending on what you want to use it for.

Explain Research different types of maps. What kind of maps have you used? Then, explore the images on the next page to learn more about different types of maps.

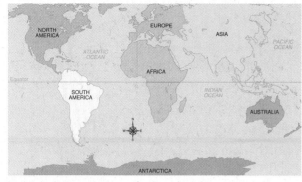

A world map shows the continents, or major land masses on Earth. It also may show mountain chains, oceans, country boundaries, islands, and lakes.

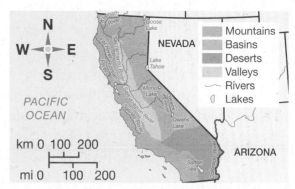

A **physical map** shows the geography of a particular area. This map is a physical map of California. Physical maps use colors and symbols to distinguish geographical marks, such as mountains, bodies of water, and valleys.

A **topographic map** shows features such as mountains or waterways that are natural or human-made. It also shows the elevation changes of the land. Contour lines show the height of features in relation to one another.

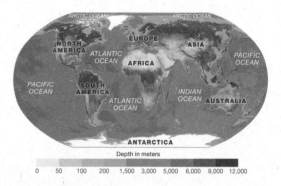

A **bathymetric map** is a type of map that shows water depths and underwater features, such as the shapes and sizes of underwater mountains and other features along the ocean bottom.

 Language SmArts **Compare and contrast** two different maps on this spread.

_____

_____

Infer Which type of map would be helpful for someone who wants to climb a mountain and needs to analyze how steep or high it is?

_____

_____

 EVIDENCE NOTEBOOK Which type of map gives information most like the one you saw at the beginning of this lesson? What kinds of information does that type of map provide? Record your findings in your Evidence Notebook.

Find Your Way

Knowing which direction on a map points north lets you use the map to find your way. A compass rose shows the cardinal directions—north, south, east, and west. Often the cardinal directions are indicated on the compass rose as N, S, E, and W. The points shown between two directions are called intercardinal directions. For example, the mark between north and west is the northwest direction.

compass rose

A Map of Washington, D.C.

Use the compass rose and the map of Washington, D.C., to answer the questions.

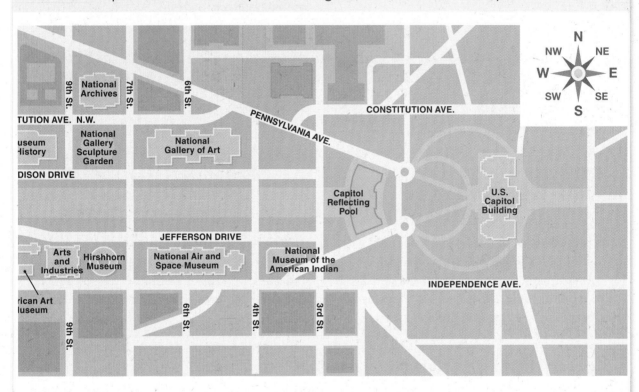

Identify In what direction must you move from the intersection of Pennsylvania Avenue and 6th Street to get to the U.S. Capitol building?

a. north

b. northeast

c. east

d. southeast

Analyze Starting at the Hirshhorn Museum, travel east along Jefferson Drive. Turn north on 3rd Street, and look to the east. What do you see?

a. National Gallery of Art

b. National Air and Space Museum

c. Constitution Avenue

d. Capitol Reflecting Pool

It's Key!

An important part of any map is the key, or tool to unlock what the map shows. The key explains the meaning of the map's symbols, colors, and lines.

Assess Why is a map key important?

_____

_____

_____

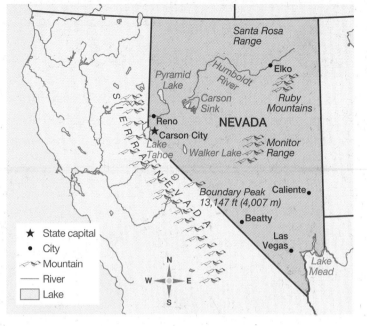

Evaluate How many lakes on the map are located within the state of Nevada? Do not count lakes that border the state.

a. 1   **b.** 3   **c.** 5   **d.** 12

World Climate

This map shows Earth's climate. Use the key to answer the questions. Place an X on all the polar climates.

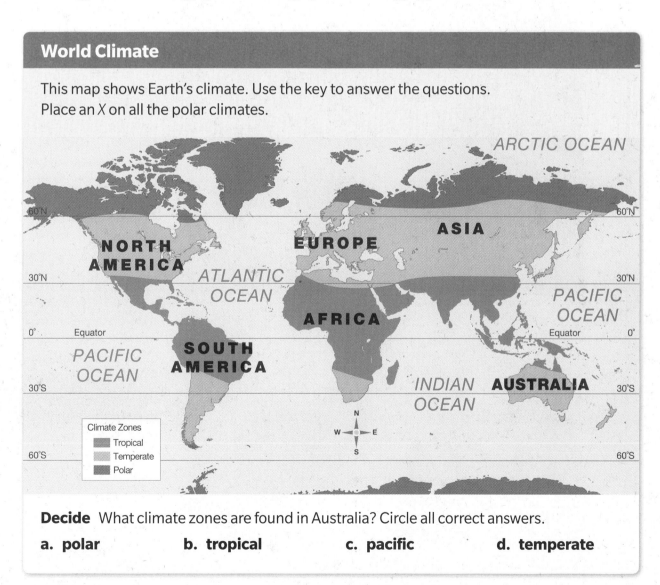

Decide What climate zones are found in Australia? Circle all correct answers.

a. polar   **b. tropical**   **c. pacific**   **d. temperate**

Do the Math

Using a Map Scale

Maps can be as small as the screen on a smartphone or as big as a dining room table. Most maps have a **scale.** The scale relates the distance on the map to the distance on Earth. Read below to learn how to use a map scale.

a.

Using the edge of a blank sheet of paper, copy the scale off the map.

b.

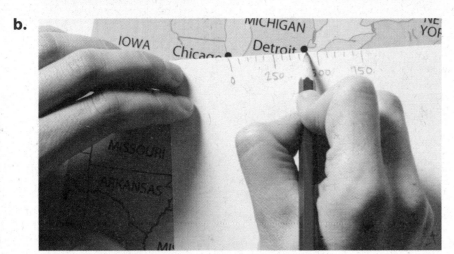

Use the scale you copied to find the distance between Chicago and Detroit. Start by placing the scale between the two city dots on the map. The distance from Chicago to Detroit is 450 km.

c.

If the distance on the map is longer than the actual scale, measure it in parts. Then add the distances together to arrive at the correct distance.

For some printed maps, you can use a ruler as a scale. In the scale below, 1 cm on the map is equal to 5 km on Earth. Multiply to find out the distances in kilometers.

Rule: 1 cm = 5 km

Measure	Distance						
cm	1	2	3	4	5	6	7
km	5	10					

The map below shows the state of Montana. The map scale shows the scaled distance on the map. Find the cities Big Timber and Roundup in the central, southern part of this state. The distance from the city Big Timber to Roundup is about 120 km. Try measuring it yourself. Then work with a partner to find two cities that are about 60 km apart.

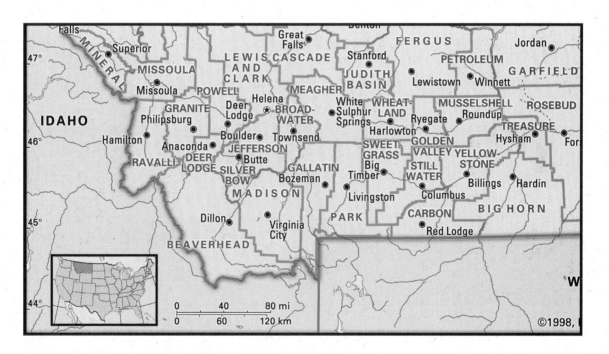

Identify Pick two cities on the map, and measure their distances using the map scale.

_____

_____

Make a Map

Draw a map of your school, including a map key that would help a map reader identify key features of the school, such as exits, water fountains, offices, and so on.

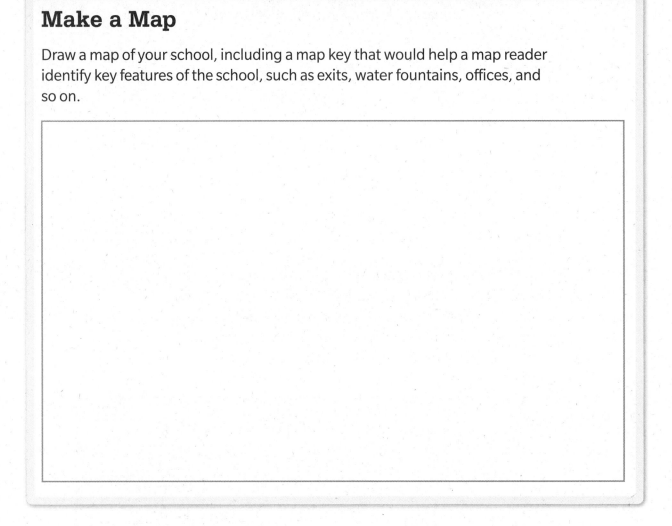

 EVIDENCE NOTEBOOK Think about the different features of maps, such as keys and scale. In your Evidence Notebook, record how these features can be used to read a map.

 Language SmArts
Make a Presentation

Analyze Make a digital presentation that shows how to use a key, scale, and compass rose to read a map. List the parts of your presentation below.

_____

_____

_____

_____

What Can Maps Show Us?

It's On the Map!

You have learned about different types of maps, keys, compass roses, and scales. Now you will learn how scientists use maps to study Earth. View the different maps for details about each map.

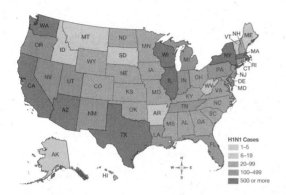

Medical Map Scientists use these maps to identify patterns, such as locations where certain diseases are more common.

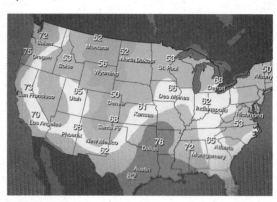

Weather Map This map shows rainfall, temperature, air pressure, and other parts of weather. A weather map usually applies to a few days.

Resource Map This map shows where resources such as gold, iron, and coal are found. Maps such as these help determine patterns of where specific resources may be located.

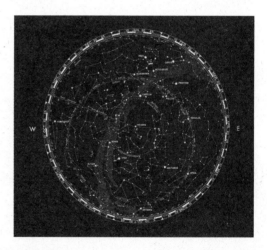

Star Map This map shows the positions of some of the stars and planets in the night sky. Star maps help scientists point their telescopes in the direction of the objects they want to observe.

Infer Work with a partner to research the kinds of maps that could be helpful for scientists. What other ways do you think scientists use maps?

_____

_____

_____

How High?

Topography is the study of the physical features of land. A topographic map uses curved lines to show a landform's change in elevation. Elevation is the height above or below the level of the sea. The contour lines mark places at equal elevations on the map. They use elevation data to display patterns that people use to understand an area's topography. The closer together the lines are drawn, the steeper the slope is of the land between them. These maps are helpful in understanding how the shape of the land can affect rivers, weather, and soil.

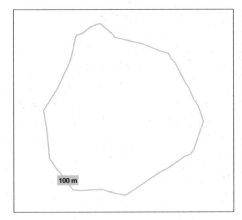
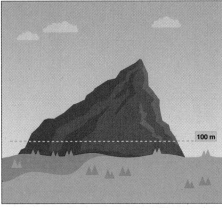

To make a topographic map of this mountain, we will begin by drawing the first contour line at 100 m. The shape of the line shows the shape of the mountain at the given elevation.

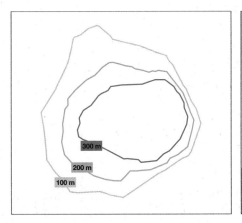
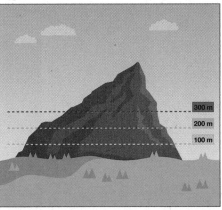

The shape of the mountain is marked every 100 m as the elevation rises. Notice that the bands are drawn closer together on the right side and wider on the left. Discuss with a partner why it is drawn this way.

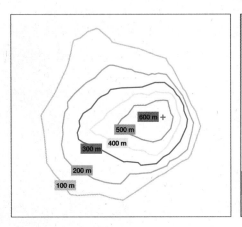
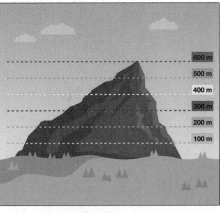

The contour lines continue every 100 m until the summit, or the highest point of the mountain, is reached. The summit is shown with a cross. How can you tell which side of the mountain is the steepest by looking at the map?

Topographic maps are useful for planning buildings and roads. They have other uses too, such as for hiking.

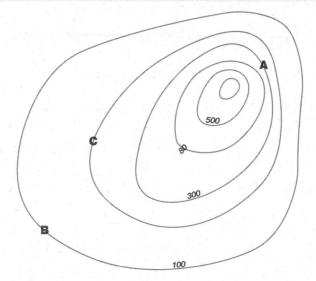

Infer A group of hikers is planning to climb the mountain shown on the map. They would like to climb the part of the mountain that is the least steep. How should they plan their climb?

a. Start below area B, then continue through area C to the top.

b. Start below area A, then climb up through area A to the top.

c. Start below area B, then cross to area A, and continue to the top.

d. Start below area A, then cross to area C, and continue to the top.

Identify Which of these points on the map has the highest elevation?

a. A   **b.** B   **c.** C

Apply What You Know

Using Topographic Maps

Predict Research some maps of your community. Predict places where you think erosion will happen the fastest. You may need to use different kinds of maps to make your prediction. A topographic map can show the steepest slopes that have the most erosion. Geologic maps can show the strength of rocks that could be resistant to erosion. Explain your prediction, and use evidence from your research.

_____

_____

Determine Write the words that complete the sentences.

> | topographic | resource | star |
> |---|---|---|
> | weather | medical | world |

Maps provide many different kinds of useful information.

A _____ map is used to show where it is raining. To study the

night sky, use a _____ map. Scientists use _____

maps to identify patterns of the flu or other diseases in an area.

Evaluate How can you tell how steep a mountain is by looking at the contour lines on a topographic map? Circle the best answer.

    a. The higher the elevation, the steeper the area.

    b. The lower the elevation, the steeper the area.

    c. The more space between the lines, the steeper the area.

    d. The less space between the lines, the steeper the area.

 EVIDENCE NOTEBOOK What do the lines and numbers on a topographic map indicate? What does it mean when the lines are close together or far apart? Record your answers to these questions in your Evidence Notebook.

 Language SmArts
Use Reasons and Evidence

Summarize You are planning a road trip across the country to do some hiking. What types of maps will be useful for your trip? Support your choices with reasons why you've chosen these maps.

_____

_____

_____

_____

_____

_____

_____

Park Designer

Objective

Collaborate to design a park. A park designer uses a map to plan where equipment and features go in the park. Think about how a park designer uses a map to do his or her job. As a park designer, you will need to include a playground area, an eating area, and rest areas. You must find ways to protect the animals that live in and around the lake. Your budget is $7,000. You must allow 90 cm minimum of walking space between objects that people must walk around. You must also include a 240 × 240 garden.

> **Materials**
> - printed park site map
> - printed park material cutouts
> - ruler
> - glue
> - scissors
> - notebook

Form a Problem: What question will you investigate to meet this objective?

_____

_____

_____

Procedure

STEP 1 Research with your group information and features of different parks across California.

STEP 2 Define the problem.
What are your criteria?

_____

_____

_____

_____

What are your constraints?

_____

_____

STEP 3 Brainstorm solutions with your group on how you can build the park and follow the requirements. Think about the features in your park. To be successful, your park will meet certain criteria and constraints. Then **evaluate** your solutions, and choose the best.

STEP 4 **Develop, test, and model:** Draw a rough draft of your park's design. Then make sure you are within your budget by listing the items you need and the cost.

_____

_____

_____

Build your park. Begin building your park on the provided map. Cut and lay out all your pieces first. Once you are happy with the placement, glue the pieces down. Use the scale to measure distances to be sure you meet the criteria and constraints. Make sure you add a key.

STEP 5 **Evaluate** your park to make sure you have met the criteria and the constraints. You might change your map several times before you have the most successful plan. Explain how you would improve your park.

_____

_____

STEP 6 **Develop and test a new model.** How could you redesign the park at a lower cost?

_____

_____

_____

_____

How does your park's design allow for the survival of the animals that live in and around the lake?

_____

_____

_____

298

How did you make sure there was enough walking space for getting around the entire park?

_____

_____

_____

_____

Communicate: Compare your park with your classmates' parks. Name one thing you designed well, and explain why you think so. Name one thing another group did well, and explain why you think so.

_____

_____

_____

_____

In your opinion, what part or area of your park would you like to change? Why?

_____

_____

_____

_____

Make a **claim** based on your investigation. Cite **evidence** from the activity to support your claim, and explain your **reasoning.**

_____

_____

_____

Think of other problems you would like to solve related to designing maps.

_____

_____

_____

_____

Discover More

Check out this path . . . or go online to choose one of these other paths.

Careers in Science and Engineering

- **Search Party**
- **Above and Below**

City Planner

To build a park, you would have worked with a city planner. City planners plan out city lands to suit the needs of the people living there. June Manning Thomas is a city planner and a Centennial Professor of Urban and Regional Planning at the University of Michigan. Throughout her career, Thomas has focused on bringing struggling urban areas back to life and establishing social equity in various cities.

June Manning Thomas is a city planner and professor who believes in urban revitalization.

City planners should have a good understanding of maps to help plan the layout of the city. Specific parts of land may be zoned, or set aside, for houses, businesses, retail stores, roads, public parks, and schools.

Thomas has also written and edited books on urban mapping and development. A lot of her work has taken place in Michigan, where she developed statewide initiatives to identify the development needs of cities like Detroit. A true visionary, Thomas is the recipient of awards for her creative solutions to development problems.

City planners like Thomas need to possess a specific set of skills to succeed in their careers. They must be able to work and communicate well with others, like politicians and builders. This is because they often have to propose and negotiate ideas. City planners must also have a good understanding of maps to help plan the layout of a city. Specific parts of land may need to be zoned, or set aside, for houses, businesses, retail stores, roads, public parks, and schools. Understanding how to interpret maps is essential to carrying out these tasks.

City planners must plan solutions to traffic and transportation problems. Buses and trains help reduce traffic and pollution in growing cities.

Infer What do you think are some advantages to zoning, or setting aside, specific parts of land within a city?

_____

_____

City planners help make laws about how land can be used. They make decisions about requirements for new buildings. For example, in an area with hurricanes, they may require buildings to withstand high winds.

City planners also must consider how to conserve, or protect, spaces for the local wildlife and plants. They may set aside a wooded area that cannot be developed or require a certain number of parks be built to preserve nature.

Analyze How do city planners use science and engineering in their job?

_____

_____

Improve Your City or Town

Suppose you want to add a new park to your city. You will have to decide what part of the city you can replace with a park. Do research to locate and print a map of your town. Use that map as a guide to draw a new map below that includes the location of your new park. Then answer the questions below.

Evaluate About how big is the park you added? How did you decide on its size?

_____

_____

_____

_____

Assess What did you remove to make room for the park? Does this change cause other problems? If you were the city planner, how would you solve them?

_____

_____

_____

_____

Lesson Check

Name _____

Can You Explain It?

1. Review the topographic map from the beginning of the lesson. What does it show? Summarize what maps show and how they are useful. Be sure to include the following:

   • names and descriptions of different types of maps

   • features that help you interpret a map's contents

   • descriptions of how maps can be used

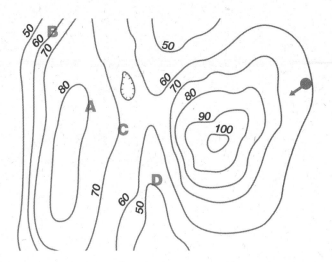

📓 **EVIDENCE NOTEBOOK** Use the information you've collected in your Evidence Notebook to help you cover each point above.

_____

_____

_____

_____

_____

_____

_____

_____

_____

Checkpoints

2. How are maps useful to scientists in their work?
   a. Maps can be used to show patterns and data to make predictions.
   b. Maps can be used to show the location of rooms in a building.
   c. Maps can be used to show the state capitals.
   d. Maps can be used to show the order of steps in an experiment.

Answer each question below about maps and their uses.

3. A team of scientists needs to collect data regarding a recent earthquake. The scientists believe that the earthquake caused the ocean floor to crack. Which kind of map would be the best for them to use to collect their data?

   a. resource map

   b. physical map

   c. bathymetric map

   d. weather map

4. Analyze the data on the map shown. What is the change in elevation between point B and point D?

   a. 10 m

   b. 20 m

   c. 30 m

   d. 40 m

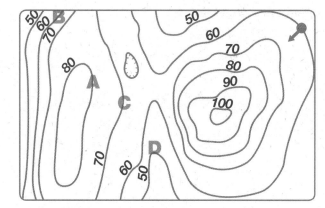

5. What is the capital of Nevada?

   a. Tonopah

   b. Carson City

   c. Las Vegas

   d. Wells

6. Using the scale on the map, about how far across is the state of Nevada at its widest part?

   a. 100 km

   b. 300 km

   c. 500 km

   d. 600 km

Lesson Roundup

A. If you wanted to determine the distance of a mountain feature on a map, what would you use?

   a. scale   **c.** compass rose

   b. keys   **d.** contour lines

B. Draw a line from each map part to match the correct description of how it is used.

a figure on a map that is used to show which way is north, south, east, and west

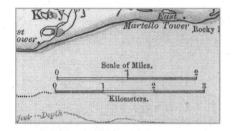

a figure on a map that shows the relationship between distances on the map and the distances on Earth's surface

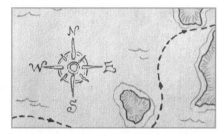

a figure on a map that explains the meaning of the map's symbols, colors, and lines

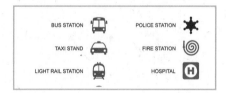

C. How can maps help you see patterns in Earth that exist under the water?

_____

_____

_____

_____

_____

Model It, Map It

A pair of three-dimensional models can contrast what something looks like before and after a change. Imagine you are working on a research team that is looking into a part of Earth's history. Your team will build two models that show how a land feature is changed by system interactions, such as wind or water, over a long period of time. Then you'll make topographic maps of your models. Your maps' keys will explain the processes that shaped the land features.

Imagine what this land area looked like before the river carved the canyon.

DEFINE YOUR TASK: Choose one of these land features to model: a changing coastline, a canyon, a winding river path, or sand dunes. Write a brief description of factors that shape and change that type of land feature.

_____

_____

Before beginning, review the checklist at the end of this Unit Performance Task. Keep those items in mind as you proceed.

RESEARCH: Review the lesson, and use online or library resources to learn about the land feature that you will model. Record notes about factors that shape the land feature. Consider how long it takes for such a feature to form and change. Look for patterns in the land features that can be used to create your "after" models.

_____

_____

_____

PLAN YOUR MODELS: Sketch rough drawings of what your before and after land feature models will look like. Decide how big you will make the models as well as the scale that you will use. List the models' dimensions and what materials you will use.

_____

_____

_____

BUILD YOUR MODELS: Use materials provided by your teacher to build the before and after models of your selected land feature. Place at least three numbers on parts of each model that you will explain in captions. What features did you number?

_____

_____

_____

MAP YOUR MODELS: Draw a topographic map of each model that locates different land and water features. Make a numbered key for each map. The numbers and features listed on your map key should match the numbers of the features on your models.

CAPTION YOUR MODELS: For each numbered feature on your models and map keys, write a corresponding caption. Each caption should describe a characteristic of the numbered part of the land feature and tell how it was formed or changed by wind or water.

COMMUNICATE: Display your models, maps, and captions for the class. Look at the models and maps made by other students. Construct an explanation of what all the models and maps have in common as well as how they differ.

_____

_____

_____

_____

✅ Checklist

Review your project, and check off each completed item.

_____ includes two three-dimensional models of a land feature

_____ models the same land feature before and after a change

_____ includes a topographic map corresponding to each model

_____ includes captions for at least three details on each model

_____ Captions explain the processes and time involved in the change shown between the two models.

Unit Review

1. Which of these can be an effect of weathering?

    a. It can make water and rainfall more powerful.

    b. It can reduce erosion and deposition.

    c. It can create better roads through mountains.

    d. It can change habitats for animals.

2. Complete the sentences using the words from the word bank.

slow-moving	**flooding**	**freezing**
fast-moving	**erosion**	**deposition**

    A glacier is a huge, _____ block or river of ice.

    Glaciers cause _____ when they are active and

    _____ when they melt.

3. Which forces cause fast rates of change? Choose all that apply.

    a. earthquakes

    b. landslides

    c. wind

    d. glaciers

4. Complete the sentences using the words from the word bank.

weathering	**erosion**	**sand**	**dirt**	**water**	**dust**

    This photograph shows one common cause of

    _____. Another cause is the freezing and

    expansion of _____ during cold weather.

© Houghton Mifflin Harcourt Publishing Company • Image Credits: ©Blulz60/iStock/Getty

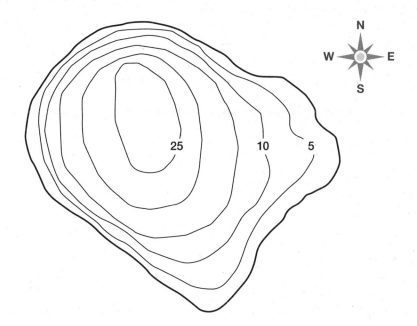

5. Use the map to answer the question. Which side of the mountain is the least steep?

   a. north

   b. south

   c. east

   d. west

6. Which choices name a specific type of map? Circle all that apply.

   a. key

   b. scale

   c. road

   d. weather

   e. topographic

7. Which phenomenon is represented in this image?

   a. deposition

   b. glacial erosion

   c. topography

   d. flooding

8. Choose the correct word or phrase to complete the sentences.

scale	key	compass rose
patterns	boundaries	lakes

A _____ relates the distance on a map to the distance

on Earth. Contour lines reveal _____ that can show

the height of a mountain. World maps can show mountain

_____ within or on the edges of continents.

9. If a scientist wants to study a trench on the ocean floor, which map would help the scientist the most?

a. topographic

b. world

c. bathymetric

d. physical

10. Which of the following played a role in the formation of the landscape shown here? Circle all that apply.

a. erosion

b. eruption

c. elevation

d. deposition

e. weathering

Earthquake Engineering

You Solve It: Build a Wave Pool As you learn about waves and earthquakes, you get to be an engineer. You will develop a wave model to explore patterns and control a pump to see how waves behave in a water theme park.

The surface of Earth changes constantly in countless ways. Much of that change is gradual. Some of it, such as volcanic activity, is abrupt and violent.

At a Glance

Name

UNIT PROJECT • Engineer It!
Wave Patterns

What are wave properties? Do all waves have the same properties? For this project, you will prepare a multimedia presentation that models different kinds of waves. You will use these models to describe patterns in terms of amplitude and wavelengths and to provide evidence that waves can cause objects to move.

Consider and plan how you will model different kinds of waves in a multimedia presentation.

Think about the kinds of waves you interact with on a daily basis. Write a question that you will investigate as you prepare your presentation and develop your models.

_____

_____

_____

Materials Think about how you will develop your multimedia presentation and models. What materials will you need? Are there multiple solutions to your problem?

_____

_____

_____

_____

Think about how you will organize your presentation. Develop an outline that includes the important points you wish to discuss. Then determine how your models can support your arguments.

_____

_____

_____

Research and Plan Make a plan for the research you will do. As you prepare your presentation, consider the following points:

- Can your claims be supported by facts and data?

- Can you show those facts and data graphically or as part of your multimedia presentation?

- What questions may others ask after viewing your presentation? How can you prepare yourself to answer those questions?

Plan how you will use multimedia in your presentation.

_____

_____

_____

_____

_____

_____

_____

_____

_____

_____

Rehearse your multimedia presentation. If you choose to record it, do so. Describe any modifications you will make.

_____

_____

_____

_____

Analyze Your Results Analyze your speech by focusing on how many of your claims are supported by facts and examples. You can include your models in your analysis.

_____

_____

_____

Restate Your Question Write the question you investigated.

_____

_____

_____

Claims, Evidence, and Reasoning Make a claim that answers your question.

_____

_____

_____

_____

Review your plan. What evidence from your plan supports your claim?

_____

_____

_____

Discuss your reasoning with a partner.

Language Development

Use the lessons in this unit to complete the network and expand understanding of the science concepts.

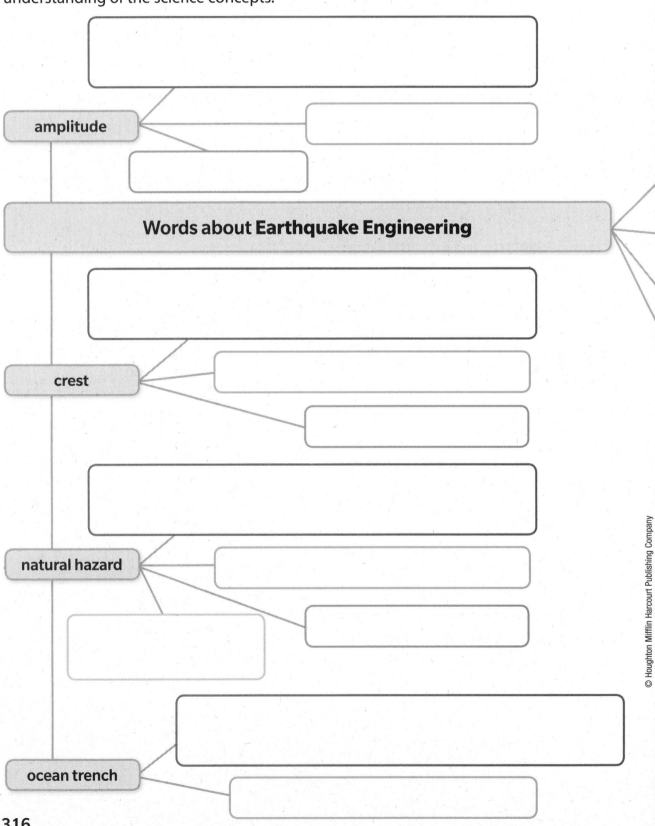

amplitude

Words about **Earthquake Engineering**

crest

natural hazard

ocean trench

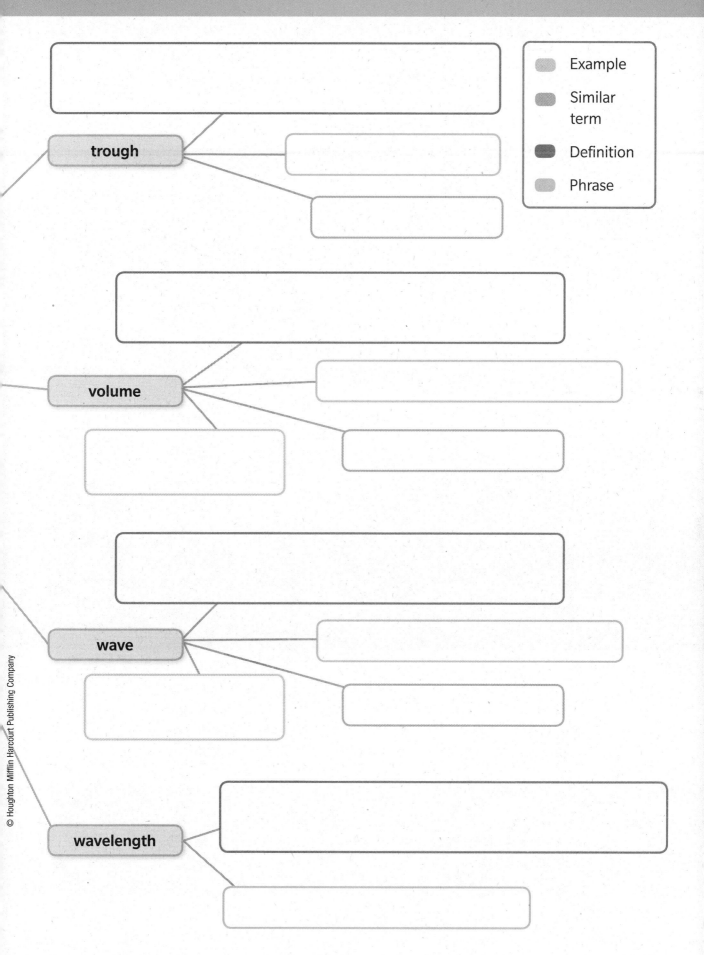

trough

volume

wave

wavelength

Example

Similar term

Definition

Phrase

What Do Patterns Tell Us About Earthquakes?

An erupting volcano is an amazing sight, especially at night. Volcanoes form when pressure below Earth's surface causes hot, molten rock called *lava* to flow onto the land. They also form when ash explodes onto Earth's surface. Volcanoes are found only in certain places on Earth. Do you know where?

Explore First

Rocking and Rolling Research to find the location of one earthquake and one volcanic eruption. Record the date and the location of each event. Find the country, state, and closest city, and plot it on the map your teacher provides.

Can You Explain It?

Explore Online

Great Rift Valley

km 0   400

mi 0   400

In 2005, a huge crack began to form in the desert of eastern Africa. This giant crack is part of the Rift Valley. A rift is a large crack in Earth's surface where the top layers of Earth are being pulled apart.

The rift in Africa is getting bigger and deeper every year. Study the map. Predict how the land and bodies of water in this area of the world might change as the rift changes.

_____

_____

_____

_____

_____

_____

_____

_____

 EVIDENCE NOTEBOOK Look for this icon to help you gather evidence to answer the question above.

By Land or By Sea

Ring of Fire

Earthquakes and volcanoes occur on land and under water all around the world. You can see patterns when they happen in the same locations again and again.

Earthquakes occur when large blocks of rock shift and release stored energy. They cause the ground to shake.

When volcanoes erupt, lava flows onto Earth's surface. Ash from volcanic eruptions can travel great distances.

Volcanic eruptions and earthquakes do not occur everywhere. One area of Earth that does experience many volcanoes and earthquakes is along the edges of the Pacific Ocean. This region is called the Ring of Fire. This includes the entire west coast of California. On the map, locate this area that rings a large part of the Pacific Ocean.

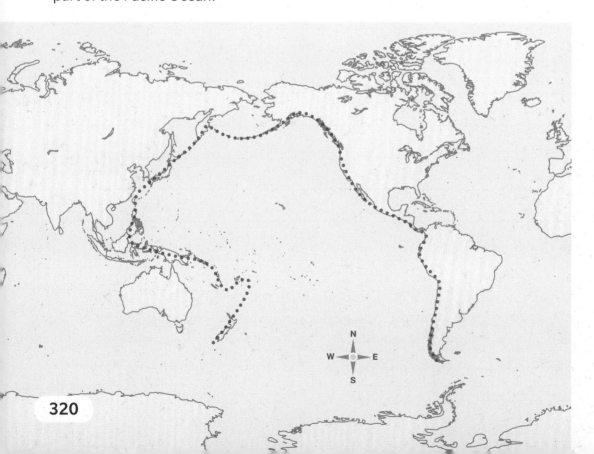

Language SmArts **Compare** and contrast earthquakes and volcanoes.

_____

_____

_____

Explain Complete the sentences.

The Ring of Fire is an area with many _____ and _____.

It is located around the _____.

> **EVIDENCE NOTEBOOK** Do any of the images remind you of the African Rift? How does this help you begin to understand what is happening in the Rift Valley?

Up and Down

Other features that can be found on Earth's surface are mountains and trenches.

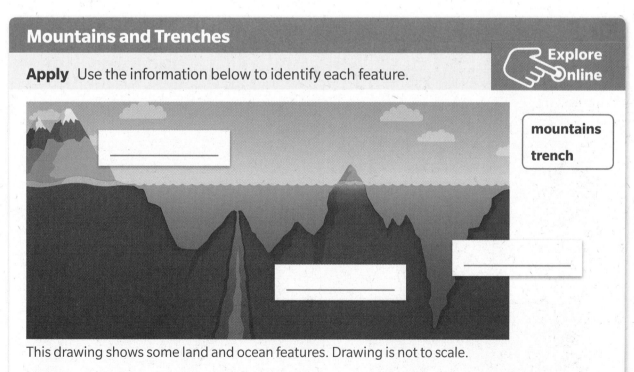

Mountains and Trenches

Apply Use the information below to identify each feature.

Explore Online

mountains

trench

This drawing shows some land and ocean features. Drawing is not to scale.

 Mountains can form on land or under water. Some are very tall and jagged, while others are smaller and rounded. Mt. Everest in the Himalaya Mountains is the tallest mountain on land. A huge mountain range called the Mid- Atlantic Ridge runs down the middle of the Atlantic Ocean.

 An **ocean trench** is a long, deep, narrow valley found on the ocean floor. The Marianas Trench in the Pacific Ocean is the deepest ocean trench.

Engineer It!
Mapping the Ocean Floor

Explore Online

The ocean floor has many interesting features—mountains, trenches, and volcanoes, just to name a few. But how do we know this?

Multibeam sonar is a technology that uses sound waves to determine how deep the ocean floor is. The signal is sent out from a ship in a fanlike pattern. The signal returns data about the features found on the ocean floor. This information is used to make ocean floor maps.

Evaluate What is an advantage and a disadvantage of using sonar to map the ocean floor?

_____

_____

Putting It Together

On each line, write whether the feature forms on *land, under water,* or *both*.

Mountains

Trench

Volcano

Earthquake

Can Maps Help Us See Patterns?

Finding Patterns on the Ocean Floor

These maps show earthquakes and other features of the ocean floor. Use your observations to answer the questions that follow.

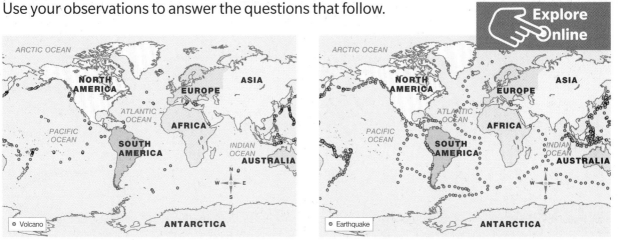

This map shows the locations of volcanoes on the ocean floor.

This map shows earthquake epicenters, or where earthquakes have started, on the ocean floor.

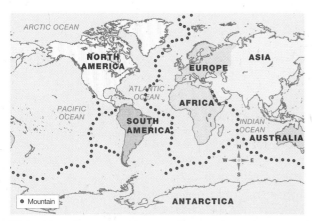

This map shows the mountains on the ocean floor.

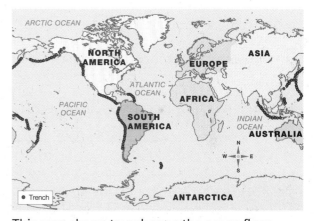

This map shows trenches on the ocean floor.

Explain Describe the pattern of ocean trenches.

_____

_____

_____

_____

_____

_____

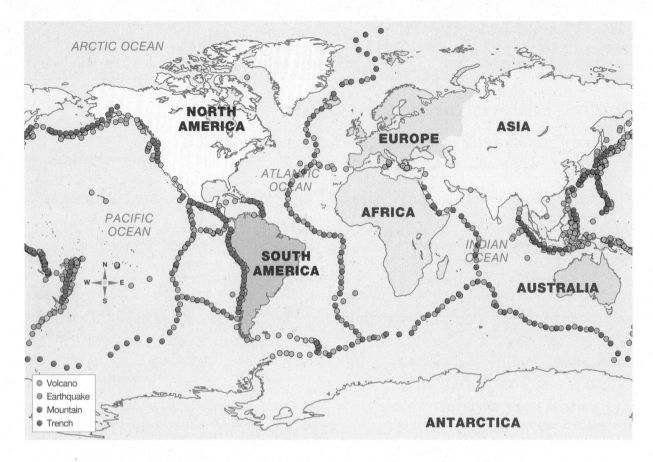

Apply Choose the word or phrase that correctly completes each sentence.

> **the centers of oceans**   **coastlines**   **islands**

Most underwater volcanoes occur near _____, and a few occur in the

middle of the ocean. Many underwater mountain ranges are found near

_____. Ocean trenches are common near _____.

Analyze Study the maps on the next page. Compare the locations of earthquakes and volcanoes. Are they the same on land as they are in the ocean?

_____

_____

_____

Argue Study the maps on the next page to contrast the locations of mountain ranges on land and the ocean floor. Are they the same on land as they are in the ocean?

_____

_____

_____

Finding Patterns on Land

You've discovered that mountains, earthquakes, and volcanoes can occur in the ocean. They also occur on land. Where on Earth are they more likely to occur?

Explore Online

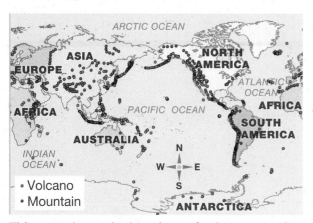

• Volcano
• Mountain

This map shows the locations of volcanoes and mountains that have formed on land.

• Earthquake

This map shows earthquake epicenters, or where earthquakes have started, on land.

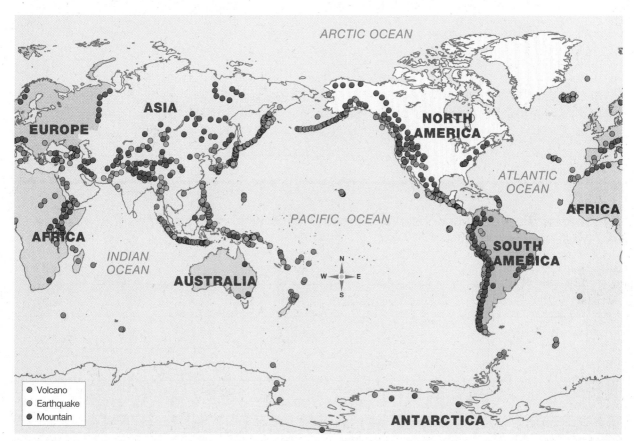

• Volcano
• Earthquake
• Mountain

Infer Choose the words or phrases that correctly complete each sentence.

> in the center
> near the edges

Earthquakes on land are most likely to occur _____ of continents. Volcanoes on land often are located _____ of continents.

Mountains on land are found _____ and _____ of continents.

325

Do the Math
California Quake Plot

An earthquake epicenter is the place on Earth's surface right above where an earthquake occurs. People mapped Earth with lines of longitude that go around Earth vertically and lines of latitude that run horizontally. Every location on Earth can be identified by the intersection of the line of latitude and longitude.

Apply Plot the epicenters of these earthquakes on the map.

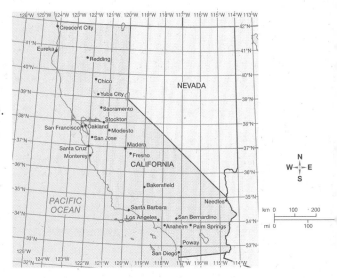

Earthquake Epicenters		
Latitude	**Longitude**	**Year**
36.20	−120.80	1857
32.55	−115.65	1892
37.70	−122.50	1906
41.12	−124.67	1980
42.02	−125.72	1991

Infer Use your map to describe the pattern of earthquake activity in California.

_____

_____

Summarize Based on your observations of the maps, what can you claim about mountains, volcanoes, and earthquakes?

_____

_____

_____

_____

HANDS-ON Apply What You Know

Modeling Features of the Ring of Fire

Use modeling clay to make a 3D model of the features of the Ring of Fire. Include locations of volcanoes, mountains, trenches, and earthquakes. Label your model.

Mark up the Map!

Use what you've discovered to draw the symbols for the locations of volcanoes, earthquakes, and mountains on the map below. Draw at least five symbols for each feature. Use colored pencils to make dots for the symbols.

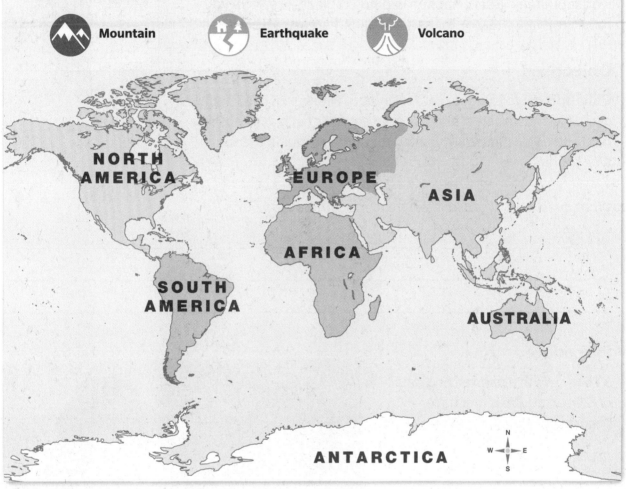

EVIDENCE NOTEBOOK How can these map patterns help you predict what is happening in the African Rift Valley?

Language SmArts
Understand Graphics

Maps are visual models used to show information more easily. Choose one of the maps from this part of the lesson. Write a few sentences that explain what the map shows.

_____

_____

_____

Tracking Quakes

In this lesson, you learned that earthquakes happen all over the world. But they usually happen in predictable places. Now you have the chance to look for patterns with real earthquakes.

Objective

Collaborate to examine data to find out where most earthquakes occur. Scientists detect about 50 earthquakes each day. Most are mild and do not cause any damage, but they occur in the same *type* of area.

What question will you investigate to meet this objective?

_____

_____

_____

Procedure

STEP 1 With a partner, find data on 20 earthquakes that have occurred during the past week.

How did you decide which earthquakes to research?

_____

_____

_____

_____

_____

_____

_____

STEP 2 For each of the 20 earthquakes, record the date, magnitude, and location. Use additional paper as needed.

What does an earthquake's magnitude indicate? Research the term, if needed.

_____

_____

_____

_____

_____

Earthquakes—Week of _____		
Date	**Earthquake magnitude**	**Location (city or country)**

STEP 3 Plot the earthquake locations on your world map. You should have one symbol for each location of an earthquake. In which part of the world did most of the earthquakes occur? Did you see a pattern in the location of the earthquakes?

_____

_____

_____

Of the earthquakes you plotted, in what type of area did most occur?

_____

_____

Compile the entire class's results into one large data table. Each group should graph the results. What patterns do you see now, and how are those patterns different from the ones above? Did having more data help you see the patterns more clearly?

_____

_____

_____

_____

_____

Make a **claim** about earthquakes. What **evidence** do you have that most earthquakes occur in certain parts of the world? Explain your **reasoning**.

_____

_____

_____

_____

What other new questions do you have about the locations of most earthquakes?

_____

_____

_____

_____

Shake, Rattle, and Roll

California Quaking

Have you ever been in an earthquake? Do you know anyone who has? Earthquakes can be devastating. The more people and structures there are in a location, the more damage is done. California has suffered major earthquakes throughout its history.

1/9/1857 8:20 a.m. Fort Tejon These are the remains of an U.S. Army outpost. They were near the epicenter of a major earthquake that ruptured about 350 km of the San Andreas Fault.

10/21/1868 7:53 a.m. Hayward This earthquake destroyed nearly every building in town and ruptured about 32 km of ground.

4/18/1906 5:12 a.m. San Francisco This quake was so severe because it struck a large city. Over 80% of the city was destroyed. Fires broke out and lasted for days.

2/9/1971 6:00 a.m. San Fernando This quake damaged sections of highways. Newer buildings that met regulations survived, but many older ones were destroyed.

Analyze Find two similarities and two differences in the pictures.

_____

_____

_____

_____

Weekly/Library of Congress Prints & Photographs Division; (bl) ©Bettmann/Getty Images; (br) ©The Art Archive/REX/Shutterstock

© Houghton Mifflin Harcourt Publishing Company • Image Credits: (tl) ©Historic American Buildings Survey/Library of Congress Prints & Photographs Division; (tr) ©Harper's

Mild and Severe Earthquakes

Possible effects of a mild earthquake

Possible effects of a severe earthquake

Earthquakes have different levels of severity. You might not even notice a mild earthquake, or you might feel a slight shake if you stand very still. If you are in a slightly more severe earthquake, you might feel a vibration or see hanging objects sway. You might hear dishes rattling.

You would know if you were in a severe earthquake. It would wake you up if you were sleeping. Objects would fall over. Windows could break. Poorly built structures would collapse. The most severe earthquakes can destroy bridges and bend train rails.

Infer Circle the effects of a mild earthquake.

1. bridges falling down
2. dishes rattling
3. Earth rupturing
4. hanging plants swaying
5. windows breaking

 EVIDENCE NOTEBOOK Think back to the picture of the African Rift Valley. Record your ideas about what type of event caused the crack in the ground.

 Language SmArts
Media Knowledge

Think about the earthquake pictures and videos you have seen. Think about what you have read about earthquakes. In your own words, use the information to explain how you could prepare for an earthquake.

_____

_____

_____

Interview an Earthquake Survivor

Think of someone you know who has lived through an earthquake. Make a plan to ask this person about his or her experience.

1. Make a list of questions to ask in your interview.
2. Have your teacher check over your questions.
3. Contact the person you want to interview.

   • Ask politely for permission to interview him or her about the earthquake experience.

   • Set a time for interview.

   • Ask permission to record the interview.

You may consider asking family or friends about their experiences with earthquakes.

4. Make sure your questions and recorder are ready before you start the interview.
5. Review your recording.
6. Share your interview with your class.

San Andreas Fault

By looking at the Ring of Fire, you can see that most earthquakes and volcanoes occur where the Pacific Ocean meets land. But some of these events happen in other places, too.

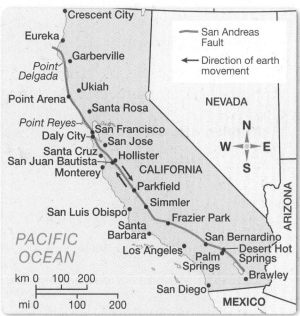

Many earthquakes occur along the San Andreas Fault. The fault is about 750 mi (1,200 km) long. The 1857 Fort Tejon earthquake and the 1906 San Francisco earthquake occurred along the San Andreas Fault.

The fault marks the boundary between giant plates of rock under the ground. The plates move very slowly in opposite directions. When enough stress builds up, an earthquake occurs.

Quake Clues

Argue Compare the map of the San Andreas Fault earthquakes to that of the Ring of Fire. Make a claim about the patterns you see in where earthquakes are located. Support your claim with evidence from the maps.

_____

_____

_____

_____

_____

_____

_____

_____

_____

_____

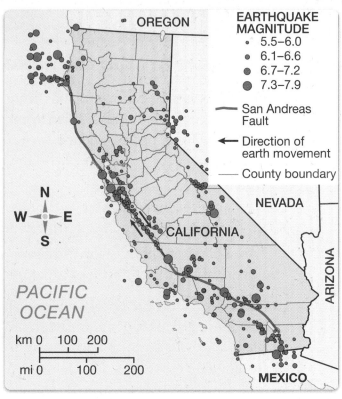

Over time, earthquake epicenters have occurred all along the San Andreas Fault line.

Putting It Together

Earthquake movements are recorded and measured. Some are mild. Some are very strong. Order the following earthquake results from 1 to 5 in order from weakest to most severe.

Number	Result
_____	Felt by all people. Heavy furniture moves. Poorly built structures are standing.
_____	Not felt except by very few people.
_____	Bridges are destroyed. Underground pipe lines are broken.
_____	Well-designed buildings are standing. Poorly built buildings are destroyed.
_____	Felt by people on upper floors of buildings. Cars rock slightly, like when a truck passes.

Discover More

Check out this path . . . or go online to choose one of these other paths.

People in Science & Engineering

- **Volcanic Islands**
- **Volcano Formation**
- **People in Science & Engineering**

Lewis, Clark, and Sacagawea

The United States purchased the Louisiana Territory in 1803. President Thomas Jefferson asked Meriwether Lewis and William Clark to find a passage through the territory. The two men were to map the terrain for future explorers. Sacagawea was a bilingual Native American woman who had knowledge of the terrain. She often acted as a diplomat between the explorers and other Native Americans they encountered.

Explore Online

Meriwether Lewis and William Clark

Sacagawea

HANDS-ON Apply What You Know

Making Mountains!

Procedure

1. Cover the bottom of the plate with a layer of shaving cream about 1 cm thick.

2. Dip the two pieces of cardboard in the bowl of water until they become soft.

3. Place the damp pieces of cardboard next to each other on top of the shaving cream.

4. Slowly push the pieces toward each other. Observe what happens to the cardboard at the edges where they smash together.

5. Draw a picture of your model, and submit it to your teacher.

Materials
- paper plate
- shaving cream
- 2 small pieces of corrugated cardboard
- bowl of water

335

Rising High

As you saw in the activity, some mountains form when two slabs of rock smash against each other. The edges of each slab crumpled and folded. Such a collision can also shove one slab of rock up over the other. This process produces some of the world's highest mountains.

Earth's crust is made up of plates, or slabs, that are always moving. Sometimes these slabs move toward each other.

When they meet, the slabs push against each other. This creates heat and pressure at the meeting point.

As the slabs continue to push against each other, mountains form and grow taller.

How do some of the world's highest mountains form?

_____

_____

_____

Lesson Check

Name _____

Can You Explain It?

1. Now that you've learned more about the features of Earth's surface, explain what is happening in the African Rift Valley. Be sure to do the following:

   • Explain what could have caused this crack.

   • Explain how you used patterns to determine what happened here.

   • Predict how the crack might change the nearby land over time.

EVIDENCE NOTEBOOK Use the information you've collected in your Evidence Notebook to help you cover each point above.

_____

_____

_____

_____

_____

_____

_____

Checkpoints

2. You learned about several features found on the ocean floor. How do those compare with the ones on land?

   a. All of them are found on land.

   b. Most of them are found on land.

   c. They do not include volcanoes.

   d. They do not include mountains.

3. Circle all the features that occur in the ocean.

    a. mountains   **c.** volcanoes

    b. ocean trenches   **d.** earthquakes

4. Circle the correct answer. Most volcanoes and earthquakes occur near the _____.

    a. middle of the Atlantic Ocean   **c.** coastlines of Africa

    b. Ring of Fire   **d.** the center of South America

5. Study the map. Which statements describe the information shown? Circle all that apply.

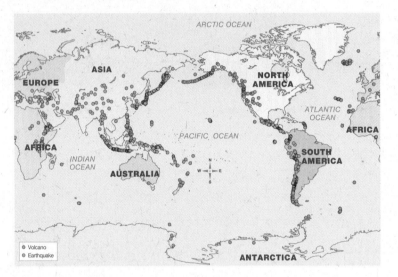

    a. It shows every volcano on Earth.

    b. It shows a pattern in the locations of volcanoes.

    c. It shows where every future earthquake will occur.

    d. It shows a pattern in the locations of past earthquakes.

6. Write the correct words to complete the sentences.

mild	plates
severe	earthquakes

Earthquakes occur along boundaries of underground _____ that

move slowly against each other. When stress builds up, _____ can

occur. Some of these events are so _____ that people barely notice

them. More _____ earthquakes cause major damage to structures.

The 1906 San Francisco earthquake was a _____ earthquake.

Lesson Roundup

A. Imagine you are piloting a submarine just above a somewhat flat area of the ocean floor. The ocean floor begins to slope downward. You cannot see the ocean floor anymore. It's as though you've glided off the peak of a steep mountain. A few minutes later, the submarine's sensors tell you the ocean floor is now 5 km deeper than your present depth. What are you and your submarine hovering over?

    a. a plain   **c.** an ocean trench

    b. a mountain   **d.** a volcano

B. What does this pattern in the Atlantic Ocean suggest?

    a. Slabs of rock are forming walls.

    b. This is the most common place volcanoes occur.

    c. Mountains are common between continents.

    d. There is an ocean trench between Europe and North America.

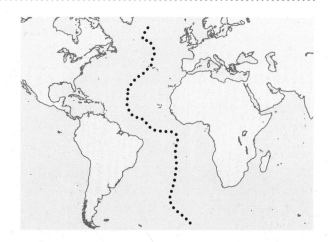

C. Why is the pattern shown on the map known as the Ring of Fire?

    a. Slabs of smashing rocks cause the Pacific Ocean to warm up.

    b. It shows a deep ocean trench, which causes warm water to rise.

    c. It is the site of earthquakes caused by volcanoes.

    d. It shows volcanoes around the Pacific Ocean.

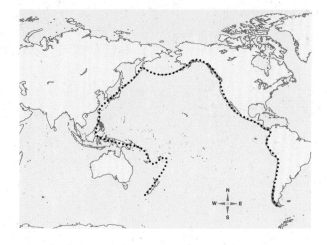

D. What do mountains, ocean trenches, volcanoes, and earthquakes have in common?

    a. They all can occur under water.

    b. They all can occur on land.

    c. They all occur in patterns at the boundaries of underground plates.

    d. They occur only in the Ring of Fire.

What Are Waves?

This American flag waves as hundreds of hands carry it across the stadium.

Explore First

Wave On Work with a partner. Hold one end of a jump rope, and have your partner hold the other. Stand close together and shake the rope up and down slowly, then quickly. Then stand farther apart and shake it again. What do you observe about the motion of the rope?

Can You Explain It?

Imagine you are at the beach and you see a bunch of surfers. They paddle out into the choppy water. When the time is right, they jump up onto their boards and ride the waves back to the beach.

How does a surfer know when to stand up on the board to "catch" a wave?

_____

_____

_____

_____

_____

_____

 EVIDENCE NOTEBOOK Look for this icon to help you gather evidence to answer the question above.

Let's Make Waves!

Objective

Collaborate to explore how waves move through different mediums.

Form a Question: What question will you investigate to meet this objective?

_____

_____

Procedure

STEP 1 Fill an aluminum pan with water. Place a table tennis ball at one end of the pan. Tap the water. Observe the ball.

What happened to the ball? What caused it to occur?

_____

_____

_____

_____

_____

STEP 2 Place a shoebox over a small speaker or a smartphone with the volume turned up. Pour a handful of puffed rice on top of the shoebox. Play music. Observe the puffed rice.

What is happening to the rice? Do you notice any patterns?

_____

_____

_____

_____

_____

STEP 3 With partners, hold the edges of a large, round cloth. Have everyone hold the cloth at a low, level height. One person should quickly raise and lower their section of the cloth. Observe what happens to the cloth. What happened to the motion in the cloth? How were your observations similar to and different from the observations you made in steps 1 and 2?

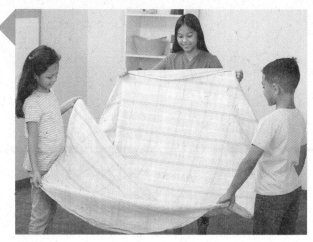

_____

_____

_____

_____

What kinds of mediums did you make waves in?

_____

_____

How did the waves move in each of your investigations?

_____

_____

_____

_____

_____

Use **reasoning** to make a **claim** about how waves affect other objects. Cite your **evidence** and explain your **reasoning.**

_____

_____

What is one new question you have about waves?

_____

_____

How Waves Transfer Energy

Waves 101

You may see or experience waves every day. A wave can be the up-and-down movement of water. Wind can make a flag wave. In science, a **wave** is a disturbance that carries energy, such as sound or light.

Apply List some other examples of waves in everyday life. How do you know if a wave is strong or weak?

_____

_____

Have you ever thrown a rock into a pond? Once the rock hits the water, it creates a bunch of ripples on the surface. Ripples form because the motion energy of the rock is transferred to the water. Waves are evidence that energy is transferred.

The size of a wave is related to the amount of energy transferred. The rock that was dropped into the pond in the photo was small.

Infer What would happen to the waves in this same pond if a larger rock were dropped into the water?

   a. The waves would be closer together.

   b. The waves would be smaller in size.

   c. There would be fewer waves with less energy.

   d. There would be larger waves with more energy.

HANDS-ON Apply What You Know

Bobbing and Waving

Get a bucket and a cork from your teacher. Fill the bucket up part of the way with water, and then drop the cork into it. Notice what happens. Then gently rock the bucket side to side to add more energy to the water. Record your observations of the water in the bucket in terms of energy.

Ocean Waves and Energy Transfer

Explore Online

Waves in the ocean can carry a lot of energy.

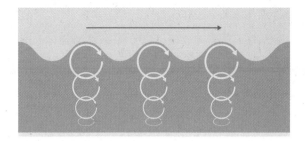

Wind transfers energy to the ocean's surface, causing a wave to form. Each circle shows the movement of water up and around in a wave. The water doesn't move forward. Only the wave energy moves forward.

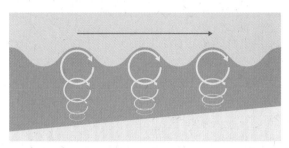

As the water becomes more shallow, the water has less room to move, forcing the water to move higher into the air. The height of the wave increases, and the energy moves forward more slowly.

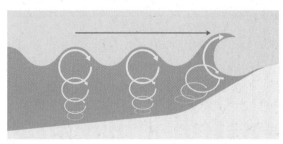

When waves get close to the beach, the back of the wave moves faster than the front, causing the wave to break. As the water crashes onto the shore, some of the energy produces sound, and some causes beach erosion.

As a wave gets closer to the beach, the land underneath the water is closer to the surface, causing the energy in the wave to force the water to rise up.

Explain Imagine you are in the ocean. The water reaches your waist. How will energy in a small wave affect you as the wave passes?

_____

_____

Sometimes, out at sea, strong winds or heavy storms create large waves that have a lot of energy. These waves can travel great distances until they find a place to release all that energy. Some buoys measure and collect data about this energy. They move up and down with the waves but do not move forward from their spots. They are often anchored to the sea floor.

Waves That Move Up and Down

Waves and energy can move in different directions.

Up and Down

Use your finger to trace the direction that energy travels. Then trace how matter moves as the wave passes.

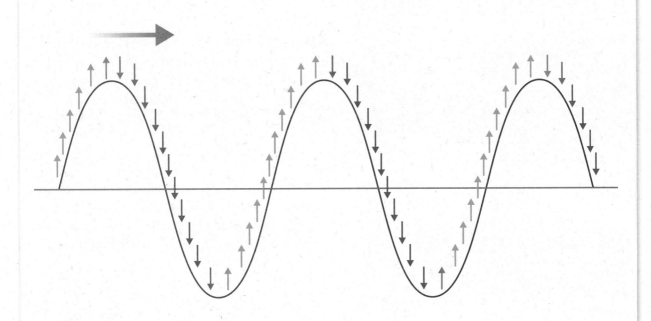

In an up-and-down or side-to-side wave, matter moves at right angles to the motion of the wave as a whole and to the direction that energy travels. Here, energy is moving to the right.

Waves that move up and down or side to side are very common. They can move through all types of matter and even through empty space!

When people do "the wave" at a game, they stand up and cheer in sequence so that it looks like a wave moving through the stands.

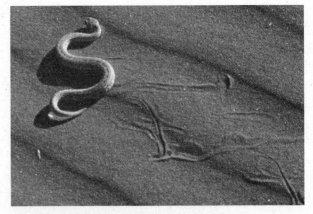

To move forward, some snakes move their bodies from side to side. This movement is called *slithering*.

The sun's light travels as up-and-down waves. Light waves can travel through space where there is no air. Sunlight that reaches Earth warms the planet and everything on it.

Signals from satellites, such as this one, travel through the vacuum of space and through clouds and the air to reach Earth's surface. These waves move at the same speed as sunlight, which moves extremely fast compared to sound waves.

A buoy bobs up and down in the water as waves pass by. If you know which way the waves are moving, you can tell which way the energy in the water is moving.

Glow sticks like these mix chemicals to make waves of light. They are cool to the touch.

 EVIDENCE NOTEBOOK In an ocean wave, what is moving toward the shore— the water or the energy? What evidence do you have to support your answer?

Summarize Write a saying that will help you remember how energy and matter move as they travel in an up-and-down wave.

_____

_____

_____

Shake Like a Quake!

BOOM! A firework goes off! There's a bright flash of light followed by the sound of the explosion. Light and sound are both waves. But with sound, matter moves differently.

Explore Online

Back and Forth

Use your finger to find the three points where the wave is the most compressed. This is the energy of the wave moving to the right.

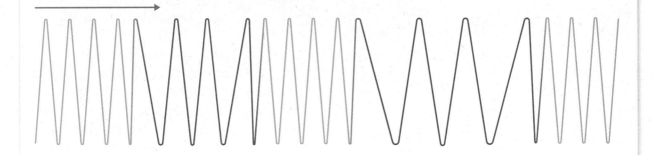

Energy transferred by back-and-forth waves moves in the direction in which the wave moves. Matter moves backward and forward, parallel to the direction the wave is traveling.

Sound is one example of a wave in which energy and matter move in the same direction. Unlike light, sound can only travel through matter. Sound travels better through water than through air. Because of this, animals that live in the ocean can hear sounds that are far away from them.

When a drum is struck, its skin vibrates. Sound waves traveling away from the drumhead compress and expand the air in bands. In this way, sound energy travels to our ears.

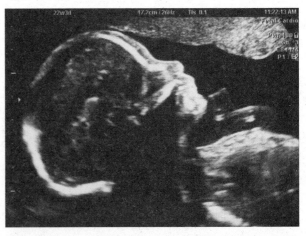

Ultrasound can be used to look inside of things—even people! These sounds move relatively slowly and can't be heard by humans. The sound waves bounce around to form images of objects.

Another type of wave that moves back and forth is one of the waves generated during an earthquake. When the ground starts to shake during a quake, different waves move through the rocks in the ground. These waves are used to figure out how strong an earthquake is.

A wave that moves through the ground is known as a *seismic wave*. Seismic waves that travel along the surface of Earth are responsible for most earthquake damage.

 EVIDENCE NOTEBOOK What types of waves are sound waves? How do they move matter and energy?

 Language SmArts
Wave Recall

Type of waves	Movements
light waves	
sound waves	
water waves	

Wave Parts

Hunks and Chunks of Waves

Waves have different parts.

Explore Online

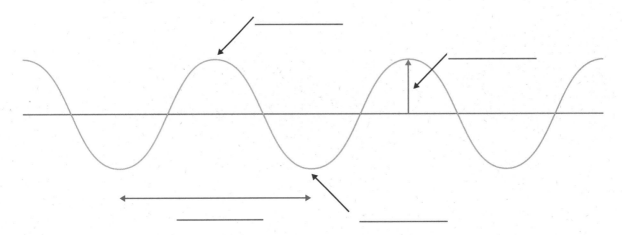

Explain Read the captions. Then label each part of the wave with the correct letter.

a. The top of a wave is called a **crest.** This is the highest point on a wave. It is where matter is moved the farthest upward.

b. The bottom of a wave is called a **trough.** This is the lowest point on a wave. It is where matter is moved the farthest down.

c. The distance between adjacent crests or troughs is called the **wavelength.** The wavelength is the distance between a point on one wave and the identical point on the next wave.

d. The height of a wave is called its **amplitude.** The amplitude is half the distance from the crest to the trough. Waves with a greater amplitude have more energy than waves with a lower amplitude.

Language SmArts

Connecting Ideas

Look at the picture above. Find two points on adjacent waves where the distance is the same. Describe these points. Then explain how the crest and trough are connected.

_____

_____

_____

_____

High and Low . . . Long and Short

Use the drawings to compare each set of waves. Choose the correct words from the word bank to complete the sentences.

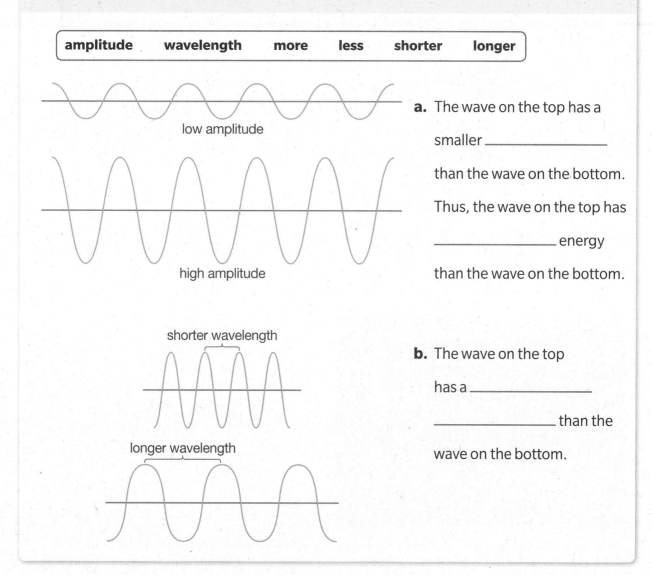

| amplitude | wavelength | more | less | shorter | longer |

low amplitude

high amplitude

shorter wavelength

longer wavelength

a. The wave on the top has a smaller _____ than the wave on the bottom. Thus, the wave on the top has _____ energy than the wave on the bottom.

b. The wave on the top has a _____ _____ than the wave on the bottom.

Explain Select the word or words that make each sentence correct.

| crest | trough | wavelength | amplitude |

a. The top of a wave is called the _____.

b. The bottom of a wave is called the _____.

c. The distance between two crests is a wave's _____.

d. A wave with much energy has a large _____.

Can You Hear This?

All waves have an amplitude and a wavelength. In a sound wave, the amplitude is related to how loud something is. Loudness is also called **volume.** Compare the sounds described on this page to learn how amplitude differs for different sounds.

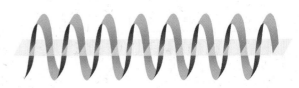

Engines on a jet produce very loud sounds. These sound waves have a lot of energy that is carried over a long distance.

The amplitude of a sound wave produced by a jet engine is very large. The distance between the crest and trough is large.

Songbirds produce soft sounds when they chirp. These sounds can only be heard over a short distance because they have a small amount of energy.

The amplitude of a sound wave produced by a songbird is small. The distance between the crest and trough is small.

Sound waves with more energy and volume have larger amplitudes. Sound waves with less energy and volume have smaller amplitudes. Compare the sounds described on the next page to learn how wavelength differs.

 EVIDENCE NOTEBOOK Write evidence from this page that sound waves have different amounts of energy.

© Houghton Mifflin Harcourt Publishing Company • Image Credits: (t) ©istock / getty

A dog whistle produces sound waves that only some animals, such as dogs, can hear.

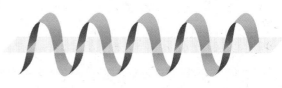

The wavelength of a sound produced by a dog whistle is short. The distance between two neighboring crests is small.

A flute produces a variety of sound waves that humans can hear.

The wavelength of a sound produced by a flute is longer than the wavelength produced by a dog whistle.

Do the Math
Compare Earthquake Models

Explore Online

These images show computer visualizations of earthquake waves as they travel across Earth's surface. They are from two different earthquakes.

What kind of earthquake does the first image represent? Explain your answer.

_____

_____

What kind of earthquake does the second image represent? Explain your answer.

_____

_____

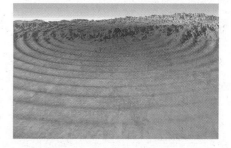

Surfing the Waves

Remember the surfer from the beginning of the lesson? Let's use what you have discovered about the parts of a wave to explain what happens when someone surfs on a wave.

Like all waves, ocean waves have amplitudes and wavelengths. Look at the photos. Which day should the surfer choose to ride? Circle your answer.

The wavelengths are small. The amplitude is low.

The wavelengths are still small. The amplitude has increased, but the crests are not very high.

The wave amplitude has increased. Crests are high, and the wavelengths are long.

The wavelengths are very short. The waves are breaking close together.

Putting It Together

Select the words that make each sentence correct.

| volume | larger | smaller | amplitude | wavelength |

All waves have _____ and _____. In a

sound wave, amplitude is related to _____. The louder a

sound is, the _____ its amplitude. Sounds that are soft have

_____ amplitudes than sounds that are loud.

Waves Interact

Harmony!

Explore Online

Waves can interact with one another. If waves combine in pleasing ways, they are said to be in harmony. Look at the photos on this page to see what happens when waves of sound or light interact.

If you have ever been to a concert, you've heard waves that are in harmony. The musicians here are playing instruments that make different sounds. When the sounds combine, music is produced.

Music is a collection of different sound waves interacting. If you listen carefully to music, you can pick out sounds and notes from each instrument in a band.

If you've been to a theater, you might have seen a dark stage at the beginning of a show. You also may have seen different lights come on, one by one, until the entire stage is lit up.

Like sound waves, light waves can interact, and when many people are seen on a stage and many lights are on, all of the light waves are interacting to showcase the actors.

Apply What are some other examples of waves interacting that you may have seen or heard?

_____

_____

_____

_____

_____

Crossing Invisible Paths

Examine the pictures and captions on these pages to see what happens when waves combine to add or cancel each other out.

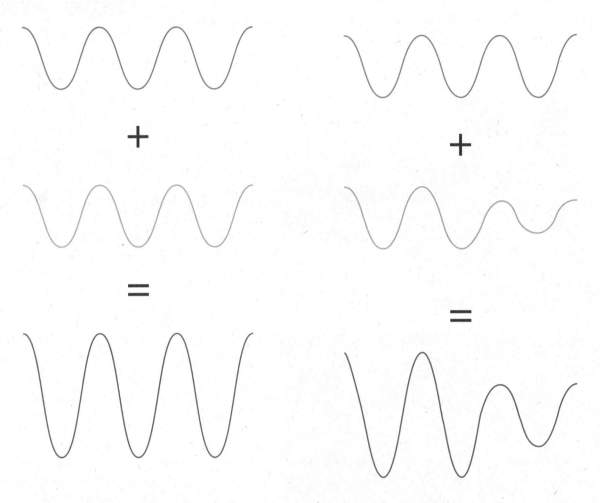

Sometimes waves join together to produce a larger or louder wave. Think about a rock band. When multiple sound waves from the instruments combine, they can create a sound with a loud volume. Waves that are able to combine in this way often have similar or the same wavelength and amplitude.

Waves can also join together to form a completely different wave. The crest of one wave might join with the crest of another wave and create a wave with twice the amplitude. Or the crest of one wave might join with another wave on its way to the trough to form a wave with a much smaller amplitude at that point.

When two waves come together, they can combine to form a wave with larger amplitude. Or they can cancel each other out. Waves can also combine to form a new wave with different characteristics than either of the source waves.

© Houghton Mifflin Harcourt Publishing Company

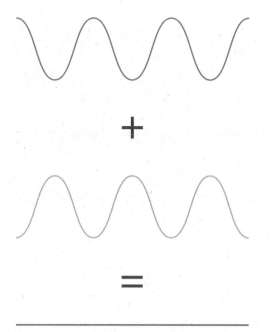

Sometimes waves can work against each other. When this happens, they can cancel each other out. Waves that completely cancel each other out are exactly opposite in amplitude. Then when the two waves join, the lows cancel out the highs and produce no sound.

Noise-canceling headphones are a type of technology that uses wave cancellation. A small microphone outside the headphones picks up background sounds. The headphones then generate a wave with the opposite characteristics. The two waves then cancel each other out. This produces a quiet environment for the user.

 EVIDENCE NOTEBOOK Apply what you've learned on these two pages to ocean waves and surfing.

 Language SmArts
Interacting through Writing

Suppose that you had an opportunity to attend an orchestra concert. Write a letter to a friend about the concert. Describe the sounds you heard. How did the instruments combine? How might you describe the sound waves that each instrument produced? Try to use the words *amplitude* and *wavelength* in your letter.

_____

_____

_____

Hear the Beat

Do you own a musical instrument? If so, then chances are that you know that you need to tune it on occasion. Read on to learn how a piano is tuned.

A piano makes sounds when a key is pressed. That key causes a hammer to hit a string. A piano tuner begins by using a tuning fork, such as the one shown in the violin image, to set the pitch for the first note. To do this, the piano tuner loosens or tightens the vibrating piano string until the sound it produces matches the pitch of the sound produced by the vibrating tuning fork. The notes in that octave, or set of notes, are tuned relative to the first note.

Tuning other notes typically involves adjusting the rate, or timing, of beats, which we hear as a series of loud and soft sounds. Beats occur when sound waves interfere, or combine, with each other in certain ways. The piano tuner plays notes together and changes the timing of the beats that are produced by loosening or tightening the strings. To help time the beats, the piano tuner may use a watch or a clock.

Tuning forks are mechanical tools.

Some instruments are tuned with electronic tuners.

Infer When piano tuners tune pianos using tuning forks, what are they trying to do? Choose the correct answer.

   a. increase the volume of the instrument

   b. decrease the volume of the instrument

   c. match the two sound waves

   d. cancel out the two sound waves

Putting It Together

Select the words from the word bank to make each sentence correct.

amplitude	louder	quieter	combine	cancel out

Noise-canceling headphones work when sound waves _____.

The headphones _____ unwanted sounds with small

_____ so that they cannot be heard. At concerts, waves can

combine to form _____ sounds.

Discover More

Check out this path . . . or go online to choose one of these other paths.

People in Science & Engineering

- **Seismic Waves and Earthquakes**
- **Theater Acoustics**

People in Science & Engineering

Christian Doppler, Debra Fischer, Wanda Diaz-Merced

Why does the siren of an ambulance or fire truck sound different as it passes you? It's the Doppler effect, of course!

Christian Doppler was an Austrian physicist and mathematician. He discovered that sound waves appear to have a higher pitch as you approach the object making the sound. Pitch is the highness or lowness of a sound. When an object giving off a sound wave is moving away from you, the sound will appear to have a lower pitch. This is called the Doppler effect.

Christian Doppler

Explore Online

Doppler's ideas are used by weather forecasters to predict oncoming storms. Using Doppler radar, they are able to see how fast storms are moving. They can also determine where the storms are going and what types of precipitation are going to fall.

Debra Fischer, an astrophysicist, is one scientist who uses the Doppler effect to find planets. Fischer uses a telescope fitted with special equipment to detect changes in the frequency of light from a star. This is caused when an unseen planet pulls the star toward, and then away from, Earth. The shifts in the frequency of light produced by these slight gravitational "tugs" are like the apparent changes in the pitch of sounds produced by objects moving toward and away from an observer.

Debra Fischer

Wanda Diaz-Merced

Imagine being able to listen to data the way that you listen to a song! Wanda Diaz-Merced is a blind astronomer who has come up with a way to do this. She developed a technique to use sound to represent large sets of data. This process is known as sonification. Sonification relies on the Doppler effect, because it analyzes pitch and other properties of sound to convey information. Today, Diaz-Merced studies and researches solar wind for NASA by listening to data. Solar wind produces a specific pitch that can be used to determine things like speed, closeness, and other properties.

On the lines below, describe the Doppler effect.

_____

_____

_____

_____

_____

Lesson Check

Name _____

Can You Explain It?

1. Now that you have learned about waves, explain how a surfer gets onto a wave. Be sure to do the following:

   • Explain how waves carry energy.

   • Identify the properties and parts of waves.

   • Identify what happens when waves interact.

EVIDENCE NOTEBOOK Use the information you've collected in your Evidence Notebook to help you cover each point above.

_____

_____

_____

_____

_____

_____

_____

_____

_____

Checkpoints

2. Choose the words that make each sentence correct.

quickly	a little	small	large	energy

   If a spring is wiggled _____, the amplitude of the waves that form is

   _____. This is because the amount of _____ of the wave

   is small.

3. Write *high* or *low* on each line to correctly describe the amplitude of each sound.

_____   _____   _____   _____

4. How do seismic waves travel? How do they cause matter to move?

_____

_____

5. Which of the following are examples of wave interactions? Select all that apply.
  a. a full orchestra playing a song
  b. moving a spring back and forth quickly
  c. having two spotlights on a performer
  d. watching a movie in surround sound
  e. tuning a piano to the correct notes
  f. wearing noise-canceling headphones on an airplane

6. Choose the words or phrases that make each sentence correct.

water waves	**sound waves**	**matter**
parallel	**at right angles**	**up and down**

Different kinds of waves cause _____ to move in

different ways. For example, _____ are up-and-down

waves. Matter moves _____ to the direction these

waves travel. On the other hand, matter moves back and forth along the direction

that _____ travel. In one kind of earthquake wave,

matter vibrates _____ to the direction the wave

travels.

© Houghton Mifflin Harcourt Publishing Company • Image Credits: (l) ©Jupiterimages/Age

Lesson Roundup

A. Which of these are evidence that ocean waves have energy? Select all of the correct answers.

    a. They can combine or cancel each other out.

    b. They need a medium in which to move.

    c. They make things wet.

    d. They crash when they hit shore.

B. Which of these are true? Select all of the correct answers.

    a. All waves move up and down.

    b. Some waves don't need a medium.

    c. All waves transfer energy.

    d. All waves move back and forth.

    e. Some waves transfer matter.

C. Label each part of the wave.

    a. crest   **c.** wavelength

    b. trough   **d.** amplitude

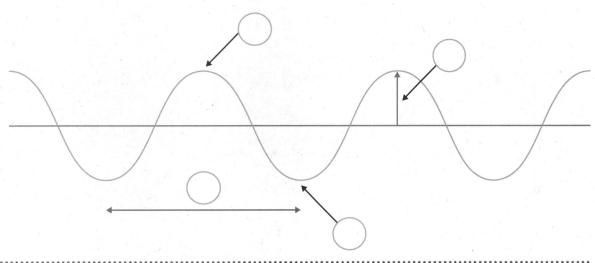

D. Scientists use a tool that records seismic waves. Suppose this tool records waves that have a very high amplitude. What can you conclude about the strength of the earthquake? Explain.

_____

_____

_____

How Can People Reduce the Impact of Natural Hazards?

A picture of a volcanic eruption is amazing. You can see the hot lava and billowing ashes and gases the volcano releases. How can people stay safe when a volcanic eruption happens?

Explore First

Nature's Hazards Look at a series of items your teacher has chosen. Work in small groups to determine which ones could be useful in a natural hazard. Be sure to name the natural hazard each item would be best used during.

Can You Explain It?

Explore Online

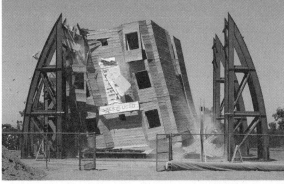

At the University of California, San Diego, engineers construct buildings to test their ability to withstand earthquakes. How do you think the tests are done?

In what ways can people reduce the impact of natural hazards, such as earthquakes?

_____

_____

_____

_____

_____

_____

 EVIDENCE NOTEBOOK Look for this icon to help you gather evidence to answer the question above.

Natural Hazards

Nature's Dangers

Earth has many processes that affect its surface. But these processes can also cause natural hazards. A **natural hazard** is an Earth process that threatens people and property.

Types of Hazards

Use the images and captions to learn about natural hazards.

 When a volcano erupts, it can release lava, rocks, ash, and poisonous gases. These can be dangerous to people and surrounding property.

 Landslides can be falling or flowing soil, mud, rocks, or snow. They can knock down trees and bury homes and other property.

 In an earthquake, the ground shakes violently. This shaking can collapse buildings and bridges. Roads and walkways can crack and crumple.

 During a wildfire, an area of forest, shrub, or grassland burns out of control. Buildings can be destroyed, and people have to leave.

 A hurricane is a strong storm with dangerous winds and heavy rains. It is not safe to be outdoors during a hurricane.

 A tsunami is a powerful type of wave. It rushes onto the ocean shore like a high flood. It can have enough force to smash buildings.

 During a drought, there is much less water than usual. People and animals struggle to have enough water.

 During a flood, water covers the land and may flood homes as well. Floodwater can ruin property and threaten people's safety.

Why is it important for people to be warned about natural hazards?

_____

_____

Make Your Own Seismometer

A seismometer detects and measures ground movement. In this interaction, you will make a seismometer.

> **Materials**
> - shoebox without lid
> - ruler
> - pointed-tip scissors
> - construction paper
> - clear adhesive tape
> - 2 rubber bands
> - fine line marker
> - yarn or string

Procedure:

a. Use a ruler to measure a 10 cm cutting line along the bottom edge of each long side of the box. Cut a slit along each cutting line.

b. Cut the paper into 9 cm wide strips. Attach the pieces together with tape to form one strip. Insert the strip of paper into the slits so that each end extends out of the slits.

c. Attach two rubber bands so that the bands are stretched wide to the sides of the two box slits.

d. Cut two pieces of yarn or string. Tie the marker into place between the rubber bands. The tip should lightly rest on the paper in the box.

e. Working together, one partner jiggles the box while the other pulls the strip through to get a reading.

Describe one way your seismometer could be improved.

_____

_____

Language SmArts

Drawing Examples from Text

Use examples to explain why understanding the causes and effects of natural hazards is important to helping people stay safe.

_____

_____

EVIDENCE NOTEBOOK In your Evidence Notebook, identify three facts about natural hazards that engineers could use to design ways to keep people safe. Explain why you included each.

Cause and Effect

The cause of every natural hazard is related to an Earth process. The effects of these events can be very destructive.

Explore Online

Causes and Effects of Natural Hazards

Read about each of the natural hazards shown here. Then complete the tables.

Volcanic eruptions occur when molten rock bursts through an opening in Earth's crust. The hot lava can cause wildfires. Falling ash can cause landslides.

Sometimes, enormous pieces of Earth's crust suddenly snap past each other, causing an earthquake. The ground shakes so hard that buildings can collapse.

Landslides can be triggered by volcanic eruption or earthquakes. Rock slides and snow avalanches occur on steep slopes, but mud can flow on even a gentle slope.

Wildfires are caused by human activities, volcanic eruptions, dry conditions, and lightning. They can destroy environments and homes as well as cause landslides.

Natural hazard	Cause and effect
	Cause—Melted rock bursts through a crack in Earth's crust.
wildfire	Effect—
	Cause—Earth's enormous rock plates grind against each other.
landslide	Cause—

A hurricane forms as the energy in warm ocean water fuels strong winds and heavy rains. It causes storm surges, flooding, landslides, and wind damage.

Droughts are caused by long dry periods. Droughts can last years. A drought's effects are related to a lack of water. Dried up plants burn easily, so droughts can lead to wildfires.

Tsunamis are a series of giant waves, caused by undersea earthquakes, landslides, or volcanic eruptions. Tsunamis move onto shore, washing away almost anything in their path.

River flooding is caused by heavy rain or snowmelt. Coastal flooding is caused by storm surges. Floodwater can damage structures and cause landslides.

Natural hazard	Cause and effect
hurricane	Effect—
	Cause—Heavy rainfall, melting snow, or a storm surge raises the water level.
tsunami	Effect—
	Effect—Plants, animals, and people do not have enough water, and the wildfire danger is high.

 EVIDENCE NOTEBOOK In your Evidence Notebook, identify how information about the causes and effects of natural hazards can be used to lessen their impacts.

Cause and Effect Choose one natural hazard, and explain both its cause and its effects.

_____

_____

Do the Math
Richter Scale

The Richter scale is used to measure and compare earthquakes. Each magnitude on the Richter scale is 10 times as great as the one before it. So a magnitude 3 earthquake is 10 times as strong as a magnitude 2 earthquake. A magnitude 3 earthquake is also 100 times as strong as a magnitude 1 earthquake.

Magnitude	Ground shaking
1–3	not felt
3–4	weak
4–5	light/moderate
5–6	strong/very strong
6–7	very strong/severe
7+	severe/violent/extreme

Apply Use the table to determine the magnitude of an earthquake in which you felt the ground shake.

_____

_____

Evaluate How much stronger is a magnitude 7 earthquake than a magnitude 5 earthquake?

    a. 2 times as strong   **c.** 100 times as strong

    b. 10 times as strong   **d.** 1,000 times as strong

Explain Use the number 1 to represent the strength of a magnitude 1 earthquake. Explain what number would be used to represent the strength of a magnitude 5 earthquake.

_____

_____

Putting It Together

What are some ways that people can apply information about water-based natural hazards to help people stay safe?

_____

_____

_____

_____

_____

Strong, Stable Structures

Objective

Collaborate as a team to investigate structures that would survive an earthquake.

What question will you investigate to meet this objective?

_____

_____

Materials
- cardboard rolls
- building blocks or sticks
- yarn or string
- tape or glue

Procedure

STEP 1 Certain kinds of buildings and building materials are better able to withstand earthquakes. What questions come to mind when you think about that sentence? On a separate piece of paper, write down as many different questions as you can. Be ready to share them with the class.

STEP 2 With your class, select the most important questions about buildings that survive earthquakes. Write down the questions your class came up with here:

_____

_____

_____

STEP 3 How can you investigate the questions your class picked as most important? Think about the materials your teacher shows you and what else you might need. Write your plan, and show it to your teacher to see if you can get the other things you need. Attach your plan to this lab sheet. If you use other things than those shown by your teacher, be sure to write them in the list above.

STEP 4 Carry out your plan, and record your results. Present your data in a way that everyone can see what you did and what happened. You might choose a table or a graph as a presentation tool. Or you might choose to make a poster with photographs.

Make a claim that answers the question or questions your class decided to explore. You may need to have a **claim** for each question. Support your claim with **evidence** from your investigation and **reasoning** to explain how the evidence supports your claim. Record your claim, evidence, and reasoning on a separate sheet of paper, and attach it to this lab sheet.

Take It Further

After your investigation, what new questions do you have about buildings that survive earthquakes? You can start your question with "What happens if . . ." or "Is this always . . ."

_____

_____

_____

Reducing the Impacts of Natural Hazards

Expect the Unexpected

You can't prevent natural hazards from happening. They are results of Earth's processes. However, you can prepare for natural hazards and plan for how to be safe when they do occur.

Preparation and Response

For each natural hazard shown, research to find out how to prepare ahead of time and respond while it is happening.

Hazard	Preparation	Response
volcanic eruption		
earthquake		
landslide		
wildfire		
hurricane		
tsunami		
flood		
drought		

Predict Circle the pictures that represent a way to stay safe during an earthquake.

Apply Select the pictures that represent a way to stay safe during a hurricane. Circle all the pictures that apply.

 EVIDENCE NOTEBOOK Engineers design technology to keep people safe during an earthquake. How might seismographs and maps showing the history of earthquakes in an area help them? Write your answer in your Evidence Notebook.

 HANDS-ON Apply What You Know

Make a Plan

For every natural hazard, there are ways to plan ahead to be safer. With a team of three or four students, choose a land-based natural hazard. Using what you learn during your research, make a safety video about that hazard. Submit your video to your teacher.

 Language SmArts Gather Information For the natural hazard you chose above, make a plan for each member of your family should that hazard occur. Carry out research by integrating information from two texts, then write your plan below.

_____

_____

_____

_____

Disaster Supply Kit

Select one type of natural hazard. Brainstorm and research what supplies would be important to include in a disaster supply kit for this type of hazard. Draw a diagram of your supply kit. Identify the type of hazard it is designed for. List the things you will include, and write an explanation of why each item is important.

Engineer It!

Earthquake-Resistant Buildings

How would you design an earthquake-resistant building? When engineers design buildings to be resistant to earthquakes, they consider many factors. Look at the picture to learn more.

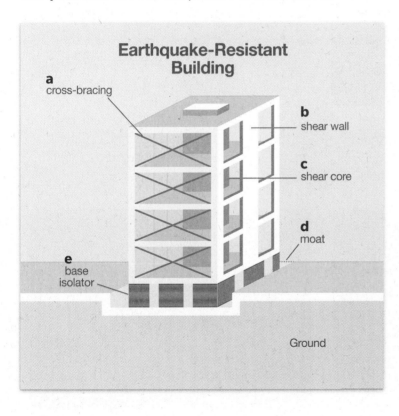

Earthquake-Resistant Building

a
cross-bracing

b
shear wall

c
shear core

d
moat

e
base isolator

Ground

a. Cross-braces are diagonal. They help reinforce the building and increase its stability.

b. Shear walls are vertical walls. They help make the building solid and stiff. They increase the ability of the structure to withstand rocking.

c. In the middle of a building, you might find a shear core. This is an inside structure made out of shear walls. You might find a shear core around an elevator.

d. A moat is an area around the outside of a building. A moat protects the building from damage by nearby buildings that are not earthquake resistant.

e. A base isolator separates the building from the ground. A base isolator is made to absorb the movement of the earthquake.

Communicate Describe two specific ways that engineers make buildings earthquake resistant.

_____

_____

What's the Pattern?

Because we can't prevent natural hazards, scientists study patterns that serve as warning signs. It's important to predict hazards so that people can get to safety or be prepared.

Patterns that Are Warning Signs

Use the pictures and captions to list warning signs for each hazard.

Scientists can predict a volcanic eruption if they see a pattern of movement of the ground, earthquakes, and release of volcanic gases. All of these can be detected by scientific tools.

Warning signs for earthquakes include past earthquakes in the area and strain in Earth's crust. Earth movement is measured using modern technology.

Landslides happen suddenly, with little warning, and are often triggered by earthquakes, volcanoes, heavy rains, and wildfires.

Wildfires occur when there is very little rainfall but heavy winds. Under dry conditions, once a wildfire has started, satellites or aircraft can find it. Then people are alerted and take action.

Tsunamis typically form when earthquakes move large volumes of water. Rising or falling water levels are a warning sign. A warning system tells countries when coasts are in danger.

Warning signs for floods include heavy rainfall, levee or dam failure, and early snowmelt. Warnings are based on past flooding patterns and readings from scientific equipment.

Scientists detect and track hurricanes using satellites and radar. Warning signs can include an increase in ocean swell, wave frequency, wind speed, and rainfall.

Weather and climate patterns, including rainfall and temperature, can help determine what areas are at risk for drought. Reservoirs can save water for periods there are droughts.

Natural hazard				
Warning signs				
Natural hazard	tsunami	flood	hurricane	drought
Warning signs				

Reducing Impacts with Technology

Humans cannot prevent earthquakes, volcanic eruptions, or other natural hazards. But technology can help us be safer from natural hazards.

 Explore Online

Minimize Impacts

Use the pictures and captions to identify the hazard for each technology in the first column. Then research other technologies that help keep us safe, and record them in the table below.

When molten rock moves upward, it tilts the ground around it. A tiltmeter records these changes, helping scientists predict eruptions.

Seismograph readings show the size and location of an earthquake's source, including how deep underground it is.

If a tsunami passes under a deep-ocean detection buoy, the buoy sends data to a warning center. The buoys help scientists predict when tsunamis might reach shore.

Piles and retaining walls are built to keep unstable rocks and soil from sliding down a hillside.

Hazard	Technology	Additional Technologies
	deep-ocean buoys	
	tiltmeter	
	piles and retaining walls	
	seismograph	

Water from a powerful tsunami can travel as far as 16 km inland if the shoreline is not elevated. A tsunami can devastate the area.

A tsunami begins with an underwater disturbance, such as an earthquake.

When the first wave reaches shallow water, it slows down. Its height increases.

A tsunami harms people and property by both the force of its impact and the amount of water it moves onto land.

After the water has drained away, many people find that their homes, schools, and businesses are destroyed.

After a tsunami, people need to clean up and rebuild.

Natural hazards, such as tsunamis, are triggered by Earth processes. They can harm many people, homes, and property, as well as animals and their habitats. What is one way people can reduce the impact of a tsunami?

Infer Imagine that scientists are monitoring an area using a seismometer. They notice patterns of small movements of Earth's surface. They also know this is an area where there is strain in Earth's crust. Which of these natural hazards could happen soon? Circle all that apply.

a. lava erupting from volcano

c. wildfire

b. landslide

d. earthquake

Explain Individual landslides cannot be predicted, but scientists know occurrence of certain hazards can make a landslide more likely. Identify one of those hazards, and explain how it can trigger a landslide.

_____

_____

_____

Predict What pattern of events is most likely to indicate that a wildfire might occur in an area?

a. low rainfall amounts

c. change in the tilt of the land in an area

b. small movements of Earth's surface

d. shifts in Earth materials on a hillside

 EVIDENCE NOTEBOOK One way to prevent landslides is to plant ground cover such as trees, shrubs, and grasses. How might this help stop a landslide from happening? Write your answer in your Evidence Notebook.

 Language SmArts
Summarizing Information

Choose the correct words to complete each sentence.

| watch | patterns | prevent | future | warning |

You cannot _____ natural hazards, but you can

plan what you will do during one. Natural hazards can't be

predicted far in advance, but studying _____

makes some advance warning possible.

Technology helps keep people safe by giving a

_____ that a hazard has begun or by reducing

the impact of the hazard in another way.

Discover More

Check out this path . . . or go online to choose one of these other paths.

People in
Science &
Engineering

- Hawaii Island Lava Hazard Zone Maps
- Debate About a Volcano Solution
- Careers in Science & Engineering

Waverly Person

Waverly Person is a seismologist, or an earthquake scientist, and geophysicist. He is an expert at understanding, predicting, and preparing for earthquakes.

From 1977 to 2006, he was the chief scientist of the United States Geological Survey's National Earthquake Information Center in Golden, Colorado. It was Person's job to construct explanations for why earthquakes happen. He also designed solutions to help communities prepare for earthquakes.

Waverly Person

When Person first started working at the Survey, it would take days of measurements to predict earthquakes. The advancements of computers and other technologies, such as seismographs, now allow scientists to detect and monitor earthquakes in real time.

Person has traveled to schools throughout the United States, encouraging an interest in geology among students.

Person watching seismographs.

Which of the following was **not** a job of Waverly Person?

   a. constructing explanations for why earthquakes happen

   b inventing machines to prevent earthquakes from happening

   c. designing solutions to help communities deal with earthquakes

   d. traveling to schools to encourage students' interest in geology

Go online to the U.S. Geological Survey website, and gather data about earthquakes of magnitude 2.5 or greater in the past year. Determine the five states that had the most earthquakes, and list the states and the number of earthquakes in the table.

State	Frequency

Use the information from the U.S. Geological Survey. Plot the location of the five most recent earthquakes in the United States on the map.

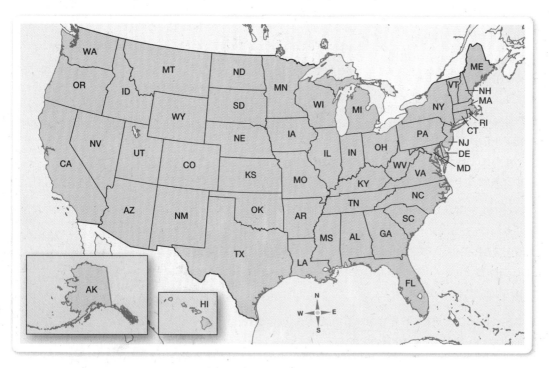

Compare your data to the data found on the earthquake frequency map shown earlier in the lesson. Explain how your results are similar to or different from the information shown in those maps.

_____

_____

_____

Lesson Check

Name _____

Can You Explain It?

1. What are some ways people can reduce the impact of natural hazards, such as earthquakes? Be sure to do the following:

   • Describe several natural hazards.

   • Describe ways that the impact of natural hazards can be lessened.

   • Explain how engineering processes can reduce the impact of natural hazards.

   • In particular, describe how the impacts of earthquakes could be reduced.

EVIDENCE NOTEBOOK Use the information you've collected in your Evidence Notebook to help you cover each point.

_____
_____
_____
_____
_____
_____
_____
_____

Checkpoints

2. Choose the correct response. Which one of these would help scientists predict when a tsunami might reach shore?

   a. daily weather report   **c.** drought monitor map

   b. tiltmeter   **d.** deep-ocean buoy

3. Match each word with the correct picture of a technology that can reduce the impact of that type of hazard.

Natural Hazards

volcanic eruption

tsunami

earthquake

landslide

4. The risks for which natural hazards are increased during time periods when there is not much rain?

 a. volcanic eruption   **c.** earthquake

 b. drought   **d.** wildfire

5. Use the word bank to write the most likely cause of each of these effects.

> earthquake   volcano   both

 a. landslide _____

 b. crumpled roads _____

 c. building collapse _____

 d. release of poisonous gases _____

6. Which natural hazards are most likely to be the direct cause of a wildfire? Circle all that apply.

 a. earthquake

 b. volcano

 c. landslide

 d. lightning strike

Lesson Roundup

A. Choose a technology from the word bank that can lessen the impact of each natural hazard.

earthquake-resistant building	**firebreak**	**retaining wall**
deep-ocean buoys	**reservoirs**	**tiltmeter**

_____

_____

_____

_____

B. What else have you learned about natural hazards in this lesson?

_____

_____

_____

Withstanding Water

You are an engineer in the United States. Your team has asked you to design a building that will keep out water during a flood.

DEFINE YOUR TASK: How will you know if your project is successful? Before beginning, review the checklist at the end of this Unit Performance Task. Keep those items in mind as you proceed.

You'll need to design a building that will keep out water during a flood.

_____

_____

_____

RESEARCH: Use online or library resources to learn about building engineering. Find out how engineers design buildings to stand up to flooding. Note the kinds of features the designs use to prevent water from entering the building. Cite your sources.

_____

_____

_____

BRAINSTORM: Brainstorm engineering design ideas. Use what you learned from your research to come up with a design that you could use to make buildings safe during floods.

_____

_____

CRITERIA: List the criteria for your design.

_____

_____

CONSTRAINTS: List the constraints for your design.

_____

_____

DESIGN: Draw a design of your model in the space below. Label the structures of your building.

PEER REVIEW: Swap your model drawing with another classmate, and review each other's work. Give the classmate feedback on his or her design.

IMPROVEMENT: Make any improvements to your design based on the feedback you got. List the improvements that you made.

_____

_____

Review your model, and decide how you will modify it based on feedback.

COMMUNICATE: Present your design to your class. Explain the reasoning behind your design, and discuss possible ways to revise and improve it even more.

✓ Checklist

Review your project and check off each completed item.

_____ includes a statement defining the task

_____ includes research of building design and cites sources

_____ includes 2–3 brainstormed ideas for the design

_____ includes design criteria and constraints

_____ includes model drawing with labels

_____ includes a list of improvements made to the design

_____ includes an oral presentation of the design to the class

Unit Review

1. Which choice names two parts of a wave?
   Circle the correct choice.

   a. size and speed

   b. crest and trough

   c. amplitude and volume

   d. wavelength and reflection

2. Classify each item as an example of back-and-forth waves (*B*), up-and-down waves (*U*), or both (*both*).

   _____ music

   _____ light from stars

   _____ satellite signals

   _____ earthquake tremors

3. What two types of waves are produced by this performance?
   Circle the correct choices.

   a. light waves

   b. water waves

   c. sound waves

   d. seismic waves

4. Match the word with its definition.

   wavelength   the lowest point of a wave

   amplitude   the distance between two crests

   volume   the loudness of a sound

   crest   the height of a wave

   trough   the highest point of a wave

5. Where are volcanoes most likely to occur on land? Circle all that apply.

   a. near coasts

   b. all over a continent

   c. near the Ring of Fire

   d. in higher areas such as mountains

   e. only in the ocean

6. What long-term natural disaster is pictured here?

Circle the correct choice.

   a. a flood

   b. a drought

   c. a tsunami

   d. a hurricane

7. Use the word bank to complete the sentences.

hurricanes	**half as strong as**	**twice as strong as**
earthquakes	**volcanoes**	**ten times stronger than**

The Richter scale is used to measure the strength of _____.

Each level of the Richter scale is _____ the

previous level.

8. Air and water at different temperatures can produce violent storms such as hurricanes. Explain how temperature, water, and air are related to a hurricane.

_____

_____

_____

_____

9. If an earthquake happens on land, where is it most likely to occur?

    a. along a fault line

    b. in the middle of the continent

    c. along the mountain ranges of the continent

    d. in the center of big cities

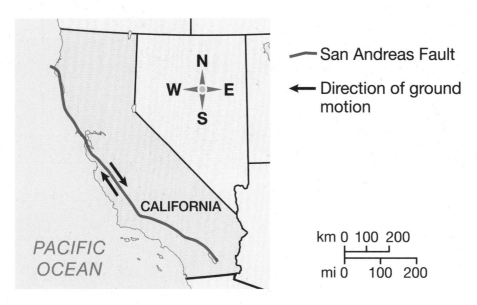

10. Look at the map. Then answer the question.

Which statements about faults are true? Circle all that apply.

    a. Fault lines can be aboveground or underwater.

    b. Fault lines only appear aboveground.

    c. Fault lines last short distances and are never long.

    d. Fault lines can cover long distances.

Plant and Animal Structure and Function

Explore Online

You Solve It: Structures and Functions
As you learn about the structures and functions of plants and animals, you get to investigate different digestive systems that are adapted to the kinds of foods animals eat. Ask your teacher for details.

Like all plants and animals, this rhinoceros has body parts, or structures, that carry out functions that keep it alive.

At a Glance

Name _____

UNIT PROJECT

Plant and Animal Partnerships

Have you ever seen a hummingbird drink nectar from a flower? Did you notice that its beak is the perfect shape and length for reaching the sweet nectar it wants? For this project, you will investigate how the structure and function of plants and animals work together to allow for pollination. You will then present your findings to the class.

Hummingbird drinking nectar

Write a question that you will investigate as you perform your analysis of plant and animal structures and functions related to pollination.

_____

_____

_____

Materials Think about how you will perform this investigation. What materials will you need?

_____

_____

_____

To carry out this investigation, decide, as a team, on the plant and animal you wish to focus on. Think about selecting plants and animals based on your interest or based on the ones that are native to your area (although you are not limited to this). Which plant and animal did your team decide on?

_____

_____

Research and Plan Make a plan for how you will carry out your investigation. As you make your plan, consider the following:

- What are the structures and functions of the animal parts?

- What are the structures and functions of the plant parts?

- Do the structures and functions work together to result in pollination?

Use Internet sources and books to complete your research.

_____

_____

_____

_____

_____

_____

_____

Review your research as a group. Write a conclusion about the structures and functions of animal and plant parts and how they work together to support pollination.

_____

_____

Review your research to draw conclusions and cite evidence.

_____

_____

_____

Analyze Your Results Look for patterns in the data you found. Based on your investigation, make an observation about animal and plant parts and pollination.

_____

_____

_____

_____

Restate Your Question Write the question you investigated.

_____

_____

_____

Claims, Evidence, and Reasoning Make a claim that answers your question.

_____

_____

_____

Review your investigation. What evidence from your investigation supports your claim?

_____

_____

_____

Discuss your reasoning with a partner.

Language Development

Use the lessons in this unit to complete the network and expand understanding of the science concepts.

fertilization

Words about Plant and Animal Structure and Function

pollination

receptors

reproduction

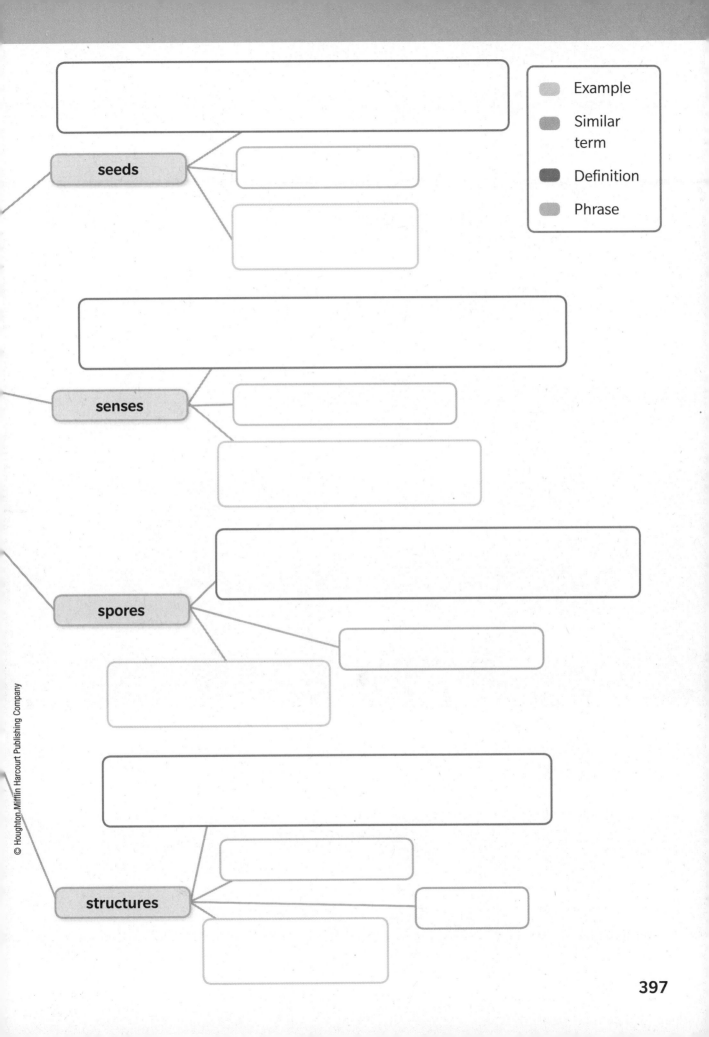

Example

Similar term

Definition

Phrase

seeds

senses

spores

structures

© Houghton Mifflin Harcourt Publishing Company

397

What Are Some Plant Parts, and How Do They Function?

Different plants have different types of structures. The structures function in ways that enable the plants to survive.

Explore First

What's Your Opinion? Which plant parts do you think are the most important for survival? Examine the plant samples your teacher provides, and identify parts that you think are important for survival. Be prepared to support your argument using evidence.

Can You Explain It?

👉 Explore Online

Examine the images above. Have you ever noticed an indoor plant leaning in one direction instead of growing straight up?

Why do you think the plants in the pictures bend in the directions that they do? How would this behavior help the plant grow and survive?

_____

_____

_____

_____

_____

_____

_____

_____

_____

 EVIDENCE NOTEBOOK Look for this icon to help you gather evidence to answer the questions above.

Plant Dissection

Do Parts Serve Purposes?

You can tell from a quick glance at a plant that it has different structures. **Structures** are the physical parts of living things. Many plants have similar structures that perform similar functions.

Functions of Plant Parts

Complete each description. Then label the plant structures with the letters.

| root | stem | leaf | flower |

a. _____ This part of the plant grows down into soil.

b. _____ This part of the plant captures sunlight.

c. _____ This part of the plant grows away from the ground and helps keep the plant upright.

d. _____ This part of the plant attracts insects.

Infer Fill in the chart below to explain how you think each of these parts is involved in plant survival.

Plant part	How is it involved in plant survival?
root	
stem	
leaf	
flower	

Part by Part

Some plants have different parts that serve different purposes. Read about the functions of these parts and how they help the different types of plants survive.

Thorns are sharp, pointed parts on some plants. Thorns protect a plant from being eaten by animals. **Flowers** attract insects and are involved in reproduction so that the plant can make new plants.

Cones are involved in the reproduction of certain kinds of plants. **Bark**, a tree's woody covering, protects it from cold temperatures and from animal damage.

Cacti live in dry areas and have **spines** instead of wide, flat leaves. Not having flat leaves reduces water loss. Spines also protect the cactus from animals.

Plants such as ferns and mosses produce **spores**, which are often released into air. When spores land in a spot where conditions are right for growth, a new plant will start to grow.

Roots help hold a plant in place. They also absorb water and nutrients from the soil. These materials are needed for a plant to survive and grow.

Leaves capture sunlight and use it to make food in the form of sugar. Plants use the food to grow. Plant **stems** support leaves and help plants stay upright.

Compare How are thorns on a flower and spines on a cactus similar? Circle the correct answer.

a. Both reduce water loss.

c. Both absorb water from soil.

b. Both protect plants from animals.

d. Both hold plants upright.

Explain Which function do roots *not* perform?

a. absorb water from soil

c. develop seeds for reproduction

b. anchor a plant in place

d. absorb nutrients from soil

Similar but Different

When you look around at different plants, you see that they often have similar structures—roots, stems, leaves, flowers, and more. But these structures do not look exactly the same in all plants. Leaves and flowers differ in shape, size, and color. Some plants have thorns. Others do not.

Different Parts, Similar Jobs

Compare how the plant structures in each set of photographs function. Write whether the parts most support protection, growth, or reproduction.

A. A **taproot** can get water from deep underground, and it does well in droughts. It can also store food.

B. **Fibrous roots** can quickly absorb water and nutrients near the soil's surface. They also stop soil erosion.

_____

C. This large, **flat leaf** captures sunlight. Having lots of large leaves in spring and summer allows the plant to absorb more sunlight and make more food.

D. The **needles** of evergreens such as pine trees gather sunlight for the plant to make food. Their shape and waxy coating reduce water loss during dry weather.

_____

E. **Woody stems** allow plants such as trees and shrubs to stay upright in strong winds. They can help trees become very tall. Tall plants get more sunlight.

F. Other plants, such as dandelions and sunflowers, have **green stems.** These stems can also capture sunlight while they hold the plants up and support branches, leaves, and other parts.

_____

402

G. Plants such as dandelions and apple trees produce **flowers**. A flower has different parts that are involved in reproduction, including petals and the pollen-producing stamen. Many flowers attract animals that move pollen from one plant to another.

H. Plants such as pine trees make **cones** instead of flowers. Male cones release pollen that pollinates female cones. Female cones then hold seeds until they are ready to be released. New plants grow from seeds that land in places with the right conditions.

I. Other types of plants reproduce through the use of **spores**. Once spores are released, they are carried by wind. If spores land in a place with the right conditions, new plants will grow.

J. Some plants, such as roses, have **thorns** with sharp, pointed ends that can injure an animal that tries to eat the plant.

K. Tough, thick **bark** prevents many animals from eating trees and shrubs. It also reduces infections caused by fungi or bacteria getting into a plant.

L. Plants, such as cacti, that live in dry areas have leaves shaped like **spines**. An animal that tries to eat a spiny plant will likely be injured.

Language SmArts
Writing Opinion Pieces

Think of the functions of the different plant parts you have explored. Recall that some plant parts have more than one function. For example, roots absorb water and minerals from the soil, but they also anchor a plant in place.

Make a **claim** about which plant part you think is most important for plant growth. Use three facts to provide **evidence** to support your claim. You may use facts from this lesson. You may also do additional research to support your **reasoning**.

Record your claim and your evidence in the table below. Then debate your claim with your classmates.

Claim	Evidence
I think that the _____ is the most important part for plant growth.	Fact 1: _____ _____ _____ _____ _____ Fact 2: _____ _____ _____ _____ _____ Fact 3: _____ _____ _____ _____ _____

What's Inside?

Slurp!

You have already learned that the roots of a plant absorb water and minerals from soil. How does the plant use the water?

before

You've seen a stalk of celery like this before.

after

Explore Online

If you put a stalk of celery that has been cut in colored water, it will look like this.

Explain Why do the leaves become the same color as the colored water? How do you think this happens?

_____

_____

_____

_____

Do the Math
Reason Quantitatively

How long does it take water to move up a plant? Suppose you have a 14 cm plant. You've observed that in this plant, colored water moves up the stem at about 0.5 cm per hour. How long would it take the colored water to reach the top of the plant?

_____

_____

It's What's Inside that Counts

Do you know why the celery's appearance changed when it was placed in colored water? Take a closer look at the inside of the stems in the two plants below. Each one will show a different system of tubes that helps the plant survive and grow.

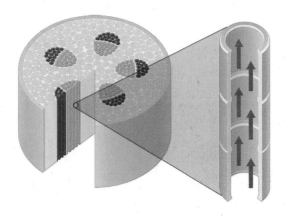 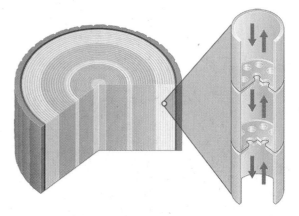

Inside a plant stem is a system of **water-carrying tubes.** Water is taken in from the roots. The water moves through the tubes into the plant's leaves. The leaves can then use the water to make food.

Sugar that is made in a plant's leaves moves through a system of **food-carrying tubes.** These tubes travel from the leaves, throughout the plant, and down to the roots. Some plant roots, such as carrots, store extra sugar produced by the plant.

Language SmArts Interpret what you see. Briefly describe the two different tube systems in a plant.

_____

_____

_____

_____

_____

_____

Identify Write the words in the order that food moves from one plant part to the next.

| roots | tubes | leaves |

_____ ➡ _____ ➡ stem ➡ _____

Engineer It!
Green Roofs

Growing grass and plants on the rooftops of buildings in cities helps solve two problems. First, it allows more space to grow plants in cities that have limited space. Second, a grass layer reduces how hot the building gets on hot summer days.

In winter, heat from inside the building keeps the grass warmer. This means the grass can grow for a longer part of the year.

Explore Online

Vegetation

Growing medium

Drainage

Water and root barrier

Thermal insulation

Roof surface

To grow grass on rooftops successfully, you need different layers of materials. First, a layer is needed to protect the roof and the plants. A layer of insulation and a layer of waterproof material keep roots from growing into the roof. Next is a layer of material that will allow water to drain away from the roof. The top layer includes the soil and growing plants.

Evaluate What are some advantages and disadvantages of green roofs? Do additional research if needed.

_____

_____

_____

_____

HANDS-ON Apply What You Know

Modeling Water Flow in Plants

Using what you can infer about water moving in celery, make a 3D model of a plant's water system. Your model does not need to function, but do use different materials to represent the different materials in the plant.

 EVIDENCE NOTEBOOK Think about the tube systems in plants and the leaning plants pictured at the beginning of the lesson. Which tube system moves substances formed in leaves? substances absorbed by the roots?

Putting It Together

Analyze What color do you see in the celery besides its normal green color? What does this suggest?

_____

_____

Reason Use the celery investigation to support the following claim with evidence.

"A celery plant has a tube system that carries water through the plant."
Circle all evidence statements that apply.

  a. I can see the tubes when the celery is cut open.

  b. I can see that the color of the tubes is the same color as the water when the celery is cut open.

  c. The color of water in the bowl got lighter. This means that water must have been absorbed by the celery.

  d. I can see that the leaves turned the same color as the water.

Hold the Soil

Objective

Collaborate to build a system to grow plants in water instead of soil.

Growing plants in water instead of soil is called hydroponics. As long as plants have the sunlight, space, water, and nutrients they need added to the water, they can grow without soil.

Imagine that a company has hired you to grow hydroponic plants. Use your knowledge of plant parts and their functions to design such a system. Your budget is $12. Your system cannot be larger than 30 cm x 15 cm x 15 cm.

Find a Problem: What question will you investigate to meet this objective?

Materials	Cost
• 5 bean seeds	$3
• plastic cup or bottle	$1 for 1 or $2 for 3
• paper towel	$1 for 2 or $2 for 5
• gravel	$2 per 113 g
• vermiculite	$2 per 113 g
• cotton balls	$1 for 3 or $2 for 10
• foam pellets	$1 per 113 g
• liquid nutrients	$2 per 50 g
• aluminum foil	$1 per ¼ sq. m
• plastic wrap	$1 per ¼ sq. m
• metric ruler	$0
• water	$0

Procedure

STEP 1 **Research** with your group how to grow seeds in water instead of soil.

STEP 2 **Define the problem.** What are your criteria?

What are your constraints?

STEP 3 **Brainstorm** solutions for your system in which to grow seeds. Then **evaluate** your solutions and **choose the best.**

STEP 4 Develop and test a model. Draw your device. Write how you will test it. Get your teacher's approval before you follow your plan.

Explain how you made sure you met the criteria and constraints in your system.

_____

_____

_____

STEP 5 Build and **test** your system. Write out the steps.

_____

_____

_____

STEP 6 Observe your system. Record results at least two times a week for four weeks. Use a ruler as a tool to measure the growth of the plants.

Observation Table

Date	Seed/plant growth (cm)	Other observations

How many of your bean seeds sprouted? Of those plants, how many survived four weeks or more? How much did they grow?

_____

_____

_____

Evaluate and Redesign your device. How well did you meet the criteria and constraints? What improvements could you make to your system's design?

_____

_____

_____

Communicate to compare your hydroponic system and results with those of other groups. Did another group's seeds grow better than yours? Why or why not?

_____

_____

_____

Make a **claim** based on your investigation. Support your claim with **evidence** from this activity. Explain your **reasoning.**

_____

_____

_____

Think of other problems you would like to solve related to designing systems to grow plants.

_____

_____

Can Plants Move?

Move and Groove

Have you ever seen a vine grow up the side of a house or wrap around a fence post? What happens if a potted plant gets knocked over on its side and keeps growing? Plants have certain behaviors that help them grow and survive.

In picture **a,** the plant was knocked over on its side and grew in one direction. Why do you think this occurred?

_____

_____

In picture **b,** the plant was placed by a window and grew in one direction. Why do you think this occurred?

_____

_____

In picture **c,** the leaves of the mimosa folded inward when it was touched. Why do you think this happened?

_____

_____

Oh, Behave!

In nature, plants live in environments where conditions change constantly. The sun is not visible all day. The temperature can change drastically. A herd of animals may rumble through the environment. Whatever the conditions, plants have to absorb sunlight, make food, grow, and survive.

How Do You Grow?

Read about plant behaviors below, and complete the activity.

Plants **respond to light.** Plants need sunlight to make food, so a house plant that sits in front of a window will grow toward the light. If the plant is not turned regularly, it will become very lopsided. Circle the image that shows what will happen if this plant is not turned at the window.

The roots of plants grow down toward the center of Earth in **response to gravity.** The stem of a plant grows in the opposite direction, away from the center of Earth. This usually results in the stem growing upward. Circle the image that shows what will happen if this plant is knocked over.

Some plants respond to touch. A leaf might curl up to protect a plant from damage or from being eaten. A Venus flytrap clasps its leaves closed if an insect touches the fine hairs on the inside of the leaves. For plants that eat insects, this is an important **response to touch.** Circle the image that shows what will happen when the fly lands on the leaf.

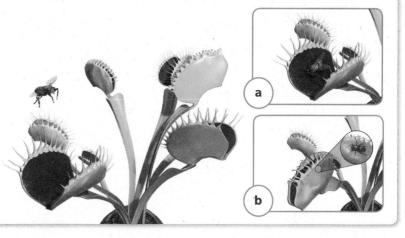

EVIDENCE NOTEBOOK Which photo on the previous page shows a plant's bending behavior similar to what you saw at the beginning of the lesson? Describe the similarities in your Evidence Notebook.

Apply What You Know

Plant Response

Choose one of the ways that a plant responds to its environment. Draw a comic strip with at least three panels showing one of the plant behaviors you learned about. Write captions for each panel you draw.

_____   _____   _____

_____   _____   _____

_____   _____   _____

_____   _____   _____

Language SmArts
Multiple Sources

Using multiple sources, explain how plant behavior helps plants survive. Cite your sources.

_____

_____

_____

_____

_____

Discover More

Check out this path . . . or go online to choose one of these other paths.

Careers in Science & Engineering

- **Burrr!**
- **People in Science & Engineering**

Botanist

Plants keep humans alive. We eat them, and animals that eat them provide us with food. Plants also produce the clean air we breathe. Without plants, our atmosphere would be filled with the gases that other animals and we produce. We could not survive in such a world.

A botanist is a scientist who studies plants. Some botanists investigate how to keep plants healthy. Others focus on certain types of plants. Still others work with plants that are important to a particular business or industry. Some botanists even work with other scientists to develop vaccines grown in plants.

Jenny Xiang (*left*) is a botanist. Much of her research focuses on how plants respond to changes in climate. She breeds plants that can grow in high temperatures and fight infections caused by other organisms.

Marie-Anne Van Sluys (*left*) and Mariana Cabral de Oliveira (*right*)

The grape industries in California produce nearly $3 billion a year. In the early 2000s, a sickness called Pierce's disease attacked California's grapevines. It was caused by tiny organisms, called *bacteria*. The bacteria block the flow of water within a plant and kill it. Two botanists, Marina Cabral de Oliveira and Marie-Anne Van Sluys, determined how the bacteria made the plants sick by studying patterns. Scientists often look at patterns to analyze or interpret data. Their research produced ways to effectively fight the disease.

415

Pedro Acevedo is a research botanist who works at the American Museum of Natural History in Washington, D.C. His research focuses on plants in the soapberry family, and he has worked on multiple plant field guides. Soapberry plants produce berries that have a soap like compound. This compound was historically used for cleaning.

Plant and field guides are books that are often used by other scientists and by environmental enthusiasts. These guides can be used to identify plants and animals.

Pedro Acevedo

Apply What You Know

How Unusual!

Suppose you are a botanist who has been asked to do a report for a television news station. You will need to research an unusual plant. Make sure to identify all of the parts of the plant and how each of these parts helps it to grow, survive, reproduce, and respond to the environment.

Now make a news report based on your research. Either record a video or use a design program to make a presentation with at least four slides about the unusual plant you researched. Share your video or presentation with classmates.

Use the space below to sketch out your plan.

Lesson Check

Name _____

Explore Online

Can You Explain It?

1. You've now learned more about plant parts and the functions they perform. Explain why a plant bends as its light source moves. Be sure to do the following:

   • Explain the relationship between sunlight and food in plants.

   • Identify the role of each plant part in capturing and using sunlight.

   • Describe how growth and food relate to better chances of survival for a plant.

EVIDENCE NOTEBOOK Use the information you've collected in your Evidence Notebook to help you cover each point above.

_____

_____

_____

_____

_____

_____

_____

_____

Checkpoints

2. Which parts of a plant are mostly involved in protecting it from animals? Circle all that apply.

   a. bark

   b. leaves

   c. spines

   d. thorns

3. Study the parts of the image. Write the letter of the correct label for the material that is carried by the system of tubes in each image. All labels may not apply.

   a. food

   b. soil

   c. water

   d. heat

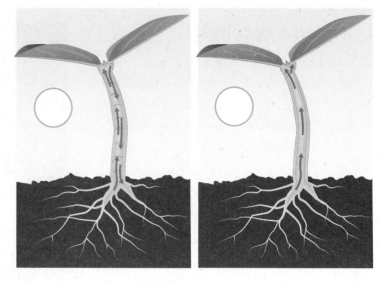

4. Support this claim with the correct evidence below: Roots are involved in plant growth.

   a. Roots absorb water, which plants need to make food.

   b. Roots capture sunlight, which gives plants a source of energy for making food.

   c. Roots help protect plants from animals.

   d. Roots are involved in plant reproduction.

5. Which answer correctly states how the food system in a plant functions?

   a. Leaves absorb water, which plants need to make food.

   b. Leaves produce food using sunlight, and food moves down the tubes to the rest of the plant.

   c. Roots absorb nutrients, and nutrients move up the tubes and turn to sugar.

6. Plants respond to _____ when they bend toward windows. Some plants respond to _____ when they trap food. In response to _____, plant parts bend so that each part is in the right position to do its special job.

   gravity

   light

   touch

Lesson Roundup

A. Write the main function of each plant part.

> growth   reproduction   protection

Stem _____

Roots _____

Flower _____

Spines _____

B. Choose all the correct descriptions about plant tube systems.

   a. Water moves from the roots of a plant to the rest of the plant through a system of tubes.

   b. Food moves from the roots of a plant to the rest of the plant through a system of leaves.

   c. Food moves from the leaves of a plant to the rest of the plant through a system of tubes.

   d. Water moves from the leaves of a plant to the rest of the plant through a system of tubes.

C. Write the letter of the type of response that each picture shows.

> **a.** response to touch   **b.** response to gravity   **c.** response to light

What Are Some Animal Parts, and How Do They Function?

Animals come in all different shapes and sizes. They move around in different ways, too. What kinds of parts does this starfish have for moving? How does it use those parts to accomplish what it needs to do?

Explore First

Functional Structures Find images of three animals using print or digital resources. Observe and identify the parts the animals use to eat and move. Draw these body parts on a sheet of paper. Think about how the animals use these body parts. How do the parts help the animals survive?

Can You Explain It?

Explore Online

Lizards are excellent climbers, expertly moving around. Most lizards climb like the one on the left. The lizard on the red wall on the right is called a gecko. How are its feet different from those of the other lizard?

What did you observe about the two lizards in the photos? You can see how the lizard on the left is moving on the grass. But how is the surface the gecko is climbing on different from the grass? How do you think the gecko's external structures are different?

_____

_____

_____

_____

_____

_____

_____

 EVIDENCE NOTEBOOK Look for this icon to help you gather evidence to answer the question above.

Body Building

It's All in the Skin

Animals that live in different environments have to deal with different conditions. These conditions can determine or limit the characteristics animals that live in those environments have to survive.

Body Coverings

Match each description with the animal covering it describes.

a. Moisture and oxygen pass easily through the thin, moist skin. The animal needs to live in a wet and warm environment.

c. A slimy substance produced by the skin keeps it from drying out in the warm environment.

b. Thick hairs trap heat produced by the animal's body to keep the animal warm in cold environments.

d. Transparent, hollow hairs of the fur appear white so that the animal can blend into its environment.

Animals have *external structures* that support survival, growth, behavior, and reproduction. External structures are structures on the outside of an organism.

Language SmArts
Compare External Structures

Look at the frog and the polar bear. Compare their external structures. How are these structures alike? How are they different?

_____

_____

_____

Time to Eat

Animals have external structures that they use to eat. Look at the photos to see how some animals get food.

Explore Online

Mountain lions have powerful jaws with very sharp teeth inside their mouths.

Antelope have mouths with flat teeth at the front. This allows them to bite grass close to the ground.

Giant tubeworms have no mouths! Tubeworms get nutrients from tiny organisms that live in them.

Eagles have very large, hooked beaks that easily tear apart flesh.

The frog has a flexible jaw that allows it to open wide to snatch food with a long, sticky tongue.

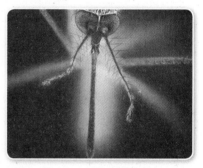

The female mosquito uses its tubelike mouth part to pierce skin and suck blood.

Classify What do you think these animals eat, based on the structures of their mouth parts? What inferences can you make?

Animal	What does it eat?	What's your evidence?
mountain lion		
antelope		
female mosquito		
golden eagle		
frog		
giant tubeworm		

423

Take Cover

Animals can be soft, hard, rough, slimy, or have spines. There are many kinds of coverings that protect the insides of an animal's body.

Explore Online

Fur insulates this alpaca, preventing heat loss in the cold mountains.

Birds have feathers to keep warm. They are also necessary for the bird to fly.

A snake's smooth scales allow it to grip and push against surfaces to move.

A hard shell covers some animals, such as tortoises, for protection.

Some animals have sharp spines on their skin to keep them safe.

A sea cucumber's leathery skin protects it from predators.

What's the Purpose?

Select the best answer from the word bank that describes each animal covering and completes the sentence.

| predators | body | scales | shells | spines |

_____ cover the length of the fish's _____.

A sea urchin has _____ for protection from _____.

feathers	fur	cool	warm
fat	wet	moist	flight

Guinea pigs are covered with _____. This helps

keep them _____.

A blue jay's _____ keep it warm. This kind of body

covering is also required in birds for _____.

 EVIDENCE NOTEBOOK Animals have many external structures that function to support survival, growth, behavior, and reproduction. Make a list of some of the other structures you see in the photos on this spread.

Apply What You Know

Design to Survive

With a group, pick an environment and describe the conditions in that environment. Then select body parts from several animals to create a new animal that would survive there. Decide what your animal eats. Design your animal on a poster, and label and describe your animal's body parts. Make sure to explain how the parts help the animal survive in its environment!

Putting It Together

Suppose you come across a picture of an animal under water with scales and a large mouth. It has no feathers or fur. Choose the argument for the animal that most likely fits the description.

- **a.** a snake because it has scales
- **b.** a lion because it has a large mouth
- **c.** a fish because it has scales and a large mouth
- **d.** a frog because it does not have feathers or fur

Inside Out

Body Language

You have learned about the external structures that animals have. They also have *internal structures* that support their growth and survival.

Look at some of the internal structures this dog has. Do you recognize some that you have, too?

The **lungs** are part of the respiratory system. They take in oxygen from the air.

The **stomach** is part of the digestive system. It breaks down the dog's food.

The **heart** is part of the circulatory system. It pumps blood throughout the dog's body.

The **liver** is also part of the digestive system. It cleans the dog's blood and stores energy the dog needs.

Internal structures are structures on the inside of an organism. The heart, lungs, and stomach are examples of internal structures.

A system is something with parts that work together. Humans and other animals have body systems. The circulatory system includes the heart, blood, veins, and arteries. The respiratory system includes the lungs, nose, and mouth. All the body's systems work together to help animals grow and survive.

 EVIDENCE NOTEBOOK Think about the lizards at the beginning of the lesson. They have similar and different external structures. List some internal structures that you think both lizards have in common.

For each image, draw a circle over the heart and a square over the lungs.

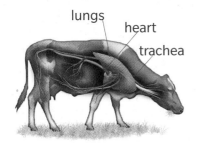

lungs
heart
trachea

A cow's heart has arteries that carry blood to the lungs and the rest of the body. Veins carry blood back to the heart.

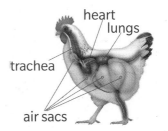

heart
lungs
trachea
air sacs

Birds, such as this chicken, have large hearts. A bird's heart helps it keep its body at the right temperature.

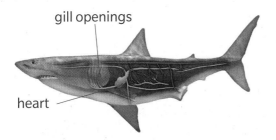

gill openings
heart

A shark's heart has two chambers. It is shaped like the letter S. Sharks do not have lungs. They have gills instead.

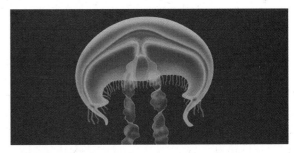

Jellyfish do not have a circulatory system. They don't have a respiratory system, either. They take in oxygen through their skin.

Do the Math
Heart Beat

Animals' hearts beat at different rates. A smaller animal's heart usually beats faster than that of a large animal. Look at the table. Then answer the questions.

Animal	Heartbeats per minute (bpm)
elephant	30 bpm
rabbit	200 bpm

How many more times per minute does a rabbit's heart beat than an elephant's?

_____

A horse's heart beats 44 bpm. A hamster's heart beats 450 bpm. How would you order the animals so they would be in order from least to most beats per minute?

_____

_____

For each image, draw a star on the esophagus, a square on the stomach, and a triangle on the intestines.

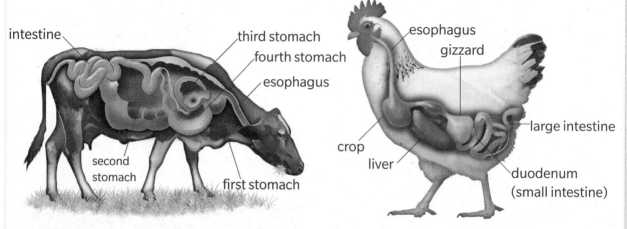

Cows have stomachs with four parts. A cow needs to chew and swallow its food several times during digestion.

Chickens have a gizzard. It is like a stomach. Some birds have a crop, which holds food until it can be sent to the digestive system.

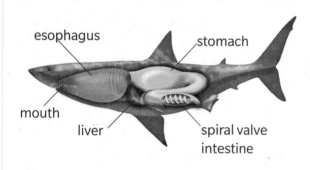

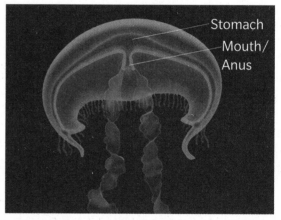

Sharks have spiral-shaped intestines and a *U*-shaped stomach to break down food that is swallowed whole!

Jellyfish do not have digestive systems. Food enters the mouth and is broken down in the body. Waste then leaves through the mouth.

Language SmArts
Compare and Contrast Body Systems

Explain one difference between the circulatory system and the digestive system.

_____

_____

_____

Dinner Is Served

Objective

Collaborate as a team to investigate external animal structures involved in animal feeding.

What question will you investigate to meet this objective?

_____

_____

Procedure

STEP 1 Different kinds of animals eat different kinds of foods. Some animals need to catch other animals in order to eat. Animals that eat other animals have external structures that allow them to catch other animals in order to survive. What questions come to mind when you think about the previous sentence? Write down as many different questions as you can. Be ready to share them with the class.

_____

_____

_____

_____

_____

_____

_____

_____

_____

_____

STEP 2 With your class, select the most important questions about external animal structures. Write down the questions your class came up with here:

_____

_____

STEP 3 How can you investigate the questions your class picked as most important? Think about the materials your teacher shows you and what else you might need. Write your plan and show it to your teacher to see if you can get the other things you need.

Attach your plan to this lab sheet. If you use other things than those shown by your teacher, be sure to write them in the materials list.

STEP 4 Carry out your plan, and record your results. Present your data in a way that everyone can see what you did and what happened. You might choose a table or a graph as a presentation tool. Or you might choose to make a poster with photographs.

Make a claim that answers the question or questions your class decided to explore. You may need to have a claim for each question. Support your claim with evidence from your investigation and reasoning to explain how the evidence supports your claim. Record your **claim**, **evidence**, and **reasoning** below.

_____

_____

_____

Take It Further

After your investigation, what new questions do you have about animal structures involved in hunting and survival? You can start your question with "What happens if . . ." or "Is this always . . ."

_____

_____

_____

_____

On the Move

Explore Online

Moving Parts

Animals have structures that help them move. Look at the pictures below. Record similarities and differences about the way these animals move.

An ant crawls along with its six legs.

The two larger hind legs of the frog are strong, allowing it to jump far.

Alike:

Different:

A bat's wings are thin, stretchy membranes made of skin that catch the air to fly.

A pigeon flaps its feathered wings to move itself up in the air.

Alike:

Different:

The tail of the shark pushes from side to side against the water, moving it along.

A dolphin pushes its tail up and down to move forward in the water.

Alike:

Different:

Moving through the Environment

Animals are *adapted* to, or fit well in, the environments in which they live. They have external body parts that allow them to move about on land, in the air, or through the water.

Land, Water, or Air?

Based on your observations, label whether the animal best moves on land, in air, or in water.

_____   _____   _____

Although most animals have structures for moving in their environment, there are some animals that don't often move from place to place. Corals, sponges, and barnacles are animals that mostly stay in one place. These animals have structures that let them catch food even though they cannot move.

 Language SmArts What do the animals moving about in each environment have in common? Look at the images on this page. List similarities in structures you observe in the animals.

_____

_____

_____

_____

_____

_____

Same but Different

As you have learned, animals use different structures for different functions. Sometimes body parts with different structures in different animals have similar functions.

Comparing Animal Parts

Examine the pictures. Then use your observations to compare and contrast each pair of animal parts in the boxes.

Bat's wing

Bird's wing

Compare and Contrast

Ant's legs

Wolf's legs

Compare and Contrast

Frog's legs

Dolphin's tail

Compare and Contrast

Find the Inspiration

What do you think the device in the photo is? What is its function?

Sometimes nature is the source for an engineer's design. Engineers may observe plant or animal parts and try to mimic their structures or functions in their designs. This device is an *ornithopter*. Research to learn more about what an ornithopter is. Determine which animal structure inspired the engineering design.

Then think of an animal that has an ability that you think would be useful. Design a device that is similar in function to the ability of the animal. Then describe the function of your design and build a model of it to present to your class.

Define a Problem. What problem do you think engineers were trying to solve when they designed an ornithopter?

_____

_____

_____

 EVIDENCE NOTEBOOK Think of an object that humans use that may be similar to a structure on the lizard's feet. Draw the object in your notebook. Then draw the animal's structure. Explain how they are similar.

Putting It Together

How might studying animal structures provide people with ideas for new inventions?

_____

_____

_____

_____

© Houghton Mifflin Harcourt Publishing Company • Image Credits: ©Kike Calvo/age

Discover More

Check out this path . . . or go online to choose one of these other paths.

People in Science & Engineering

- Careers in Science & Engineering
- Balanced Parts
- Careers in Science & Engineering

Henry Gray and Vanessa Ruiz

Henry Gray is famous for publishing a book titled *Gray's Anatomy* in 1858. In the book, Henry Gray gave detailed written descriptions of human body structures and systems. The book also included many illustrations. The illustrations, which were drawn by Henry Vandyke Carter, showed human body systems in a detailed way. The book is still used as a medical reference today.

Explore Online

Henry Gray was an English doctor who studied anatomy.

Vanessa Ruiz is a medical illustrator and artist who combines medical illustration and contemporary art. Her images of human body structures and systems are published and shown in public spaces. She hopes to show people that medical art can be interesting. She also hopes to increase people's awareness of the structures of the human body.

Vanessa Ruiz is an artist known for her work in anatomy.

Animal Anatomy

Research the structure of different animal hearts. Find information about the structure of two-, three-, and four-chambered hearts. Then research the circulatory and respiratory systems of at least six different animals. When you have completed your research, write and illustrate a booklet titled "Anatomy of Animal Systems." Include detailed written descriptions and accurate illustrations. Be sure to list your name as author and illustrator!

Animal	Number of chambers

Lesson Check

Name _____

Can You Explain It?

1. Think back to the lizards from the beginning of the lesson.

- What structures do the animals have in common?

- How do the structures function similarly?

- How do the structures function differently?

- Explain how the gecko climbs vertical surfaces.

 EVIDENCE NOTEBOOK Use the information you've collected in your Evidence Notebook to help you cover each point above.

_____
_____
_____
_____
_____
_____
_____
_____

Checkpoints

2. An octopus can change the color and pattern of its skin to match the environment while hunting prey. What does this help the animal to do?

  a. swim   **c.** play

  b. feed   **d.** breathe

Answer the following questions about animal structures and functions.

Choose the best answer.

3. Which of the following structures best function to protect an animal from predators?

   a. sharp spines   **c.** colorful feathers

   b. short legs   **d.** thick fur

4. Write the name of each internal structure in the correct column.

| heart   lungs   stomach   arteries   intestines   liver   veins |

Circulatory system	Digestive system

5. Draw lines to connect the structures on the left to the functions they perform on the right.

| a seagull's wings |

| a snake's fangs |

| an ant's mouth parts | | feeding |

| a tiger's padded feet | | movement |

| a frog's tongue |

| an ostrich's long legs |

6. Which internal structure does a shark use to digest food?

   a. stomach

   b. crop

   c. gizzard

   d. heart

Lesson Roundup

A. Label the structures with whether they function in *movement*, *eating*, or *covering* the animals.

_____

_____

_____

_____

_____

_____

B. Write the correct words to complete the sentences.

| arteries | veins | heart | lungs | circulatory | digestive |

The body system that moves blood through an animal's body is called

the _____ system. The _____ pumps

blood. Then _____ carry blood to the rest of the body. Blood

returns to the heart through an animal's _____.

How Do Plants and Animals Grow and Reproduce?

As with animals, plants also grow and reproduce. Whether the plant is a tree, a kind of grass, or a flower, it begins its life as a seed. Under the right conditions, the seeds in this picture will grow into different kinds of plants.

Explore First

Seeing Seeds Look at the fruit your teacher gave you. It is cut in half so that you can see the seeds inside. Compare the fruits and seeds. Talk with your group about how they are alike and different. Predict what would happen if you planted each seed.

Can You Explain It?

Explore Online

Madison was excited about a fruit tree in the backyard of her new home. As spring began, she observed the tree every day and noticed several bees near the tree.

A couple of months later, Madison noticed some of the flowers started to swell, while others began to wither and turn brown. She wondered what was happening.

Gradually the bulges left over from the flowers got bigger. Slowly but surely the fruit grew and grew. Eventually, the tree was covered in ripe apples.

How did the one flower turn into fruit? Why did some of the other flowers not turn into fruit?

_____

_____

_____

_____

_____

_____

_____

_____

 EVIDENCE NOTEBOOK Look for this icon to help you gather evidence to answer the questions above.

Why Do Plants Have Flowers?

Flower Power

Have you ever looked closely at a flower? There are structures inside a flower that allow the plant to reproduce.

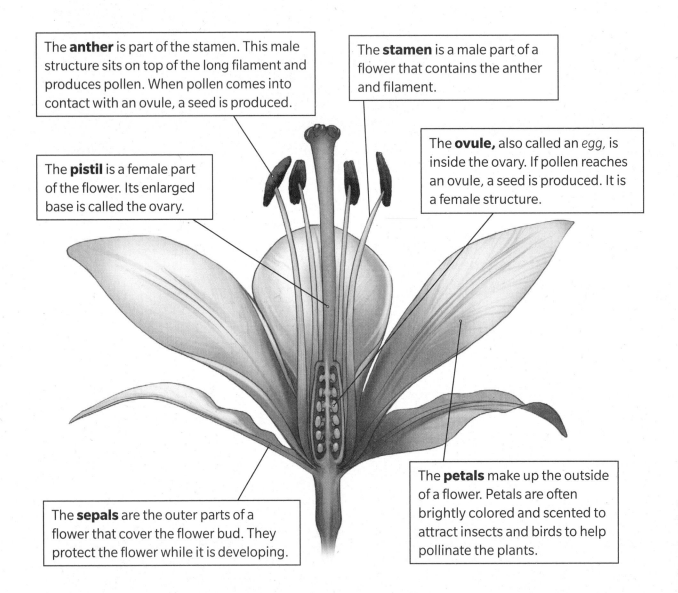

The **anther** is part of the stamen. This male structure sits on top of the long filament and produces pollen. When pollen comes into contact with an ovule, a seed is produced.

The **stamen** is a male part of a flower that contains the anther and filament.

The **pistil** is a female part of the flower. Its enlarged base is called the ovary.

The **ovule,** also called an *egg,* is inside the ovary. If pollen reaches an ovule, a seed is produced. It is a female structure.

The **sepals** are the outer parts of a flower that cover the flower bud. They protect the flower while it is developing.

The **petals** make up the outside of a flower. Petals are often brightly colored and scented to attract insects and birds to help pollinate the plants.

Describe Choose the correct words from the diagram that complete the sentences.

The _____ cover and protect the flower bud. The _____ is where

pollen is produced. If pollen comes into contact with an _____, a

seed is produced.

Where Did the Pollen Go?

You have likely seen yellow dust coating the top of a car during the spring or summer. This is pollen. Pollen is necessary for the reproduction of flowering plants.

Explore Online

Pollination is the transfer of pollen from one flower to another. Animals, such as hummingbirds, are attracted to the flowers to feed on their nectar. As an animal feeds on the nectar some of the pollen sticks to its body.

When the hummingbird moves to another flower, it transfers pollen to the top of the pistil. Next a pollen grain forms a tube that grows down to an ovule within the ovary and the egg is fertilized. **Fertilization** is the process when male and female reproductive parts join together.

 Language SmArts **Summarize** the process a flowering plant goes through for fertilization using the words *pollination* and *fertilization*.

_____

_____

_____

Reproduction occurs when a living thing makes new living things. Sometimes pollen has to move from one plant to another for reproduction to occur. Some animals are attracted to the scent or color of a plant's flower. They pick up pollen when they touch the flower. Sometimes pollen is carried by wind.

When pollen reaches an ovule, a **seed** begins to develop. A seed is a structure that contains the beginnings of a young plant. The seed will be moved from the flower to a new location. It will then grow into a new plant.

Some animals, such as these, move pollen between plants.

Some flowers can self-pollinate. This means that the pollen made by the anther is the same pollen that fertilizes the ovule. The pollen does not come from another plant.

Evaluate Which choices are ways pollen can move from one flower to another? Select all that apply.

   a. insects   **b.** birds   **c.** rain   **d.** wind

 EVIDENCE NOTEBOOK Now that you've learned how pollination occurs, think about the image from the beginning of the lesson. What pollinators did you see? What were they doing to the flower? How does the flower change as a result of their visit?

 HANDS-ON Apply What You Know

Pollination Models

Make two models of flowers using cups to represent the flowers. Place a cotton ball in each. One cotton ball represents an anther, and the other represents the top of a pistil. Sprinkle some powder on the "anther" to represent pollen. Using a pipe cleaner to represent a bee's leg, how can you model moving pollen from one flower to the other?

Try it!

How did you model pollination? What is another way you could model pollination using these materials?

_____

_____

The Steps of Reproduction

You have now learned the steps of pollination and fertilization. Describe what is happening in each image, and number the images in the correct order.

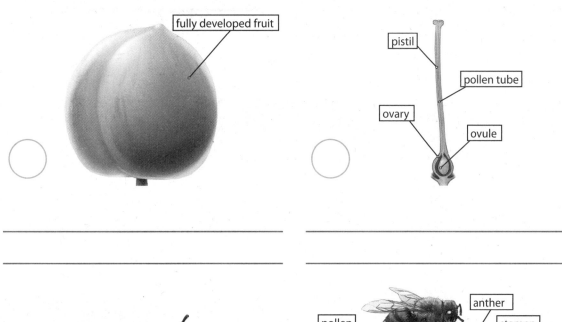

fully developed fruit

pistil

pollen tube

ovary

ovule

○

○

_____

_____

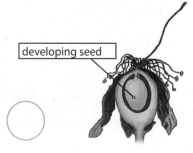

developing seed

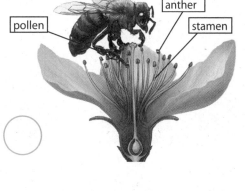

pollen

anther

stamen

○

○

_____

_____

_____

_____

 EVIDENCE NOTEBOOK You learned that apples grow from flowers. Construct an argument to prove that apples grow on apple trees as part of the tree's life cycle. Present the apple tree as a system. Identify the parts of the system and how they change during the life of the tree. Record your argument in your Evidence Notebook.

How Do Seeds Get Around?

It is usually best for seeds to be moved away from their parent plant. How do seeds get around?

Explore Online

Agents of Dispersal

Each of the structures in the top row either contains seeds or is a seed. Draw a line to the photo on the bottom row that shows how each seed is moved. These are just some of the ways seeds spread.

Explain your answers. How did you decide which way each seed would be moved from one place to another?

_____

_____

_____

Putting It Together

This is a coconut. Believe it or not, a coconut is a seed! They are large, but they do not weigh very much. Look at the picture. How do you think a coconut moves from place to place?

_____

_____

446

What If Plants Don't Produce Flowers?

Flowerless

Not all plants produce flowers. The fern and the pine tree shown in the images are examples of plants that do not produce flowers.

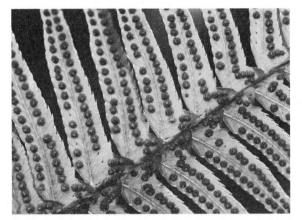

A fern has spores.

A pine tree has cones.

Describe How do you think plants reproduce without flowers?

_____

_____

_____

 HANDS ON Apply What You Know

Pinecone Parts

Get a pinecone from your teacher, and put it on a paper plate. Explore the pinecone to see its different structures. Draw what you see in detail. Dissect some of the seeds, and draw the structures you see inside. Is the pinecone male or female? What evidence do you see to support your decision?

_____

_____

_____

Ladies and Gentlemen

 Explore Online

The pine tree you just saw does not produce flowers to reproduce. Instead, it produces cones. View the timeline to learn more about how pine trees and other trees like it, such as fir trees, reproduce.

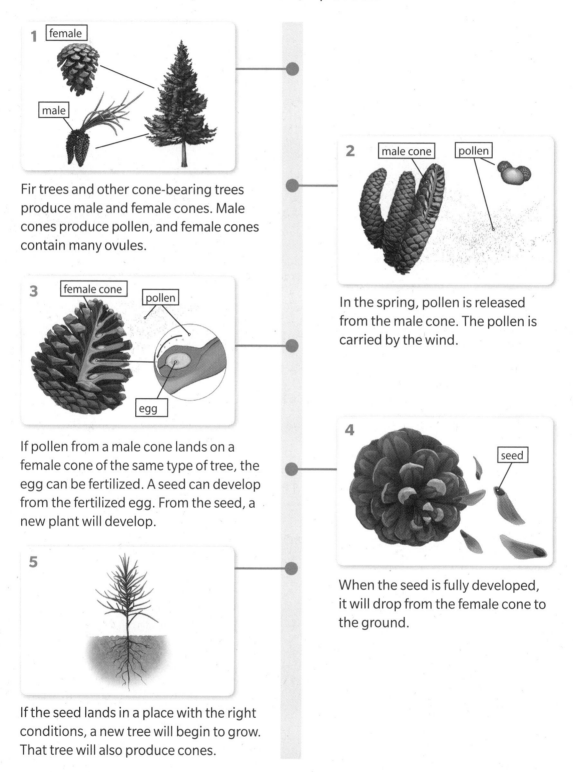

1 female / male

Fir trees and other cone-bearing trees produce male and female cones. Male cones produce pollen, and female cones contain many ovules.

2 male cone / pollen

In the spring, pollen is released from the male cone. The pollen is carried by the wind.

3 female cone / pollen / egg

If pollen from a male cone lands on a female cone of the same type of tree, the egg can be fertilized. A seed can develop from the fertilized egg. From the seed, a new plant will develop.

4 seed

When the seed is fully developed, it will drop from the female cone to the ground.

5

If the seed lands in a place with the right conditions, a new tree will begin to grow. That tree will also produce cones.

Define Which structure, or part, of a fir tree holds the pollen needed for reproduction?

   a. the female cone   **b.** the male cone   **c.** the male and female cones

How Unique!

Besides cones, there is another way that plants reproduce. Some plants produce spores, which fall to the ground or are carried on the wind. **Spores** are the reproductive part of certain types of plants. If they land in a place where conditions are right, a new plant will begin to grow.

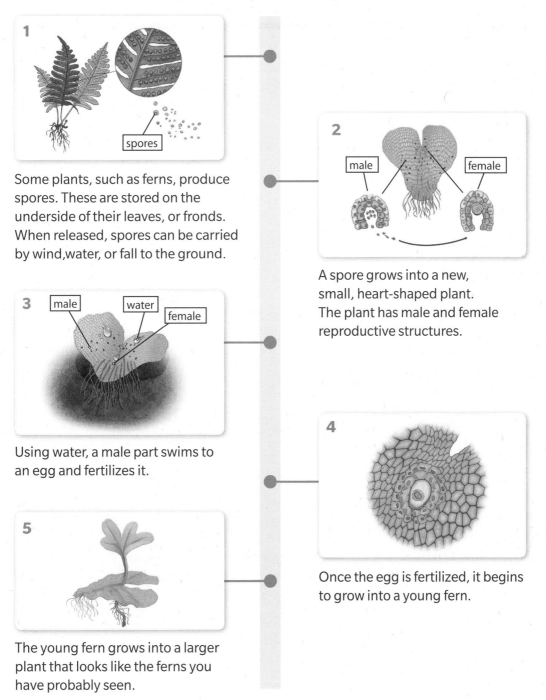

1 Some plants, such as ferns, produce spores. These are stored on the underside of their leaves, or fronds. When released, spores can be carried by wind, water, or fall to the ground.

spores

2 A spore grows into a new, small, heart-shaped plant. The plant has male and female reproductive structures.

male   female

3 Using water, a male part swims to an egg and fertilizes it.

male   water   female

4 Once the egg is fertilized, it begins to grow into a young fern.

5 The young fern grows into a larger plant that looks like the ferns you have probably seen.

Evaluate Choose the correct answer. What is the function of a spore?

a. Spores fertilize eggs, which then make new ferns.

b. Spores become small plants that have female and male structures.

c. Spores fertilize sperm cells, which then make new ferns.

Which Is True?

Look at the pictures of plants at the top of the chart, and compare them. Put a check mark for each true statement about the plant.

uses insects to pollinate			
produces a seed			
produces a spore			
produces a cone			
has male and female structures			

 EVIDENCE NOTEBOOK What type of reproductive method and structure did Madison's apple tree have? What evidence supports your answer?

 Language SmArts
Using Evidence

A man wants to plant a garden with a few plants and let them reproduce to fill up his backyard. He lives in an environment that gets very little rain and is very windy at times. There are some birds but not many flying insects. Based on the scenario, Chantelle thinks plants that reproduce with spores would do well here but flowering plants and cone-bearing plants would not. Do you agree or disagree? Support your answer with evidence. Write your answers on the lines below. Then debate with your classmates.

_____

_____

_____

_____

© Houghton Mifflin Harcourt Publishing Company • Image Credits: (l) ©Pefkos/Fotolia;

How Do Animals Reproduce?

Birds and Fish

You have learned that plants have structures for reproduction. Animals have reproductive structures, too. Some of these structures are internal, or inside animals. Some are external, or on the outside of animals. Different animals reproduce in different ways.

Female birds have internal structures to grow and lay eggs. A male bird fertilizes the eggs while they are in the female bird. The young then develop in the eggs outside of the female birds' bodies. Most adult birds care for their young until they are old enough to leave the nest.

A female fish also has an internal structure that helps her form and lay eggs. In many species, a male fish fertilizes the eggs after they are laid. Most fish do not care for their young. A female salmon can lay thousands of eggs!

Language SmArts
Form an Opinion

A bird and a fish have different methods of reproduction. What are some benefits to each method? What are some drawbacks? Which method do you think works best?

_____

_____

_____

_____

451

Other Animals

Explore Online

Many animals besides fish and birds lay eggs. Other animals' young develop inside their bodies before being born live. Parents often behave in different ways depending on their reproductive structures.

Many reptiles lay eggs. Others have structures that allow young to grow inside their bodies. Some reptiles care for their young, and some do not. Turtles do not typically protect their eggs and care for their hatchlings.

Most insect species lay eggs and do not provide any further care. Others, such as ants and bees, care for their developing young. In an ant colony, worker ants feed larvae to help them grow.

An adult mollusk releases reproductive structures into the water. These structures may or may not be fertilized. The fertilized structures eventually grow into young mollusks.

Mammals have structures that allow their young to develop inside their bodies. When the animal is born, its parents feed it and care for it until it is bigger, stronger, and can find its own food.

Do the Math

One Fish, Two Fish

A bluegill is a kind of fish that lives in lakes and ponds. Bluegill are small in size, but they can lay an average of 30,000 eggs at one time!

Suppose a bluegill reproduces two times per breeding season. How many eggs will the bluegill lay altogether? _____

Now suppose a bluegill lays eggs twice in the spring and once in the fall. If all of the eggs hatch, how many offspring will the bluegill have? _____

Song and Dance

Reproduction usually requires a male and a female. So how does an animal choose a mate? Some of them put on a show! A peacock spider does a dance. Often, animals with fancier dances are more likely to reproduce. A male quetzal shows his brightly colored feathers. In birds, it is often the male bird with more colorful feathers that is more likely to reproduce. These behaviors increase these animals' chances to reproduce.

Work with a partner. Research other animals that use displays to find a mate. Choose two animals. Then make a multimedia presentation about them for your class. Remember to use pictures and videos to make it more interesting.

EVIDENCE NOTEBOOK How is the fruit growing on the apple tree similar to an animal laying an egg? What had to occur for each event to take place?

Putting It Together

Choose the correct word or phrase to complete each sentence.

> pollinates   eggs   live young   reproduction   fertilizes
>
> external structures   internal structures   pollination

When animals make a new animal, _____ occurs. Animals reproduce in

different ways. Some animals, such as fish, lay eggs. A male fish then _____

the eggs. Fish usually do not care for their young. Other animals, such as mammals, have

_____ that allow offspring to grow inside their bodies. They give birth

to _____ and care for them after they are born.

Flying High

Objective

Collaborate Design and test a device that disperses a seed using wind.

A company has hired you to build a device to disperse a seed using wind. Use your knowledge of how seeds are dispersed by wind to design the device. Your budget is $10. The seed must travel at least 30 cm using only the wind.

Find a Problem: What question will you investigate to meet this objective?

_____

_____

Materials

• corn kernels for seeds	$3
• balloons	$1 for 1 or
	$2 for 3
• tissues	$1 for 2
	$2 for 5
• paper clips	$1 for 5
• rubber bands	$2 for 2
• straws	$1 for 3
• paper bag	$1 for 2
• yarn	$2 per m
• ribbon	$1 per m
• aluminum foil	$1 per ¼ sq. m
• tape	$1 per roll
• cotton balls	$1 for 2
• craft sticks	$1 for 2
• pipe cleaners	$1 for 2
• fan	$0
• meterstick	$0

Procedure

STEP 1 **Research** with your group to find more information about how seeds are dispersed by wind.

STEP 2 **Define the Problem** What are your criteria?

_____

_____

What are your constraints?

_____

_____

STEP 3 **Brainstorm** solutions for your device. Then evaluate your solutions, and choose the best.

What method of seed dispersal will your device model?

_____

_____

STEP 4 **Develop and test a model.** Draw your device. Write how you will test it. Get your teacher's approval before you follow your plan.

_____

_____

_____

_____

_____

_____

_____

STEP 5 Build and test your device. Record your results.

Trial	Distance seed traveled (cm)	Other observations:
1		
2		
3		
4		
5		
6		

STEP 6 Evaluate your test. What was the normal distance your seeds traveled? Do you think they could travel farther if you improved your device? Explain how you would improve your device.

_____

_____

_____

_____

STEP 7 Develop and test a new model. What improvements did you make to your design?

_____

_____

_____

STEP 8 Communicate to compare your device to other groups' devices and their results. Did their seeds travel farther than yours? Why or why not?

_____

_____

_____

Make a **claim** based on your investigation. **Cite evidence** from your design and other designs to support your claim. Explain your **reasoning.**

_____

_____

_____

Think of other problems you would like to solve related to seed dispersal.

_____

_____

_____

Discover More

Check out this path . . . or go online to choose one of these other paths.

Careers in Science & Engineering

- **Wait, There's More!**
- **It's What's on the Inside**

Pomologist

The science of growing fruit is known as *pomology*. Scientists who study how to grow fruits are known as *pomologists*.

Janine Hasey is a pomologist and master gardener who specializes in finding better ways to grow fruits and nuts, such as kiwi and walnuts. Pomologists also perform tests to grow larger, better tasting fruits.

One thing that is essential to growing fruit is having a flower pollinated. In certain plants, after a flower is pollinated, it produces a fruit around the seeds. The fruit helps protect the seeds and also helps with seed dispersal.

Explore Online

Hasey researches ways to control pests and diseases that harm fruits and nuts. She studies the difference between animals that are pollinators and animals that are pests.

Explain What does a pomologist do?

_____

_____

_____

_____

Pollinator Project

In this activity, you will research three or four animals that pollinate plants or disperse seeds. Make a booklet of your findings. Include a drawing or photo of the animal, the type of plants it pollinates, or the way it carries seeds from place to place, and its importance to the reproduction of plants. Submit your booklet to your teacher.

Comparing and Contrasting

Similarities	Differences
_____	_____
_____	_____
_____	_____
_____	_____
_____	_____
_____	_____
_____	_____
_____	_____

Compare Which animals were similar? What did they have in common?

_____

_____

_____

Summarize Compare and contrast your findings with those of your classmates. What similarities and differences did you observe?

_____

_____

_____

Lesson Check

Name _____

Can You Explain It?

1. Look back at the images from the beginning of the lesson. Think about what you have learned about plant reproduction.

- Explain how plants develop from seeds to a fully grown plant.
- Explain the difference between flowering and nonflowering plants.
- Describe how seeds spread out and why.

📋 **EVIDENCE NOTEBOOK** Use the information you've collected in your Evidence Notebook to help you cover each point above.

_____

_____

_____

_____

_____

_____

_____

_____

Checkpoints

2. Plant parts work together as a system for reproduction. Number the steps of the system in the correct order.

_____ The seed develops and drops to the ground.

_____ The egg is fertilized.

_____ A new tree can begin to grow.

_____ It lands on the female cone.

_____ Pollen is released by the male cone.

3. How does the pine tree in the picture reproduce?

   a. by producing flowers

   b. by producing cones

   c. by producing spores

4. Which plant structures are used in reproduction? Circle all that apply.

   a. leaves

   b. spores

   c. flowers

   d. wind

   e. cones

5. Read the evidence below, and then choose the best claim.

   • Wind blows pollen.

   • Flies can pollinate plants.

   • Some plants use cones to reproduce.

   • Spores produce male and female parts.

   a. Pollinators are the best way to pollinate plants.

   b. There are many ways for plants to reproduce.

   c. Water is the quickest way for seeds to move.

   d. Spores use wind to reproduce.

6. Choose the word or phrase that completes each sentence.

fertilized	pollinated	care for	male
ovule	female	larvae	adults

Like plants, most animals need both

_____ and _____

structures to reproduce. Queen ants

lay _____ eggs in a nest. These

eggs hatch into _____. Adult worker

ants _____ the offspring until they are

fully developed.

Lesson Roundup

A. Match each flower part to its description by filling in the blank.

anther	ovary	ovule	pistil	pollen	stamen

a. _____ the part of a flower that contains the anther

b. _____ the part of the flower where pollen is produced

c. _____ When this comes into contact with the ovule, a seed is produced.

d. _____ the part of the flower that contains the ovary

e. _____ the part of the flower that contains ovules

f. _____ If pollen reaches this structure, a seed is produced.

B. Study the illustrations below. Match each plant to the description of how it reproduces.

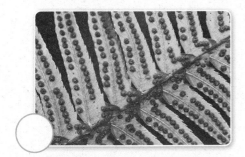

a. This plant produces spores that, if they land in the right place, grow into a heart-shaped structure. This structure grows and produces male and female structures.

b. This plant produces cones. In the spring, pollen is released from the male cone. If pollen from a male cone lands on a female cone of the same type of tree, the egg will be fertilized.

C. Which animals have internal structures that help them give birth to live young?

a. mollusks   **b.** fish   **c.** birds   **d.** mammals

How Do Senses Work?

A peacock mantis shrimp has very complex eyes. Humans have three kinds of receptors to detect light. A peacock mantis shrimp has twelve! It uses its eyesight and other senses and traits to improve its chances of survival.

Explore First

Sensory Sensation! When you go outside, what do you see? hear? smell? How do your senses allow you to learn about the environment? As a group, follow your teacher's instructions. You will explore the outdoor environment. You will then make claims supported with evidence about which senses you think are the most important for survival.

Can You Explain It?

Explore Online

Animals use their senses to obtain and process information about their environment. Dolphins often swim and search for food in dark or murky water where they cannot see using their eyesight.

How do dolphins find food in dark water if what they are looking for does not make any noise? What other sense might they use to "see" without using their eyesight?

_____

_____

_____

_____

_____

 EVIDENCE NOTEBOOK Look for this icon to help you gather evidence to answer the questions above.

Touchy, Feely

Body Senses

Have you ever touched something hot with your hand? How did you react? You probably responded by pulling your hand back very quickly! Your body has **senses** that allow you to receive information about your environment.

The Skeletal and Nervous Systems

Look at the image showing systems in your body that work together, then match the description to the part it describes.

a. Humans and many other animals have a **skeletal system** made mainly of bones. The skeletal system gives structure, support, and protection to the softer parts of the body.

b. The **nervous system** contains the **brain,** the spinal cord, and the nerves. The brain is the central processing organ and is protected by the skeletal system.

c. The nervous system contains two kinds of **nerves**: those that send information to the brain or spinal cord, and those that send information from the brain and spinal cord to the rest of the body.

d. The **spinal cord** is a bundle of nerve fibers and tissues that connect the parts of the body to the brain. It is protected by the backbone. The brain and the spinal cord make up the central nervous system.

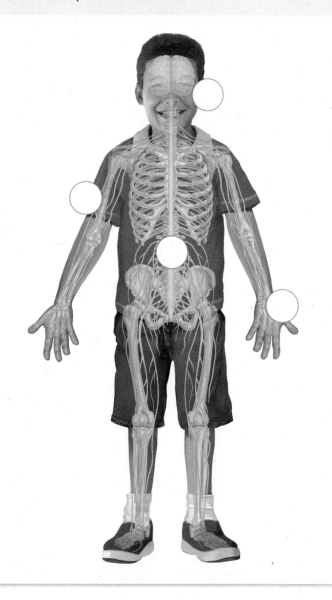

Skin Deep

The largest organ in your body is your skin. It provides protection by covering your entire body. Skin also contains special structures called **receptors**. Receptors respond to changes inside and outside the body and report them to your nervous system. These changes may form perceptions and memories that could guide your actions.

The ability to touch is one of your senses. Nerve endings in animals can receive different kinds of information that comes to the skin, or other surfaces, from the environment. This information is processed by the brain, where it can form perceptions and memories. Then these perceptions and memories can be used to guide actions.

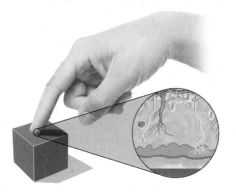

Touch and pressure receptors react to how hard, soft, rough, or smooth an object is. When you touch something such as a wood block, receptors send nerve signals to your brain. The brain processes these signals so that you know what you are holding.

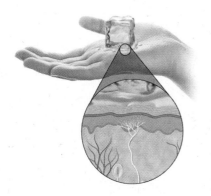

If you are holding an ice cube, you quickly realize that your hand is freezing! This is because temperature receptors in your skin react to the temperature of the ice cube and send nerve signals to the brain.

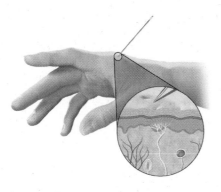

When the skin feels intense pressure or is injured, pain receptors send information about the pain to the central nervous system. The central nervous system processes the signals and causes the muscles to try to move away from the source of the pain. The body's reaction to pain is immediate.

Humans aren't the only *organisms*, which are living things, that have a central nervous system for controlling the body. All mammals, fish, insects, and birds rely on a central nervous system. Simpler animals have a more basic kind of nervous system.

Feel It

Test your understanding of how skin works by answering each of the questions below.

Identify A friend places a warm rock in your hand. Which types of information about the rock will your skin receptors most likely receive? Circle all that apply.

    a. color

    b. taste

    c. weight

    d. temperature

Analyze In most cases, where does the information sent from skin receptors in your hand get processed?

    a. in the brain

    b. in the hand

    c. in pain receptors

    d. in the tips of the fingers

Assess Which kind of receptor do you think would relay the message to your brain if you were cut? Circle your answer.

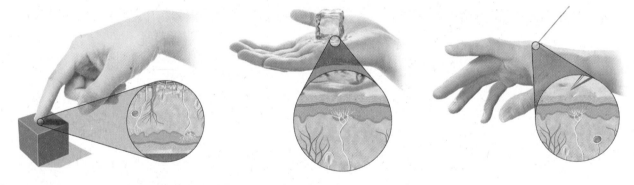

Language SmArts

Identifying Main Ideas and Details

How do your senses react to things in your environment?

_____

_____

_____

_____

© Houghton Mifflin Harcourt Publishing Company • Image Credits: (tr) ©harpazo_hope/

Knee-Jerk Response

Not all sensory information travels to the brain to be processed. Has your doctor ever checked your reflexes?

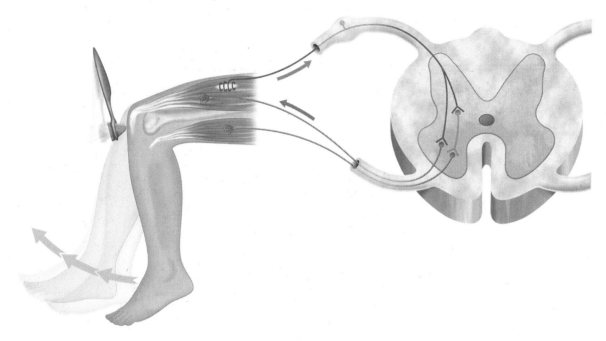

Certain body parts have receptors that send information to the spinal cord. From the spinal cord, a response is immediately sent back to the muscles. The brain is not involved. These reactions are called reflexes. Reflexes are important to the survival of many animals because they allow animals to respond more quickly to their environment.

 EVIDENCE NOTEBOOK Think about how dolphins might use their sense of touch to catch food.

Putting It Together

Show what you've learned about the different kinds of sensory receptors. Compare and contrast touch receptors, temperature receptors, and pain receptors.

_____

_____

_____

_____

_____

_____

Touch Test

Objective

Collaborate to investigate how receptors work in your body. The sensory receptors in your skin are not arranged evenly across your body. Some parts of your body may have more of one kind of receptor but fewer of another. Find out which parts of your body are more sensitive to touch and pressure.

Materials
- 2 paper clips bent into a V-shape
- metric ruler
- pencil or pen

Form a question: What question will you ask to meet this objective?

_____

_____

_____

Procedure

STEP 1 Open and bend the paper clip into a V-shape so that its ends are about 2 cm apart. Use a metric ruler to measure the distance. Make sure the two halves of the V-shape are the same length.

STEP 2 Ask your partner to rest his or her hand, palm side down, on a flat surface. Tell your partner to look away.

STEP 3 Lightly press both ends of the paper clip into the back of your partner's hand. Do not press too hard! Make sure both ends touch the skin at the same time.

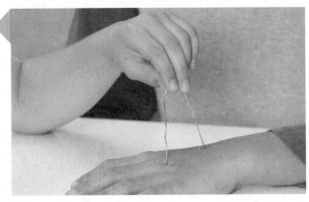

Why do you not want to press down too hard with the paper clip?

_____

_____

_____

STEP 4 Ask your partner if he or she felt one or two pressure points. If your partner feels one point, spread the ends of the paper clip apart and test again. If your partner feels two points, push the ends a little closer together and try again. When your partner FIRST feels two points, record the distance between the paper clip's ends.

Think back to step 1, in where you made sure both halves of the V-shaped clip were the same length. Why was that important?

_____

_____

STEP 5 Repeat steps 3 and 4 two more times. Record your results for all three trials by writing the smallest distance at which your partner reported feeling two points.

STEP 6 Repeat steps 3–5 on the right calf, the right shoulder, and the inside of the right forearm. You can use another data table and repeat the procedure with your partner doing the testing using a new paper clip.

	Distance		
	Trial 1	Trial 2	Trial 3
Hand			
Shoulder			
Calf			
Forearm			

What was the shortest distance record on your data table?
What was the greatest distance?

_____

_____

On what part of the body were the two points of the paper clip felt at the shortest distance?

_____

On what part of the body were the two points felt at the greatest distance?

_____

On what part of the body did it take the most tries to feel two distinct points of the paper clip?

_____

_____

How did your results compare to your partner's results?

_____

_____

_____

Based on your results, which of the four parts of the body tested is the most sensitive on your partner? on you?

_____

_____

Compare results with other groups in the classroom. How are they similar? How are they different?

_____

_____

_____

Make a **claim** about senses. Support your claim with **evidence** and **reasoning** from your observations in this activity.

_____

_____

_____

Think of other questions you would like to ask about senses.

_____

_____

_____

_____

Is That Something I Want to Eat?

How the Nose Knows

You've learned about the receptors in your skin. But did you know that you also have receptors in your nose? Your ability to smell is also one of your senses.

Every time you breathe air into your nose, receptors inside the nose sense different chemicals in the air. These smell receptors are attached to nerves that send signals to the brain about those chemicals. This is how you are able to smell odors and aromas in the air.

Identify Write the word that best completes the sentence.

You are able to smell odors and aromas because

you have smell receptors in your _____.

HANDS-ON Apply What You Know

Name That Scent!

Try a simple activity to test your sense of smell. Blindfold your partner and see how many smells he or she can identify correctly. Hold a scented item in front of your partner's nose. Keep track of your results. Switch with your partner and repeat.

Did your results surprise you? Why or why not? Which scents did you guess correctly?

_____

_____

_____

_____

_____

Need Salt?

Like your skin, your tongue has receptors to receive information from its environment. The tongue's environment is the mouth and whatever is in it. The tongue has receptors that allow you to taste and feel what you eat and drink. Your ability to taste is one of your senses.

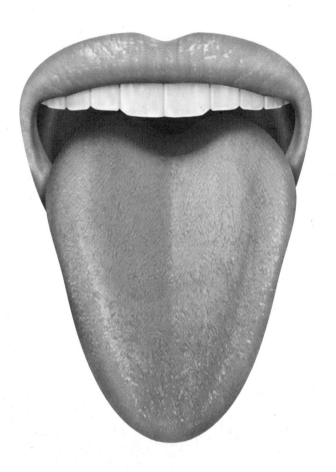

Which Receptor?

Explore Online

Explore how the sensory receptors of your tongue work. Then match the adjectives to the receptor they describe.

Taste isn't the only characteristic of food that's important. Touch receptors on your tongue let you know about the texture of what you eat and drink. Some things are smooth, some things are lumpy, and some things are rough.

It's also important to know the temperature of your food. The temperature receptors of your tongue send signals to your brain letting you know the temperature of your food or drink.

The taste buds are the receptors on your tongue that sense salty, sweet, bitter, sour, and umami (savory) flavors. Taste buds send signals to the brain to let you know how your food or drink tastes.

Occasionally, you might eat or drink something that's too hot, too spicy, too cold, or too sharp. Pain receptors on your tongue let your brain know if your food needs to cool down, warm up, or be avoided.

sour	smooth
sweet	cold
boiling	spicy
grainy	warm

Taste	Touch	Temperature	Pain

© Houghton Mifflin Harcourt Publishing Company

472

HANDS-ON Apply What You Know

No See, No Smell, No Taste?

Your nose is more important than you might think, especially when it comes to tasting foods.

Surprisingly, much of your ability to taste comes from your smell receptors. Your taste buds react to salty, sour, sweet, savory, and bitter flavors. However, it's your smell receptors that allow you to specifically identify a particular food.

Blindfold a partner, then give him or her four different foods to eat. Have your partner hold his or her nose. Ask him or her to identify the food. Switch with your partner, and repeat using four different foods.

What are your results? How do you think your daily life would change if you could not smell?

_____

_____

_____

Discuss the results with your partner. Talk with your classmates about the ways in which we use smell in our daily lives.

 EVIDENCE NOTEBOOK Dolphins are mammals, just like us. However, they don't have a sense of smell. Why do you think the sense of smell wouldn't be useful to dolphins? Record your ideas in your notebook.

 Language SmArts
Cause and Effect

Is there a food you avoid because of the way it smells or tastes? How might an animal in the wild benefit from a strong smell or taste response?

_____

_____

_____

_____

Sights and Sounds

Eye See!

Along with the skin, tongue, and nose, there are also sensory receptors in the eyes. Many animals have specialized receptors that receive different types of information through the eyes. Your ability to see is also one of your senses.

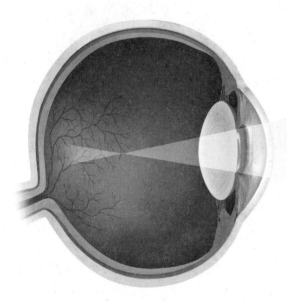

Light bounces off an object. It then enters the eye through an opening at the center. After passing through the opening, light strikes the back of the eye. At the back of the eye is an area where there are light receptors. These receptors react to the light and send nerve signals along a pathway to the brain, where the information is processed.

But How Does It See?

Circle the structures that allow each animal to "see."

Pigeons see color just like humans. But they can also see ultraviolet light, unlike humans.

Dogs and cats can see with their eyes, but they rely more on scent and sound for their survival than on vision.

Some snakes see in two ways. They see color and have vision pits in their faces that allow them to *see* heat.

Here's to the Ears!

There are sounds everywhere, but you wouldn't be able to hear any of them without the hearing receptors in your ears. As you have learned, senses allow humans and other animals to receive different kinds of information. This information is carried by nerves to the brain. The brain processes the information, causing the body to react and respond to the information in different ways.

Animals have different levels of sensitivity to sound. Many animals are able to produce and hear lower or higher sounds than humans can hear.

All Ears

Explore the image that shows the parts of the ear and their functions. Match the caption to the part of the ear it describes.

a. The *outer ear* is the part of the ear that you can see. The shape of the outer ear funnels sound into the ear, through the ear canal, and toward the middle ear.

b. The ear drum separates the outer ear from the *middle ear*. The middle ear is an air-filled area with three small bones: the hammer, the anvil, and the stirrup.

c. The *inner ear* contains the fluid-filled cochlea and the semicircular canals. The sound vibrations from the middle ear cause the fluid, as well as the thousands of tiny hairs inside the cochlea, to move.

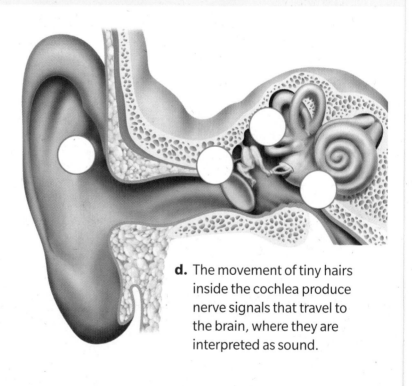

d. The movement of tiny hairs inside the cochlea produce nerve signals that travel to the brain, where they are interpreted as sound.

Language SmArts
Opinion

How do you feel when you hear music? To answer, associate words that describe your memories of music and sound with words that describe feelings.

"Seeing" By Hearing

Bats are the only flying mammals. As they fly at night, bats send out sounds through their mouth and nose. When the sounds hit an object, the sounds bounce back, or echo, and are funneled into the bat's ears. As in humans, the sound vibrations move through the ear and are converted to signals sent along nerves to the brain. There the information is processed. Bats use echolocation to locate food, navigate while flying, and find their way home.

Analyze How do you think bats use echolocation to tell the difference between small objects and large objects?

_____

_____

_____

_____

 HANDS-ON Apply What You Know

Test It!

Blindfold your partner. Make clicking noises in front of, to the left of, to the right of, and behind your blindfolded partner. Observe how your partner uses the clicking noises to locate your position.

 EVIDENCE NOTEBOOK How do you think dolphins might use sound to find their prey in murky water? Record your ideas in your notebook.

Putting It Together

Think about what you've learned about how animals see, hear, and smell.

Why is it important for their survival that animals use their senses and process information in different ways?

_____

_____

_____

_____

Discover More

Check out this path . . . or go online to choose one of these other paths.

Extreme Senses

- **Careers in Science & Engineering**
- **What Colors Do You See?**
- **People in Science & Engineering**

Extreme Senses

Explore Online

The greater wax moth is one of the favorite food sources of bats. Fortunately for the moth, it is often able to use its extreme sense of hearing to escape being eaten.

Greater wax moths can hear sounds in the same range as the bats who are trying to catch them. The moths then move in a way that makes it difficult for the bats to find them. This makes it much easier for the moths to avoid being eaten—and survive.

Mantis shrimp are about 10 cm long, but they are one of the strongest animals in the world. They use pincers shaped like clubs to punch their prey at very high speeds. This incredible force is important for hunting food and to protect itself and its home.

The mantis shrimp is not a mantis, nor is it a shrimp. It is more closely related to lobsters and crabs. It has special structures in its eyes that scientists believe allow it to see and process information quickly.

Greater wax moth

Mantis shrimp

Language SmArts
Present It!

Research 5–10 other living things that have extraordinary senses. Find out how these senses are used for survival. Present your findings to the class in a multimedia presentation, and submit your presentation to your teacher.

Use the chart below to record your notes for your presentation.

Extreme Creatures	
Organism	**Extreme senses**

Analyze What did you learn about extreme senses? Which was your favorite? If you could have an extreme sense, what would it be?

_____

_____

_____

_____

_____

_____

Lesson Check

Name _____

Can You Explain It?

1. Think back to how bats use their senses to receive and process information about their environment. How is the dolphin's environment like that of a bat's? How do you think a dolphin uses its senses to "see" its surroundings without using its eyes? Be sure to do the following:

- Discuss the internal structures the dolphin might use.

- Describe the receptors that might be involved.

- Step through the whole process the dolphin uses, ending with it eating a fish.

EVIDENCE NOTEBOOK Use the information you've collected in your Evidence Notebook to help answer these questions.

_____

_____

_____

_____

_____

_____

_____

_____

Checkpoints

2. Suppose you mistakenly rest your hand on a hot stovetop. What are some ways your nervous system will respond? Select all answers that are correct.

    a. Your nervous system will tell your arm muscles to pull the hand away.

    b. Your nervous system will wait for your muscles to respond.

    c. Your brain will remember that stovetops can be hot.

    d. Your brain will cause you to perceive the pain.

3. Match each situation to the kind of receptor that reacts.

seeing a green lizard running	pain receptor
sweet piece of fruit	sight receptor
hand is poked by a sharp object	taste receptor

4. Use the image to help you choose the correct answer.

The eyes contain _____ receptors that react to light.

5. What do you predict will happen if you hold your nose while eating your lunch? Circle the best answer.
   a. My lunch won't taste as good.
   b. I'll eat my lunch more quickly.
   c. My taste buds won't be able to function.
   d. The food in my lunch won't look the same.

6. How do sounds get from the inner ear to the brain? Circle all that apply.
   a. They pass through the eardrum.
   b. They make tiny hairs move in the cochlea.
   c. They are translated by receptors into nerve signals.
   d. They cause fluid to move in the outer and middle ear.

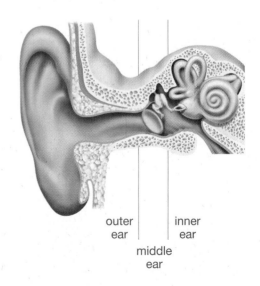

outer ear   inner ear

middle ear

Lesson Roundup

A. Choose the correct words that complete each
sentence.

> **skeletal system**   **nervous system**
>
> **brain and spinal cord**   **central nervous system**

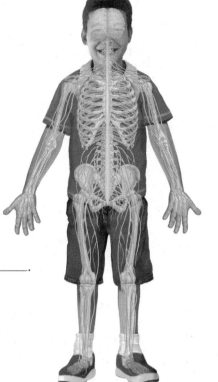

The _____ includes the brain,

spinal cord, and all the nerves in the body. The central

nervous system includes just the _____.

Sensory receptors are constantly reacting to things

inside and outside the body. The reactions are sent to the

_____ as nerve signals.

B. Choose the correct words that complete each sentence.

> **taste**   **sight**   **smell**   **hearing**   **touch**

You use your sense of _____ to choose your favorite

meal. A cheetah uses its sense of _____ to spot the

weakest zebra in a herd. A bat uses its sense of _____ to

fly at night, searching for food. A hungry grizzly bear uses its sense of

_____ to find the most fragrant berries to eat.

C. Choose the sense that reacts to each example. Place the example in the
correct column.

> **red**   **bumpy**   **spicy pepper**   **scent of pencil shavings**
>
> **smooth**   **pin dropping**   **lion roar**   **sour cherry**

Touch	Taste	Smell	See	Hear

Flower Parts

You work for a nursery that is putting together a botanist's handbook. Your team is tasked with making an educational illustration of a specific flower. To do that, you'll need to dissect the flower and identify its individual parts. Then you'll need to draw those parts separately and write a caption for each that names it and explains its function.

A flower has many parts, and each has a function of its own.

DEFINE YOUR TASK: What will your completed assignment look like?

_____

_____

_____

Before beginning, review the checklist at the end of this Unit Performance Task. Keep those items in mind as you proceed.

RESEARCH: For this project, your teacher will play the role of your company's project coordinator, assigning your team its flower. Your team will be the only one in class with your specific flower. Use online or library resources to identify your flower and learn its parts. Cite your sources.

_____

_____

MAKE A PLAN: Consider the questions below as you plan your procedure for dissecting your flower and examining, illustrating, and describing its parts.

1. What tools and equipment will we need to dissect our flower?

_____

_____

2. What parts will we look for as we dissect our flower?

_____

_____

3. What materials will we need to make our illustrations?

_____

_____

_____

4. How large should we make our illustrations, and how thoroughly should we describe the parts of our flower?

These students are looking closely at the different parts of a flower.

_____

_____

5. How should we arrange our illustrations? Should we include one illustration of the complete flower?

_____

_____

_____

DISSECT AND ILLUSTRATE: Dissect your flower. Draw, label, and describe each part of your illustrations as described in your plan.

COMMUNICATE: Give a short presentation to your class about your team's flower, what you learned from dissecting it, and what your team's illustrations teach the viewer. If there is time, the entire class can discuss similarities and differences among their different assigned flowers.

☑ Checklist

Review your project, and check off each completed item.

_____ All questions on the page are answered.

_____ An educational illustration of the parts of your team's flower is included.

_____ Demonstration and oral report about your team's procedures and illustration are included.

Unit Review

1. Support this **claim** with **evidence,** and support your **reasoning:**
   A leaf's function is to make food for the plant.

   _____

   _____

   _____

   _____

   _____

   _____

2. Which of the following must combine for a seed to form? Circle all that apply.

   a. bark

   b. roots

   c. pollen

   d. ovule

   e. thorns

3. The pine tree is an example of a plant that reproduces

   using _____ instead of flowers.

   a. flowers

   b. cones

   c. spores

   d. ferns

4. Which of the following qualities demonstrates how a frog's skin is adapted to its environment? Circle all that apply.

    a. It is thin.

    b. It is slimy.

    c. It is warm.

    d. It is moist.

5. Classify each structure as mostly involved in protection (P) or motion (M):

    _____ fur

    _____ fins

    _____ legs

    _____ wings

    _____ shells

    _____ spines

6. Which sense does this animal sometimes use to "see" in murky water? Circle the correct choice.

    a. taste

    b. touch

    c. smell

    d. hearing

7. Sophia plays basketball at her elementary school. She uses her brain, eyes, and nerves to play the sport. Explain how these three parts of her body work together to manage her movements when she's trying to catch the ball.

_____

_____

_____

_____

8. Which feature is part of an animal's internal structure? Choose all that apply.

    a. lungs

    b. heart

    c. claws

    d. tail

9. Choose the correct term to complete the sentence.

spores	seeds	flowers

Ferns produce _____ instead

of _____.

10. Describe behavioral responses that plants have.

_____

_____

_____

_____

_____

_____

_____

Animal Senses

Explore
Online

You Solve It: Species Search As you learn about animal vision, you will discover how different animals see and explore their environments. You will investigate how different technologies mimic animal sight.

Virtual reality technology allows us to visually interact with a location without being there.

At a Glance

UNIT PROJECT • Engineer It!

Code Breakers!

Think about the different methods of communication that you interact with or use on a daily basis. While one method you use may be speaking with someone face to face or watching your teacher write on the board, you can't always see the origin of the message. For this project, you will use the engineering process to investigate and develop a way to send a coded message to the rest of your group from around a corner.

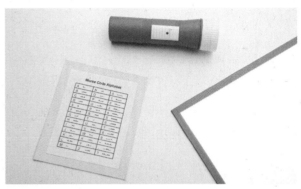

Use materials to develop a way to send a coded message to a friend who cannot see you.

Write a question that you will consider as you come up with your coded method of communication.

_____

_____

_____

Materials Think about how you will develop your coded method of communication. What materials will you need?

_____

_____

To develop your coded method of communication, identify the method you wish to communicate through. Would you prefer to communicate using light, sound, or some other sort of media? What are some initial ideas you have about the code you would like to develop?

_____

_____

_____

Research and Plan Make a plan for the research you will need to do and how you will come up with your predictions. As you make your plan, consider the following:

- Consider structures or other items that could block your method of communication.

- What sort of code will you be using?

- How will the rest of the group translate your code to determine your method?

- What are the criteria for designing your coded communication method?

- What are your constraints?

Use print or digital resources to conduct research and make your plan.

_____

_____

_____

_____

_____

_____

Swap designs with another team, and attempt to communicate your message. Provide constructive feedback. Then swap your designs back and think about the feedback you received on your design. Will you make changes to your design? Why or why not?

_____

_____

_____

_____

_____

Analyze Your Results Look for patterns in your method of communication. Make two observations about how your message was communicated.

Once you have developed your method of communication, test it to find out if it is effective.

_____

_____

_____

_____

_____

_____

_____

Restate Your Question Write the question you investigated.

_____

_____

_____

Claims, Evidence, and Reasoning Make a **claim** that answers your question.

_____

_____

_____

What **evidence** from your analysis supports your claim?

_____

_____

Discuss your **reasoning** with a partner.

Language Development

Use the lessons in this unit to complete the network and expand the understanding of the science concepts.

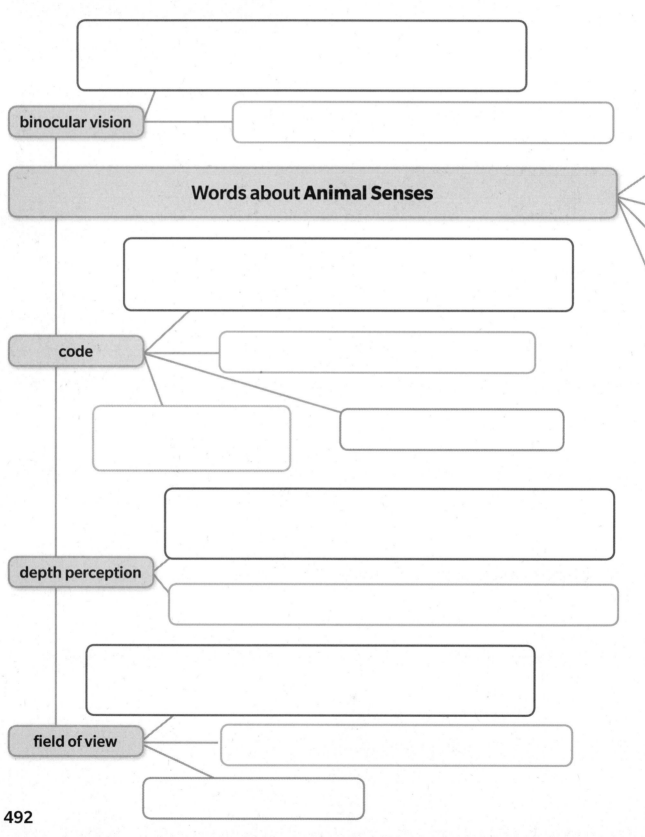

binocular vision

Words about Animal Senses

code

depth perception

field of view

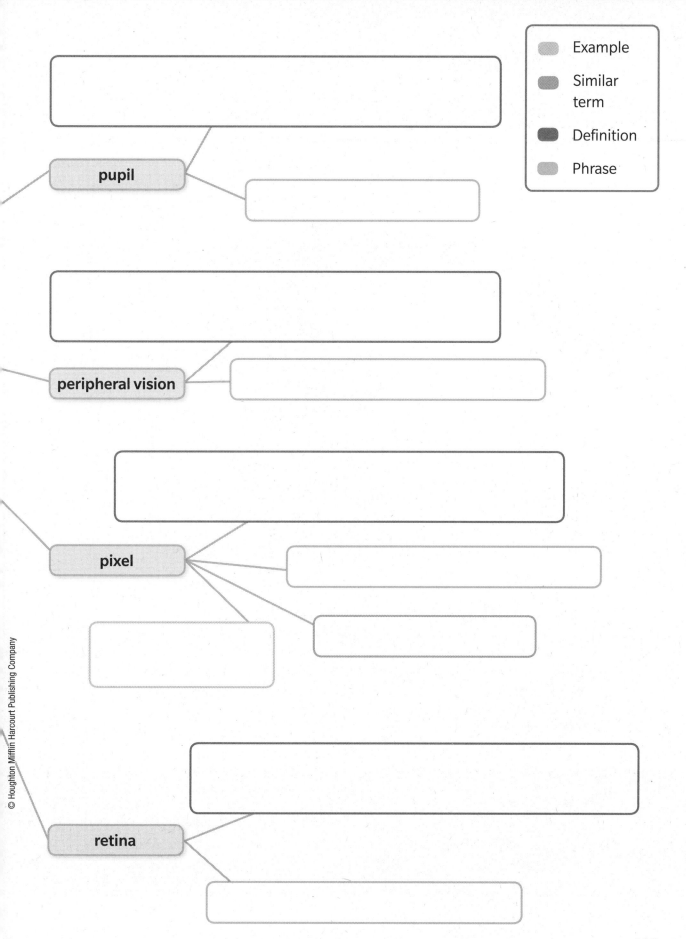

pupil

peripheral vision

pixel

retina

What Processes Are Involved in Sight?

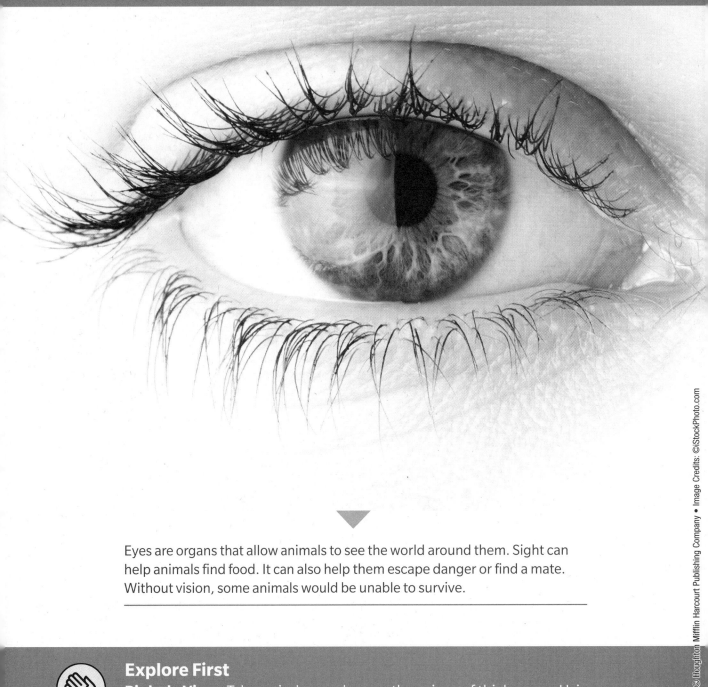

Eyes are organs that allow animals to see the world around them. Sight can help animals find food. It can also help them escape danger or find a mate. Without vision, some animals would be unable to survive.

Explore First

Pinhole View Take an index card or another piece of thick paper. Using a paper clip, punch a hole in it. Hold the index card up to one of your eyes, and look through it. What do you see? How is it different from what you see when you do not use the index card?

Can You Explain It?

Explore Online

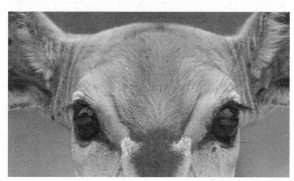

Different kinds of animals have different kinds of eyes. These are all mammals, yet they don't all have the same kind of eye.

Why do you think each of these animals has a different kind of eye? How might the differences in the structure of their eyes affect the way they live?

_____

_____

_____

_____

_____

_____

_____

EVIDENCE NOTEBOOK Look for this icon to help you gather evidence to answer the questions above.

Eye for Survival

Eyes for the Occasion

Explore
Online

Different organisms live in different environments. Their eyes are adapted so they can survive in their environments. Light transfers information. Receptors in eyes pick up light and send that information to the brain, which interprets it. Eyes allow organisms to hunt for food or escape danger.

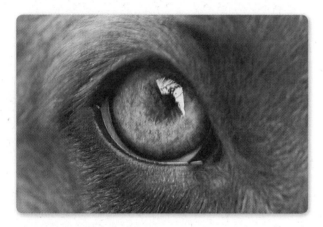

Dogs' eyes are adapted for seeing well in the dark. Their eyes are also developed to detect movement.

Spiders can have up to eight eyes. Spiders that spin webs usually do not have very good eyesight. Those that hunt prey, or other animals, on foot usually have very good eyesight.

Compare and Contrast How are the eyes in the photos similar? How are they different?

_____

_____

_____

Record Each organism's eyes have specific characteristics. Some are bigger in relation to their bodies than others. Some may be colorful, while others are not. In the table below, list the characteristics for each type of eye.

Dog's eyes	Spider's eyes

Binocular Vision

Roll a piece of paper into a narrow tube. Then hold one end of it to your eye. Now hold your free hand next to the tube in front of your other eye. Leave both eyes open. Look through the narrow tube with one eye.

Describe What do you see?

_____

_____

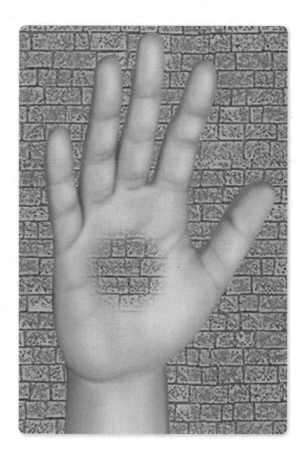

Most organisms have more than one eye. This allows some to have binocular vision. **Binocular vision** occurs when two eyes see the same thing from a slightly different angle. This results in depth perception. **Depth perception** is the ability to see the world in three dimensions. It also allows organisms to judge how far away an object is.

Having two or more eyes allows the brain to better process visual information. By being able to judge how far away something is, animals can hunt for prey more easily. People can avoid dangers such as oncoming traffic or holes in the ground.

HANDS-ON Apply What You Know

Judging Distances by Sight

With a partner, select a small, lightweight object such as an eraser or a paper clip. Face your partner. One partner should cover his or her eye with one hand, and the other partner should drop the small object. The partner with the covered eye should try to catch the object with the other hand. After doing this several times, switch positions and start over. Was catching the object easy or difficult? Discuss ways you could improve your performance.

What made catching the object difficult?

    a. too much visual information   **c.** seeing in three dimensions

    b. lack of depth perception   **d.** being too close to the object

Field of view

Field of view is how much of an area you can see at any one moment. Without turning your head, look around the room in front of you. What can you see? What prevents you from seeing farther?

Many things prevent you from seeing parts of the world around you. Walls prevent you from seeing outside. Furniture prevents you from seeing what's behind it. Because your eyes are in the front of your head, you can't see what's behind you unless you turn your head.

Peripheral vision is how far you can see to each side of you when your eyes are focused straight ahead.

To help you understand your field of view, perform the following activity. Sit or stand on a hard surface selected by your teacher. Use chalk or tape to draw a protractor on the ground.

Have a classmate try to sneak up behind you on your left. Once you can see your classmate out the side of your eye, state, "NOW!" Your classmate should mark that spot on your protractor while you are still looking straight ahead.

Record Where on your protractor did you first see the person sneaking up on you?

_____

_____

_____

Describe Stare straight ahead. Without moving your head to the right or to the left, describe the object farthest to your right. What about the object is difficult to see?

_____

_____

_____

_____

Do the Math
Big Field, Small Field

Explore Online

Not all animals have the same field of view. Some animals, such as horses, cattle, and many fish, have eyes on the sides of their heads. Others, such as cats, dogs, and some birds, have eyes in the front of their heads.

Animals with eyes in the front of their heads have a smaller field of view than animals with eyes on the sides of their heads. Animals with eyes on the sides of their heads have poorer binocular vision but do have better peripheral vision. The horse can see about 357° of its surroundings. The owl can see a total of about 110° of its surroundings.

Look at the images of the owl and the horse.

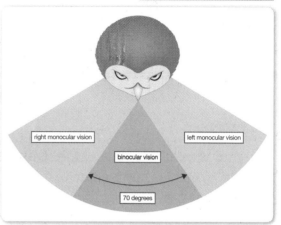

Record Which animal has the greater field of view?

_____

Solve What is the difference in degrees between the animals' fields of vision?

_____

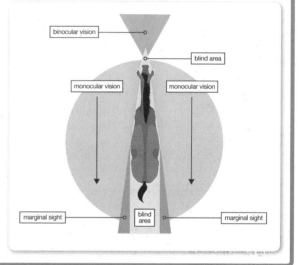

 EVIDENCE NOTEBOOK Look back at the animals in the Can You Explain It? activity at the beginning of this lesson. In your Evidence Notebook, list whether each animal is a predator—an animal that hunts other animals—or is prey—an animal that is hunted.

 Language SmArts
Making Connections

Why do animals with eyes on the sides of their heads have a better chance of escaping predators?

_____

_____

_____

See and Be Seen

Objective

Collaborate as a team to investigate how eye location and structure affect how organisms see the world.

Procedure

STEP 1 Eye location and structure greatly affect how organisms see the world. What questions come to mind when you think about that sentence? Be ready to share them with the class.

_____

_____

_____

_____

_____

_____

STEP 2 With your class, select the most important questions about eye location and structure. Write down the questions your class came up with here:

_____

_____

_____

_____

_____

_____

_____

_____

_____

STEP 3 How can you investigate the questions your class picked as most important? Think about the materials your teacher shows you and what else you might need. Write your plan and show it to your teacher to see if you can get the other things you need. Attach your plan to this lab sheet. If you use things other than those shown by your teacher, be sure to write them in the materials list.

STEP 4 Carry out your plan, and record your results. Present your data in a way that everyone can see what you did and what happened. You might choose a table or a graph as a presentation tool. Or you might choose to make a poster with photographs. Make a claim that answers the question or questions your class decided to explore. You may need to have a claim for each question. Support your claim with evidence from your investigation and reasoning to explain how the evidence supports your claim. Record your claim, evidence, and reasoning on a separate sheet of paper, and attach it to this lab sheet.

Take It Further

After your investigation, what new questions do you have about eye location and structures? You can start your question with "What happens if . . ." or "Is this always . . ."

_____

_____

_____

_____

_____

_____

_____

Eye Structure

The Parts of the Eye

Match the caption to the part of the eye it describes.

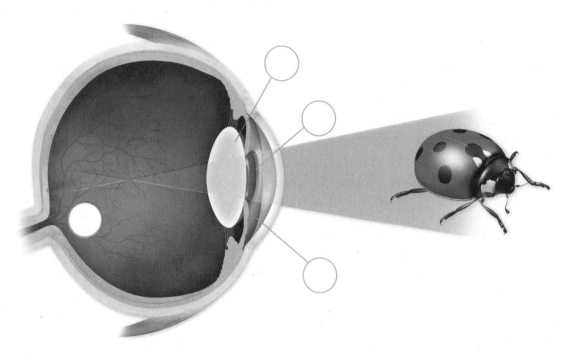

a. The iris is the part of the eye that has color.

b. The **pupil** is an opening in the eye that allows light to enter.

c. After passing through the pupil, light passes through the lens before it strikes the back of the eye.

d. At the back of the eye is an area called the **retina,** where there are light receptors. These receptors react to the light and send nerve signals along a pathway to the brain, where the information is processed.

Identify List the order in which light moves through the eye to the brain.

_____

 EVIDENCE NOTEBOOK Look back at the animals in the Can You Explain It? activity. In your Evidence Notebook, tell where on their heads their eyes are located. Describe the shape of each iris and pupil.

Front and Side

Apply Circle the animals that have eyes on the sides of their heads.

Foxes have forward-facing eyes with vertical openings in their pupils. This controls the amount of light that enters while hunting during the day or night.

Big horn sheep have side-facing eyes with horizontal pupils. This enables them to get more light from the side and see predators that may be stalking them.

Owls have forward-facing eyes with large, round pupils. Owls hunt for food at night. Their eyes allow them to search for prey in low-light conditions.

Hummingbirds have side-facing eyes with large, round pupils. This helps them distinguish color. It also helps them to avoid bumping into things when they change direction quickly.

Lobster eyes are on stalks that can move. Each eye has many parts that reflect light, enabling it to see in dark or cloudy waters.

Flies have compound eyes that are so big that they cover the front and sides of their heads. This gives them an almost 360-degree view of the world around them.

Explain What is true of most organisms that have forward-facing eyes? Circle all that apply.

    a. They have an overlapping field of view.

    b. They have strong peripheral vision.

    c. They are usually predators.

    d. They are usually prey.

Engineer It!
The Camera Eye

Eyes transmit information to the brain, which then stores that information for later use. A camera can be used as a model for the way vision works because it collects and stores images as well. It does this much like the brain is able to store images. You see an object and it is stored in your brain. Then, the next time you see that object, you know what it is.

Because the camera pictured here has only one "eye," it makes optical illusions possible. Without two eyes, a camera takes a picture that is similar to what an animal sees when it does not have binocular vision. However, some cameras can make perspective images that are similar to what animals see with binocular vision.

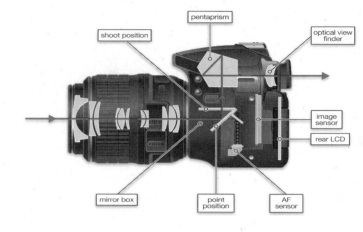

Cameras can be used to model an eye.

Explore Use online resources to find a few perspective images. How do they imitate depth perception?

_____

_____

_____

_____

Language SmArts
Draw Conclusions

Explain Why would an animal with forward-facing eyes be a better hunter than an animal with side-facing eyes? Explain your answer.

_____

_____

_____

_____

_____

Eye on Art

In the box, draw an animal based on the evidence provided below. Apply what you have learned in this lesson about the position of an organism's eyes and how it affects the organism's survival.

An animal lives on a grassy plain. It walks on four legs and travels in a herd. It eats grasses to survive and must be careful to avoid predators.

Putting It Together

Use the word bank to complete the sentences. Not every word will be used.

processes	lens	pupil	retina	rejects	light

_____ enters the eye through the _____. After light passes

through the lens and into the _____, a signal goes to the brain. The brain

_____ the signal, and you see an image.

How Eyes See

Comparing Eyes

Examine each image closely. How are the eyes similar? How are they different?

Foxes have eyes that give them better depth perception.

Bighorn sheep have eyes with wider fields of vision.

Record List the characteristics of each animal's eyes in the table below.

Fox	Bighorn sheep

Reflections of Light

Draw how our eyes use light to see objects.

When there is little light in a room, it is difficult to see objects inside that room. That's because eyes process light that is reflected or emitted from objects.

When there is plenty of light in a room, it is much easier to see objects inside that room. Eyes transmit the light they see to the brain as information.

HANDS-ON **Apply What You Know**

Vertical versus Horizontal

Work with a partner. Your teacher will dim the lights. One partner should hold the flashlight while the other holds a reflective surface. Shine the flashlight against a mirror. What happens? Do this again with a different surface. Then trade objects with your partner and start over. Discuss why different surfaces reflect light differently.

Materials
- flashlight
- various reflective surfaces
- cardboard with a vertical slit cut in it
- cardboard with a horizontal slit cut in it

Next, we will model how pupil shape changes how light enters the eye. The slits in the cardboard represent pupils. Imagine the wall is the retina. Shine the flashlight through the horizontal slit at the wall. How did the light appear on the wall? Shine the flashlight through the vertical slit. How did the light appear on the wall? How did the shape of the slit affect the field of view?

Select an animal of your choice. If necessary, use online resources to describe its pupil shape and how light allows the animal to see objects. How does this enable it to survive in its environment?

_____

_____

_____

_____

Explore Online

© Houghton Mifflin Harcourt Publishing Company

507

EVIDENCE NOTEBOOK Think about the animals in the Can You Explain It? activity. In your Evidence Notebook, describe the eye size and pupil shape of each animal.

Identify Draw a line matching each set of eyes to the correct type of animal. At least one pair of eyes can be matched to both *predator* and *prey*.

predator

prey

Putting It Together

Look at the image. Add a light source. Then draw how the light moves to enable the eye to see the object.

Discover More

Check out this path . . . or go online to choose one of these other paths.

Careers in Science & Engineering

- **Optical Illusions**
- **Illusion vs. Illusion**
- **People in Science & Engineering**

Ophthalmologist

Eyes are important organs that help people to see. You have already learned about some parts of the eye. But there's another part that helps protect it from danger. It's called the cornea. It covers the iris and the pupil to help keep out dirt, debris, and germs. When the cornea or other parts of the eye become damaged or diseased, a special doctor has to treat the eye. These doctors are known as ophthalmologists.

Ophthalmologists treat serious eye problems. For example, sometimes a cornea can become so damaged that it no longer does its job. In these cases, ophthalmologists may have to transplant a cornea from one eye to another. A transplanted cornea is donated by an organ donor.

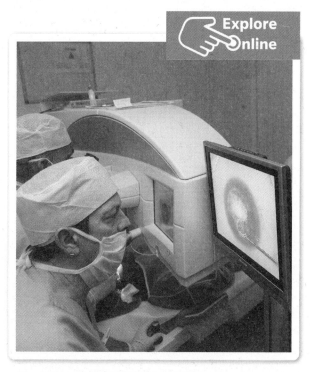

Explore Online

Doctors who perform surgeries on eyes are called ophthalmologists.

Dr. Renelle Lim is an ophthalmologist who works in New York. She focuses her research and work on eye cancers and other advanced diseases. As an ophthalmologist, Dr. Lim is always doing research on the eye and new procedures that can be safely used to treat eye problems.

Dr. Renelle Lim is an ophthalmologist who performs advanced surgeries and procedures on people with serious eye conditions.

Modeling the Eye

Build a model of the eye. Your model should include the cornea, iris, lens, pupil, and retina. To begin, select the materials you are going to use to build your model. After your teacher has approved the materials, sketch your model in the space below. After you have completed your drawing, build your model.

Once you've designed your model, you get to build it. Think about materials you will need to make your eye.

Explain It

On the lines below, explain what each part of your model represents and how it works.

_____

_____

_____

_____

Lesson Check

Name _____

Can You Explain It?

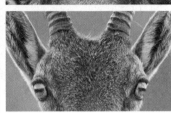

1. Why do you think each of these animals has a different kind of eye? How might the differences in the structure of their eyes affect the way they live? Be sure to do the following:

- Describe the different kinds of eyes.

- Describe where different kinds of eyes are usually located.

- Explain how animals use their eyes to survive.

- In particular, describe whether each type of eye belongs to predators or prey.

 EVIDENCE NOTEBOOK Use the information you've collected in your Evidence Notebook to help you cover each point.

_____

_____

_____

_____

_____

_____

_____

_____

Checkpoints

2. Which statements are correct about eyes? Circle all that apply.

a. They transfer information.

b. They take in light.

c. They store information.

d. They help organisms to survive.

3. Draw a line to match each term with its definition.

field of view		when two eyes see the same thing from a slightly different angle
depth perception		the ability to judge an object's distance
peripheral vision		how much of an area an animal can see at any one moment
binocular vision		how far you can see to each side of you when your eyes are focused straight ahead

4. Write the letter for each part of the eye shown in the image.

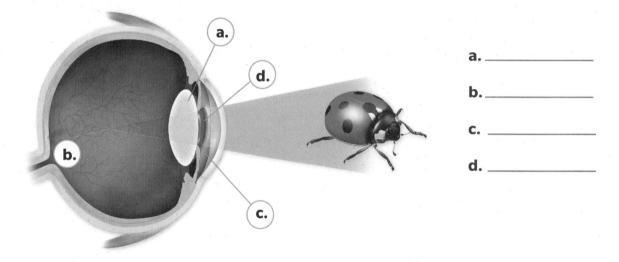

a. _____

b. _____

c. _____

d. _____

5. Which feature do you need to be able to see in three dimensions?
   a. a wide field of view
   b. binocular vision
   c. peripheral vision
   d. human vision

6. Which label describes the area this animal cannot see?
   a. monocular vision
   b. field of view
   c. blind area
   d. binocular vision

Lesson Roundup

A. On the line by each image, write whether the eyes shown belong to a predator, prey, or both.

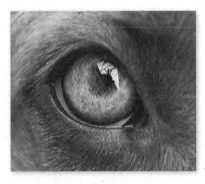 _____

 _____

 _____

 _____

B. Choose the best words from the word bank to complete the sentences.

compound	side-facing	forward-facing

Animals with _____ eyes have better depth perception.

Animals with _____ eyes have a wider field of view.

Animals with _____ eyes have an almost 360-degree view

of the world around them.

C. How are eyes able to see?

_____

_____

_____

_____

How Is Information Transferred from Place to Place?

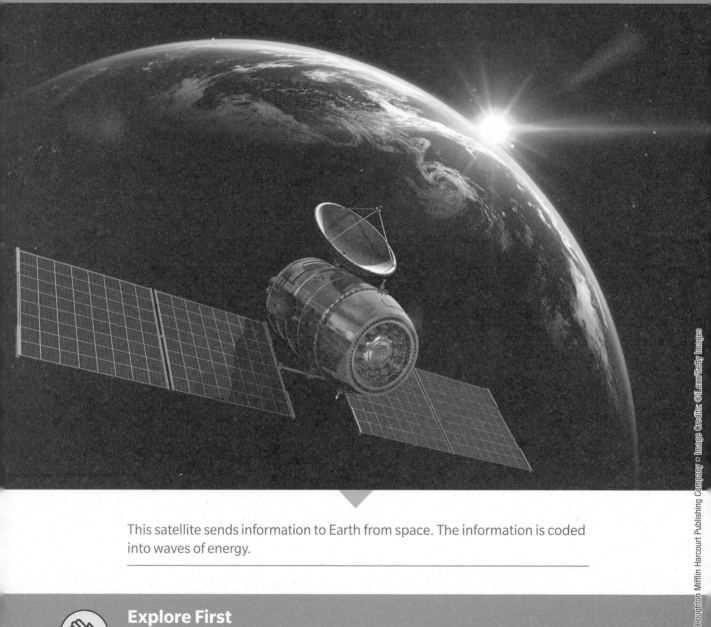

This satellite sends information to Earth from space. The information is coded into waves of energy.

Explore First

Code Breaker Can you break a code? Using the materials your teacher provides, find clues around the classroom that you can use to figure out the coded message your teacher writes on the board. Work with your group to decipher, or figure out, the message.

Can You Explain It?

Explore Online

How times have changed! 30 years ago, televisions were large pieces of furniture and telephones had wires. Today, we have televisions that have hundreds of channels and phones that can take photos and surf the web.

How has the way we receive information changed over the years?

_____

_____

_____

_____

_____

_____

_____

_____

_____

_____

 EVIDENCE NOTEBOOK Look for this icon to help you gather evidence to answer the question above.

History of Information Transfer

The Old Ways

Humans always have needed to communicate. As you've discovered, one of the oldest methods of information transfer is information captured by the senses. Light and sound are two ways information and messages can be shared. Before talking, ancient people probably sent messages by pointing, grunting, or hand gestures. As people spread out, they needed to communicate over distances. Also, it became common for ancient cultures to record their histories using pictures.

One of the earliest recorded forms of communication used *pictographs*. These drawings are often painted in caves. They are very fragile but have lasted because they are painted in places that are protected from the weather. Pictographs recorded events, such as important ceremonies and good hunting areas.

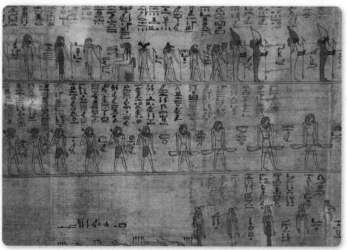

Ancient Egyptians communicated using *hieroglyphics*. Hieroglyphics are symbols for ideas, words, or letters. For example, a drawing of a lion might represent the letter *L*. Egyptians made papyrus, an early form of paper, so that ideas were not limited to the size of a wall. They passed on information about ceremonies. Because hieroglyphics could be written on paper, they could be carried from place to place.

 Language SmArts Interview an older adult. How have the ways they communicate changed over time?

How can people send messages long distances without making any noise? In ancient China, there were often battles that involved soldiers from faraway places. Soldiers used smoke signals to communicate across long distances.

Native Americans on the plains in the Midwest also used smoke to send signals. The smoke signals served as a "universal language" between the tribes.

A talking drum has two heads. It can be tuned to different notes but usually produces low wavelengths. Drums were used to tell stories, send messages, and lead ceremonies. Drums are an ancient form of communication, and they are still important to the cultures of West Africa.

"One if by land. Two if by sea." So goes the story of Paul Revere's ride, letting people know that the British were coming. Using the lanterns in the Old North Church, colonists were able to send simple messages to many people at once.

Explain Choose the words or phrases that make each sentence correct.

| hieroglyphics | lanterns | talking drums | smoke signals |

One of the earliest ways of sending messages was through the use of

_____. This involved drawing pictures on paper. To send signals

across long distances, the ancient Chinese used _____ to alert

the troops that enemies were coming.

Newer Ways

With the discovery of electricity, signals could be sent over much greater distances, thousands of miles away. A device called the *telegraph* was invented that allowed information to travel all over the world along wires. The telegraph was invented in the 1830s. A man named Samuel Morse invented a "language" that could be used to send messages using the telegraph.

International Morse Code

Character	Morse code	Character	Morse code	Number	Morse code
A	·—	N	—·	1	·————
B	—···	O	———	2	··———
C	—·—·	P	·——·	3	···——
D	—··	Q	——·—	4	····—
E	·	R	·—·	5	·····
F	··—·	S	···	6	—····
G	——·	T	—	7	——···
H	····	U	··—	8	———··
I	··	V	···—	9	————·
J	·———	W	·——	0	—————
K	—·—	X	—··—		
L	·—··	Y	—·——		
M	——	Z	——··		

A **code** is a system of letters, numbers, or symbols that are used in place of words or letters. The telegraph code is called *Morse code*. It is a series of dots and dashes, each making up a letter. An operator in one place taps out a message. It travels through wires to another location. A second operator decodes the message. Operators needed to be skilled so that messages could be sent quickly and accurately.

 Language SmArts Telegraph messages were very popular, but not always reliable. Name some ways a message might be miscommunicated or misunderstood.

_____

_____

_____

_____

Using the telegraph, messages were sent all over the world. When it was first invented, cables were laid across the Atlantic Ocean to Europe. This was beneficial during the world wars to keep track of enemies. The last telegraph message was sent in 2013.

Explore Online

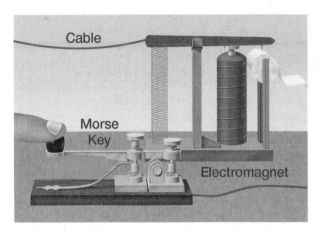

A battery, an electromagnet, a telegraph key, and a cable make up a telegraph. By tapping the key, an electric pulse is sent through the cable.

The telegraph operator uses a code called Morse code. It is a series of dots and dashes, each making up a letter.

The signal moves along the cable to a machine on the other end.

The electric pulse is transformed into sound. The operator listens and decodes the dots and dashes to make words from them.

Apply In the space below, write your name in Morse code.

© Houghton Mifflin Harcourt Publishing Company

519

Codes

Think about sending a signal. Each message needs a sender and a receiver. Chances are that you talk to or text your friends using a phone or that you have a face-to-face chat in the lunchroom at school.

How do you make your message clear? Sometimes, using text messages does not always get the correct message across. If you use shorthand such as symbols or emojis, the receiver may not know what you mean.

Sometimes you want to send a message that's meant for only one person. How do you keep it a secret? In this case, you want to be sure only the receiver can understand the message. You could use a secret code. Secret codes have been around for hundreds of years. They're useful to protect important information, such as bank accounts or personal information on websites.

Analyze Can you think of some times in history when a secret code would have been needed? What makes a good code?

_____

_____

_____

_____

During World War II, the United States government needed a way to encode special messages. They recruited Navajo people to speak their complex native language to serve as code talkers.

Another tool used to send secret messages is the *Enigma machine,* a device that looks a lot like an old typewriter with a keyboard and some wheels sticking out of the top. The Germans developed the Enigma machine during World War II.

 EVIDENCE NOTEBOOK Why was the Navajo language perfect for a code to use against the Japanese in World War II? Record your answer in your Evidence Notebook.

As you have seen, there are many different codes. Codes and different ways to send codes have been around for thousands of years. But codes don't have to be very complicated, and they can be fun to use. Look at the images to see some more codes.

Flags can be used to relay coded messages, especially between ship and shore or two people too far away to hear each other.

A **scytale** is another tool that can be used to send a coded message. A strip is wrapped around a tube. A message will be added, then the tube removed.

 HANDS-ON Apply What You Know

Make a Scytale

Get some paper, scissors, tape, pencil, and paper towel tube from your teacher. Cut the paper into long strips. Tape one end of the strip to the side of the tube. Wrap the rest of the strip around the tube. Write a message from one end of the tube to the other. Then add a bunch of other letters around the ones you wrote to fill in the space. Take off the strip of paper, and trade it with a classmate to see if they can figure out what you wrote.

Putting It Together

Suppose you wanted to send a secret message using Morse code. Circle the things you need to send a complete message. Select all that apply.

  a. a sender

  b. a microphone

  c. a series of dots and dashes

  d. a pile of papers

  e. a tablet

  f. a receiver

HANDS-ON ACTIVITY
Pixels to Pictures

Objective

Have you ever looked closely at a picture using a magnifying glass? If so, you may have seen that the image was made up of millions of tiny dots. Each dot that makes a picture is called a **pixel.** When there are a lot of pixels in an image, it will be very sharp. If there are few pixels, the image will be blurry.

Materials
- pencil/pen
- paper
- ruler
- markers

Collaborate to discover how pixels work.

Form a question: What question will you investigate to meet this objective?

_____

_____

Procedure

STEP 1 Use the ruler to draw a grid on the paper. It should have 7 columns and 11 rows.

STEP 2 Fill in the boxes with ones and zeros as seen in the illustration on the next page.

STEP 3 Color in the boxes that have ones in them to see what the message says.

STEP 4 What does the message say?

_____

_____

0	0	0	0	0	0	0
0	0	0	0	0	0	0
0	1	0	1	0	1	0
0	1	0	1	0	0	0
0	1	0	1	0	1	0
0	1	1	1	0	1	0
0	1	0	1	0	1	0
0	1	0	1	0	1	0
0	1	0	1	0	1	0
0	0	0	0	0	0	0
0	0	0	0	0	0	0

Each box in the grid represents one pixel. What was the hardest part about making an image using pixels? What was the easiest?

_____

_____

_____

How are the ones in your grid used to represent something else?

_____

_____

Using a new grid, make a message for a friend to decode. To show more details, should you include more boxes in the same-size grid, or fewer?

_____

_____

Use **reasoning** to make a **claim** about pixels. Cite **evidence** to support your claim.

_____

_____

_____

What are some other questions you have about pixels?

_____

_____

Bits and Bytes

Bits of Code

In our digital world, everything needs to be changed into code. Pictures, words, and numbers on our devices are converted into codes of ones and zeros that can be sent as electronic signals. This collection of ones and zeros is called *binary code*. Each number of the code is a *bit*. This is the smallest piece of information that can be stored by a computer. Binary code is a little tricky at first. However, once you get the hang of it, it is pretty easy.

Binary code

Binary code is needed to store information in a computer. If you were to look at the software that runs your phone, gaming system, or laptop, you would find nothing but a very, VERY long chain of ones and zeros.

HANDS-ON Apply What You Know

Make Your Own Code

Using what you learn about binary code, make your own set of binary cards. Get index cards from your teacher, and then draw a different number of dots on each one. The first card should have one dot. The second card should have two dots, and so on, up to 16. With a partner, make binary code for a number and then decode what it is.

Learn Binary Code

1

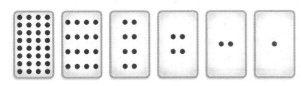

Look at the cards. Starting with 1 on the right, the next card would be 2, then 4, then 8, then 16, then 32, then 64, and so on.

2

If the first card is showing its dot, it is a one. If the card is not, it is a zero. An example with four digits of a binary code would be 0001.

3

The binary number for two would be 0010. Here, the two-dot card would be flipped over showing its dots. All the others are hidden.

4

The binary number for three would be 0011. Here, both the two-dot card and the one-dot cards are flipped.

Do the Math
Code Blue

In the table below, turn each blue number into binary code.

Number	\multicolumn{5}{c}{Number of "dots" per bit}	Binary code
	16	8	4	2	1	
1	0	0	0	0	1	00001
3	0	0	0	1	1	00011
5						
10						
13						
19						
21						

Connecting the World

Today, a lot of what we do is made easier by wireless technology. We are able to talk on a cell phone. We can "stream" movies to our TVs from wireless Internet modems or to our handheld devices. We can even listen to music that is relayed as signals from satellites.

All of these things rely on electronic signals transferring bits of code from one place to another. However, these signals can be interrupted. If you have ever had a dropped cell phone call or an Internet video that would not play, you have experienced an interrupted digital code.

The number of bits a device can move or process is a constraint. If a signal has too much information for the network to move, it slows down or stops. This is why you hear about the need for an Internet connection to be high speed.

Today we listen to music on our phones and other small devices.

Infer What types of things can cause the picture to buffer on the computer or TV?

_____

_____

_____

_____

Language SmArts Think about two criteria and two constraints to a device that can surf the Internet.

_____

_____

_____

_____

526

What is happening here? Error messages appear often on computers and tablets. Sometimes it means that there was a communication problem between parts of the system. Other times it means that the stream of bits of code needs to catch up.

Find the Cause

Draw a line from the issue to the possible cause. Find a cause for each issue.

too much traffic online

too far from
cell tower

| error message | computer speed is
too slow | lost signal |

too many phones
being used at once

 EVIDENCE NOTEBOOK How do you know when your cell phone signal strength is low? What can you do to improve it?

Code, Computers, and Networks

Explore Online

Humans communicate with words, letters, numbers, and pictures. Computers and other devices do not know what these are. Instead, they need to translate them into code (remember binary code?).

Now picture how signals are sent between computers. First, you input the words on the keyboard. Then, the computer translates them into binary code. If you are sending an email or a text to a friend, the computer needs to be able to "talk" to the Internet. The way computers talk to the rest of the world is with a device called a *modem*.

Next, the modem sends the signals to and from your computer. When you send an email, the pathway goes from your computer to the modem. It then goes to another modem, then to your friend's computer.

Kesha just sent an email to her grandma. The signal goes from the computer to the modem. It goes across the lines to grandma's modem and then to her computer.

Grandma is waiting for the email. To get to her, the signal comes from her modem. It takes very little time for the message to be received.

How Computers Help Us Communicate

Suppose you want to send an email. How does it work? The sending computer translates a message into codes that can be sent.

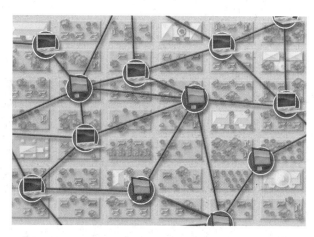

The codes are first sent through your local area network, or LAN, made up of all the modems in a virtual neighborhood.

The LAN sends the signals to all the computers that make up the Internet.

The signals containing coded words and pictures are decoded clearly by the receiver. Your message can now be read.

 Language SmArts Put these steps in order of how a message would get from Kesha's computer to Grandma's computer.

Kesha's modem	keyboard	Grandma's modem

_____   _____   _____

Grandma's computer	Kesha's computer

_____   _____

Explain Choose the correct words to complete each sentence. You may use a term more than once.

> binary code   modem   computer

When signals are sent from a computer, they need to be in

_____. The computer sends the digitized signal to a

_____. This puts the signal on the Internet. The message

first comes to the receiver's _____ before it gets to

their _____.

Sounds in the Air

When you talk on a cell phone, you use radio waves. A cell phone converts your voice (sound waves) into radio waves. These waves then get sent to a cell tower. From here, the waves are relayed to other towers. Finally, a tower sends the radio waves to a receiving phone. This entire process happens almost instantly.

 HANDS-ON Apply What You Know

The Phone Is for You!

Choose one classmate to be the leader. The leader should write down a message before telling it to the first student. The first student tells the second student the message. The second student tells the third student the story. This is repeated until all the students have heard the message. After the final student has been told, he or she should say the message aloud. Compare it to what was written down.

 HANDS-ON Apply What You Know

Make a Wave

Can you use a spring toy to send a message? Using binary code, send a short message to a classmate. "0" is represented by moving the spring back and forth. "1" is represented by moving the spring up and down. Have your classmate say the message aloud. Compare it to what was written down. Are they the same? What might improve your ability to send a message more accurately?

_____

_____

_____

How Cell Phones Help Us Communicate

1

When you talk on a cell phone, the sound waves of your voice are converted into digital code. The code is then sent as radio waves through the air.

2

The sender's radio waves reach cell phone towers, which exist in a network around the world.

3

The waves are relayed from tower to tower to satellites and then to other towers.

4

The radio waves are received by a cell phone, which converts them back into sound.

Apply Choose the correct words to complete each sentence. Some terms can be used twice.

sound waves	**light wave**	**radio waves**
microwaves	**tower**	**trough**

Cells phones convert _____ into _____.

They are then sent to a cell _____. From here, they relay

to other towers. They eventually arrive at a _____ near

another phone.

Bits of Color

Pixels are important. Remember that each picture or image you see on a screen is made of pixels. The more pixels there are, the clearer and more crisp the image will be. Back in the 1980s, video games and TVs had a lower resolution than they do today. This means that the number of pixels on the screen was smaller. Today's TVs feature many more pixels. This makes the pictures much clearer and the colors brighter. This is called high resolution, or high definition. You might have heard it called HD.

Explore Online

Does this image really look like an apple? This image has very low resolution. This means that there are very few pixels that make it up. The edges look fuzzy. And the texture of the picture looks grainy. This is how television and computer pictures looked many years ago.

Here is an image with slightly higher resolution. Notice how much clearer it is. The image also looks much smoother and more realistic. Most people today like to see higher-resolution images. This is because they look more realistic than low-resolution images.

Putting It Together

Choose the correct words to complete each sentence.

light pulses	**a system of ones and zeros**
Morse	**binary**

An image on a TV is like the image made in the grid activity because

both rely on _____ to create images. All digital

devices use _____ code to transmit signals.

Discover More

Check out this path . . . or go online to choose one of these other paths.

Elephant
Communication

- **People in Science & Engineering**
- **Wave That Flag**
- **Careers in Science & Engineering**

Elephant Stomp Sounds

There are all kinds of sounds. All sound waves have amplitude and wavelength. As humans, we can only hear things that are within a certain range of wavelengths. Some animals can hear sounds that we can't. Elephants are adapted to make and hear sounds with longer wavelengths than humans can hear. These sounds are called *infrasounds.* They can travel over great distances, which is very helpful to elephant herds. The sounds can alert them to dangers or a new food source. The ability to hear in this range has been studied a lot in three species of elephants.

Explore Online

Elephants are the largest land animals. Their size makes them fairly safe from predators. They live in large social groups and constantly "talk" to one another. Most of their sounds are made with their voice boxes or trunks. However, they are able to make deep rumbling noises within their bodies. These rumbles cannot be heard by humans.

Elephants may be able to hear through their feet as well as their ears.

It has been found that these sounds, called *infrasonic,* are felt by the elephants. They are used as a form of long-distance communication.

Think about where elephants live. Living on the open savanna has many challenges. Infrasonic calls are ideal for living here. Being able to avoid danger is important. Using infrasonic calls lets the elephants stay in touch even if they are not close. Because the signals are heard and felt, scientists believe that the elephants take them in through their feet as well as their ears.

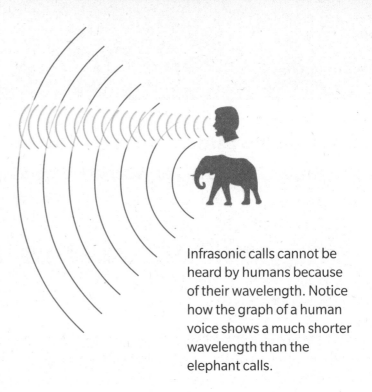

Infrasonic calls cannot be heard by humans because of their wavelength. Notice how the graph of a human voice shows a much shorter wavelength than the elephant calls.

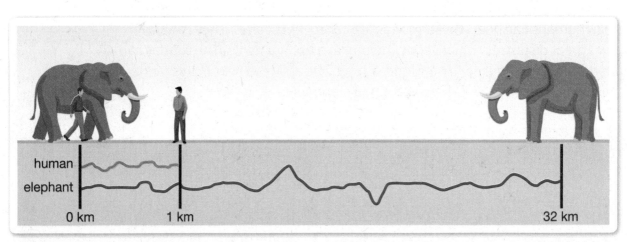

An infrasound made by an elephant can travel large distances. Human speech has shorter wavelengths that don't travel nearly as far.

Evaluate How is the way elephants use infrasonic sounds to communicate alike and different from the way we use cell phones?

_____

_____

_____

_____

_____

© Houghton Mifflin Harcourt Publishing Company

Lesson Check

Name _____

Can You Explain It?

1. How has the way we rely on information transfer changed over the years? Be sure to discuss the following:

- ways in which information has been transferred historically

- how energy transfer plays a role in information transfer

- how information is encoded, moved long distances, and then decoded without losing any of the information

- criteria and constraints of information technology

EVIDENCE NOTEBOOK Use the information you've collected in your Evidence Notebook to help answer the question.

_____

_____

_____

_____

_____

_____

_____

Checkpoints

2. Which of these methods use technology to transfer information? Circle all that apply.

a. Morse code

b. flags

c. scytale

d. infrasonic elephant sounds

e. texts to a friend using your phone

535

3. Suppose you wanted to describe African drums to a classmate. You want to tell her how they are used as a form of sending signals. Which of these would you say? Circle all that apply.

   a. The drums send signals you can hear.

   b. The drums have a very high wavelength.

   c. The drums have a very low wavelength.

   d. The drums are used for religious ceremonies.

4. Choose the correct words to complete each of the sentences.

The ancient Egyptians used _____ as a means of storytelling and recording their history. Soldiers in ancient China used _____ to send silent messages a long distance. The most famous use of _____ signals was during Paul Revere's ride. The "one if by land, two if by sea" signals told the colonists that the British were coming.

> hieroglyphics
> **Morse code**
> drums
> **smoke signals**
> lantern

5. Put these steps in order of how a message would get from your cell phone to your friend's cell phone.

| **tower near your friend's cell phone** | **tower close to your cell phone** | **friend's cell phone** |

_____ _____ _____

| **your cell phone** | **relay** |

_____ _____

6. Use the code key below to decode the message (hint: it is six words long). The message is:

9 12 5 1 18 14 5 4 13 1 14 25 20 8 9 14 7 19 1 2 15 21 20 19 9 7 14 1 12 19

1	2	3	4	5	6	7	8	9	10	11	12	13
A	B	C	D	E	F	G	H	I	J	K	L	M

14	15	16	17	18	19	20	21	22	23	24	25	26
N	O	P	Q	R	S	T	U	V	W	X	Y	Z

Lesson Roundup

A. Which of these describe the use of hieroglyphics and pictographs in ancient times? Circle all that apply.

   a. They were often drawn on walls.

   b. They are a form of signal that can be heard.

   c. They record events and cultural histories.

   d. They were made using modern art tools.

B. How are cell phone signals transferred? Circle the best answer for the question.

   a. They go from the tower to the phone to another phone.

   b. They go from the receiver's phone to the sender's phone.

   c. They go from sender to tower to relay to tower to receiver.

   d. They go from tower to receiver to sender to relay back to the receiver.

C. Decide if each phrase is describing signal transfer using coded or uncoded communication. Some may go into more than one category.

coded	Morse code	uncoded
	talking on the phone	
	scytale	
	text message	
	talking face to face	

D. Why are codes used to relay messages? Circle all that apply.

   a. They do not depend on understanding a language.

   b. Everyone can understand them.

   c. They can be encoded and decoded digitally and sent by waves.

   d. They are short.

Communication of the Wild

You are a scientist working on a team that studies animals. Your team has been asked to study the way that certain groups of animals communicate. You need to choose an animal to study and find a way to figure out how that animal uses its senses to communicate with its group.

DEFINE YOUR TASK: How will you know if your project is successful? Before beginning, review the checklist at the end of this Unit Performance Task. Keep those items in mind as you proceed.

_____

_____

_____

RESEARCH: Use online or library resources to learn about your chosen animal and how that animal communicates. Find out whether that animal has special senses for sight, sound, or smell and how that animal uses those senses. Cite your sources.

_____

_____

_____

BRAINSTORM: Brainstorm ways to study animal communication. What kinds of things and patterns would you be looking for? Remember, humans have many different ways of communicating. See what can be applied to studying animals.

_____

_____

_____

_____

© Houghton Mifflin Harcourt Publishing Company • Image Credits: ©PhotoDisc/ Getty

PLAN YOUR PROCEDURE: Consider the questions below as your group plans its animal communication strategy. Be sure to address the resources you will need and your overall goals and limits. Write a few sentences below to briefly summarize your strategy.

1. What kind of system or device should you build to study how animals communicate?

2. Where will you plant the system or device?

3. What kinds of costs do you need to consider?

4. How much time will you need to get a good amount of data on the animals?

5. What are some possible setbacks or limitations that you might have?

_____

_____

_____

REPORT: Make a document that details your animal communication strategy. Describe any concerns and how they will be addressed. List steps to complete the study. Be specific and complete.

COMMUNICATE: Present your plan to the class orally and with multimedia. Explain the reasoning behind your plan, and discuss possible ways to revise and improve it.

✅ Checklist

Review your project, and check off each completed item.

_____ includes a statement defining the task

_____ includes research into various ways animals communicate

_____ includes sources cited

_____ includes a list of concerns to be addressed

_____ includes a plan of action for the study, including possible limitations or setbacks

_____ includes an oral presentation with multimedia support

Unit Review

1. Choose the correct term or phrase to complete the sentence.

> **depth perception**   **binocular vision**   **field of vision**   **peripheral vision**

How much of an area you can see at any one moment is known as

_____.

2. What did the ancient Chinese use as means of communicating over long distances?

a. smoke signals

b. hieroglyphics

c. Morse code

d. lantern signals

3. What discovery did Morse code use to send signals over long distances?

a. electricity

b. pixels

c. bytes

d. gravity

4. Which kinds of communication are considered coded? Circle all that apply.

a. Morse

b. scytale

c. text messaging

d. speaking

5. Which of the following gives animals better depth perception?

   a. peripheral vision

   b. field of view

   c. bird's-eye view

   d. binocular vision

6. Choose the words or phrases to complete the sentence.

in front of their heads	**on the side of their heads**
on the backs of their heads	**better** **worse**

Animals with eyes _____ can detect predators

_____ because they will have a larger overall field of vision.

7. Why are animals with eyes that are closer together better predators than animals with eyes that are farther apart?

   a. They have stronger parts of the eye.

   b. They have better depth perception.

   c. They have better fields of vision.

   d. They have better peripheral vision.

8. Match the structure of the eye with its description.

| iris |
| lens |
| pupil |
| retina |

| the part that senses light |
| the part that focuses light |
| the colored part of the eye |
| the opening in the iris where light enters |

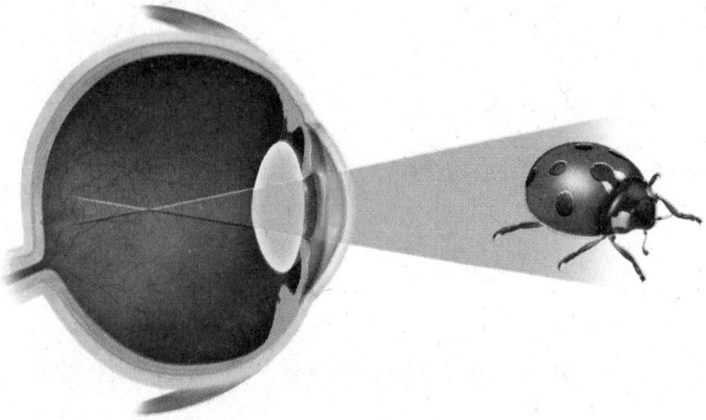

9. Which types of waves occur when you speak to someone with a cell phone?

   a. light waves

   b. radio waves

   c. sound waves

   d. speaking

10. Why were Navajo soldiers important during World War II?

_____

_____

_____

_____

_____

Interactive Glossary

As you learn about each item, add notes, drawings, or sentences in the extra space. This will help you remember what the terms mean. Here's an example:

fungi (FUHN•jee) A group of organisms that get nutrients by decomposing other organisms.

hongos Un grupo de organismos que obtienen sus nutrientes al descomponer otros organismos.

Mushrooms are a type of fungi.

Glossary Pronunciation Key

With every glossary term, there is also a phonetic respelling. A phonetic respelling writes the word the way it sounds, which can help you pronounce new or unfamiliar words. Use this key to help you understand the respellings.

Sound	As in	Phonetic Respelling	Sound	As In	Phonetic Respelling
a	bat	(BAT)	oh	over	(OH•ver)
ah	lock	(LAHK)	oo	pool	(POOL)
air	rare	(RAIR)	ow	out	(OWT)
ar	argue	(AR•gyoo)	oy	foil	(FOYL)
aw	law	(LAW)	s	cell	(SEL)
ay	face	(FAYS)		sit	(SIT)
ch	chapel	(CHAP•uhl)	sh	sheep	(SHEEP)
e	test	(TEST)	th	that	(THAT)
	metric	(MEH•trik)		thin	(THIN)
ee	eat	(EET)	u	pull	(PUL)
	feet	(FEET)	uh	medal	(MED•uhl)
	ski	(SKEE)		talent	(TAL•uhnt)
er	paper	(PAY•per)		pencil	(PEN•suhl)
	fern	(FERN)		onion	(UHN•yuhn)
eye	idea	(eye•DEE•uh)		playful	(PLAY•fuhl)
i	bit	(BIT)		dull	(DUHL)
ing	going	(GOH•ing)	y	yes	(YES)
k	card	(KARD)		ripe	(RYP)
	kite	(KYT)	z	bags	(BAGZ)
ngk	bank	(BANGK)	zh	treasure	(TREZH•er)

A

amplitude (AM•pluh•tood) Half of the distance from the crest to the trough of a wave. p. 350

amplitud La mitad de la distancia desde la cresta hasta la depresión de una ola.

B

binocular vision
(BI•nah•ku•lur VIH•shuhn) Vision in living things having two eyes that function together enabling them to see. p. 497

visión binocular Visión en seres vivientes que tienen dos ojos que funcionan juntos permitiéndoles ver.

C

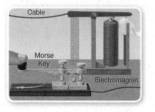

circuit (SER•kuht) The closed path or loop that an electric charge flows through. p. 85

circuito cerrado La trayectoria cerrada o el bucle cerrado a través del cual la carga eléctrica fluye.

code (KOHD) A system of words, numbers, or other data used in place of other words or letters. p. 518

código Un sistema de palabras, números u otros datos utilizados en lugar de otras palabras o letras.

collision (kuh•LI•shuhn) The result of two objects bumping into each other. p. 110

colisión Resultado del choque entre dos objetos.

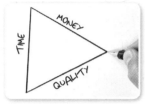

constraint (kuhn•STRAYNT) Something that limits what you are trying to do. p. 13

restricción Algo que limita lo que se está tratando de hacer.

continent (KON•tn•uhnt) One of the seven largest land areas on Earth. p. 287

continente Una de las siete áreas terrestres más grandes de la Tierra.

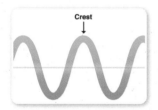

crest (KREST) The top part of a wave. p. 350

cresta Parte superior de una onda.

C

criteria (kry•TEER•ee•uh) The desirable features of a solution. p. 12

criterios Características deseables de una solución.

D

deposition (dep•uh•ZISH•uhn) The dropping or settling of eroded materials. p. 217

deposición Caída o asentamiento de materiales erosionados.

depth perception (DEPTH per•CEP•shuhn) The ability to see the world in three dimensions. p. 497

percepción de profundidad La capacidad de ver el mundo en tres dimensiones.

drawback (DRAH•bak) A disadvantage or inconvenience. p. 171

inconveniente Desventaja o problema.

electric current (ee•LEK•trik KER•uhnt) The flow of electric charges along a path. p. 81

corriente eléctrica Flujo de cargas eléctricas a lo largo de una trayectoria.

elevation (el•uh•VEY•shuhn) The height above or below the level of the sea. p. 294

elevación Altura de la tierra sobre o debajo del nivel del mar.

energy (EN•er•jee) The ability to do work and cause changes in matter. p. 76

energía Capacidad de realizar una tarea y causar cambios en la materia.

energy transfer (EN•er•jee TRAZ•fuhr) The movement of energy from place to place or from one object to another. p. 133

transferencia de energía Movimiento de energía de un lugar a otro o de un objeto a otro.

energy transformation

(EN•er•jee TRANZ•fuhr•may•shuhn) A change in energy from one form to another. p. 133

transformación de la energía Cambio en la energía, de una forma a otra.

engineering

(en•juh•NEER•ing) The use of science and math for practical uses such as the design of structures, machines, and systems. (p. 11)

ingeniería El uso de las ciencias y las matemáticas para usos prácticos como el diseño de estructuras, máquinas, y sistemas.

environment

(en•VEYE•ruhn•muhnt) All the living and nonliving things that surround and affect an organism. p. 223

medio ambiente Todos los seres vivientes y no vivientes que rodean y afectan a un organismo.

erosion (uh•ROH•zhuhn) The process of moving sediment from one place to another. p. 217

erosión El proceso de mover el sedimento de un lugar a otro.

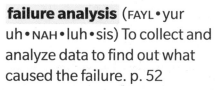

failure analysis (FAYL•yur uh•NAH•luh•sis) To collect and analyze data to find out what caused the failure. p. 52

ensayo de fatiga Coleccionar y analizar datos para averiguar lo que causó el fallo.

fair test (FAYR TEST) To conduct an experiment by changing only one thing at a time making sure all other conditions remain the same. p. 35

prueba controlada Conducir un experimento donde cambias una cosa a la vez y aseguras que todas las otras condiciones permanecen igual.

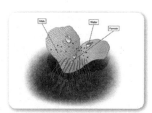

fertilization (fur•tl•uh•ZEY•shuhn) The process when male and female reproductive parts join together. p. 443

fertilización Proceso en el que se unen los órganos reproductivos del macho y la hembra.

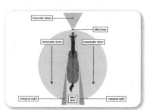

field of view (FILD UHF VU) The area where an image can be seen clearly. p. 498

campo visual El área donde una imagen se puede ver con claridad.

F

fossil (FAHS•uhl) The remains or traces of an organism that lived long ago. p. 268

fósil Restos o vestigios de un organismo que vivió hace tiempo.

H

heat (HEET) The energy that moves between objects of different temperatures. p. 140

calor Energía que se mueve entre objetos con temperaturas distintas.

M

motion (MOH•shuhn) A change of position of an object. p. 77

movimiento Un cambio en la posición de un objeto.

N

natural hazard (NACH•er•uhl HAZ•urd) An Earth process that threatens to Harm people and property. p. 366

peligro natural Proceso terrestre que amenaza con dañar a personas y bienes.

natural resource (NACH•er•uhl REE•sawrs) Materials found in nature that people and other living things use. p. 160

recurso natural Materiales que se encuentran en la naturaleza y que las personas y otros seres vivos utilizan.

nonrenewable resource (nahn•rih•NOO•uh•buhl REE•sawrs) A resource that, once used, cannot be replaced in a reasonable amount of time. p. 161

recurso no renovable Recurso que, después de haber sido utilizado, no podrá ser reemplazado en un tiempo razonable.

O

ocean trench (OH•shuhn TRENCH) A long, narrow valley found on the ocean floor. p. 321

fosa oceánica Un valle largo y angosto que se encuentra en el suelo del océano.

optimize (AWP•tim•iz) To make the most effective use of something. p. 55

optimizar Hacer el uso más efectivo de algo.

P

peripheral vision
(puh•RIF•er•uhl VIH•shuhn)
The edge of the field of vision.
p. 498

visión periférica El borde del
campo de visión.

pixel (PIK•suhl) A small unit of
color or brightness that when
put together with other units
forms an image. p. 522

pixel Una pequeña unidad de
color o luminosidad que cuando
se junta con otras unidades,
forma una imagen.

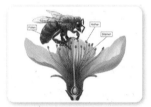

pollination
(pol•uh•NAY•shuhn) The
transfer of pollen in flowers or
cones. p. 443

polinización Transferencia del
polen en flores o conos.

pollution (puh•LOO•shuhn)
Waste products that damage an
ecosystem. p. 169

contaminación Todo
desperdicio que daña
un ecosistema.

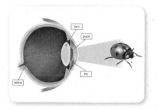

pupil (PYOO•puhl) The opening at the center of the iris where light enters the eye. p. 502

pupila La apertura en el centro del iris por donde la luz entra al ojo.

R

receptors (ree•SEP•turs) Special structures that send information about the environment from different parts of the body to the brain. p. 465

receptores Células nerviosas especiales que envían información acerca del ambiente desde distintas partes del cuerpo hacia el cerebro.

relative age (REL•uh•tiv AYJ) The age of one thing compared to another. pp. 265—266

edad relativa Edad de una cosa al compararla con otra.

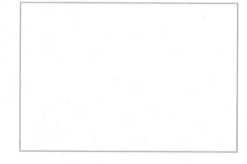

renewable resource (rih•NOO•uh•buhl REE•sawrs) A resource that can be replaced within a reasonable amount of time. p. 181

recurso renovable Recurso que puede ser reemplazado en un tiempo razonable.

R

reproduction
(ree•pruh•DUHK•shuhn) The process by which a living thing makes a new living thing. p. 443

reproducción El proceso por el cual un ser viviente tiene o genera un nuevo ser viviente del mismo tipo.

resource (REE•sawrs) Any material that can be used to satisfy a need. p. 160

recurso Cualquier material que pueda ser utilizado para satisfacer una necesidad.

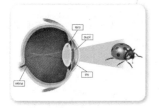

retina (RIH•ta•nuh) Lining of the inner eyeball that is connected to the brain by light receptors. p. 502

retina Revestimiento del globo ocular interno que está conectado al cerebro por receptores de luz.

S

scale (SKEYL) The part of a map that compares a distance on the map to a distance in the real world. p. 290

escala Parte de un mapa que compara la distancia en el mapa con la distancia en el mundo real.

seed (SEED) The part of a plant that contains a new plant. p. 443

semilla Parte de la planta que contiene una planta nueva.

senses The ability to receive information about the environment. The five senses are sight, hearing, smell, taste, and touch. p. 464

sentidos La capacidad de recibir información sobre el ambiente. Los cinco sentidos son la vista, la audición, el olfato, el gusto y el tacto.

spore (SPOR) A reproductive structure of some plants, such as mosses and ferns, that can form a new plant. pp. 401, 449

espora Estructura reproductiva de algunas plantas, como los musgos y los helechos, que puede generar una nueva planta.

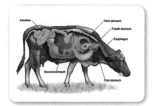

structures (STRUK•churz) Things made of parts assembled in a certain way. p. 400

estructuras Cosas hechas de partes que están ensambladas de cierta manera.

T

trough (TROF) The bottom part of a wave. p. 350

depresión Parte inferior de una onda.

V

volume (VAHL•yoom) How loud or soft a sound is. p. 352

volumen Cuán alto o bajo es un sonido.

W

wave (WAYV) The up-and-down movement of surface water. It can also be a disturbance that carries energy through space. p. 344

ola Movimiento hacia arriba y hacia abajo de la superficie del agua.

onda Alteración que transporta energía a través del espacio.

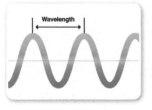

wavelength (WAYV•length) The distance between a point on one wave and the identical point on the next wave. (p. 350)

longitud de onda Distancia entre un punto en una onda y ese mismo punto en la próxima onda.

weathering (WETH•er•ing) The breaking down of rocks on Earth's surface into smaller pieces. p. 217

desgaste Descomposición de las piedras de la superficie terrestre en piezas más pequeñas.

Index

I19

light reflection and, 503, 506, 507

ophthalmologists and, 509

optical illusions, 504

peripheral vision, 498–499, 500–501

pupils in, 502, 503, 507–508

usefulness of, 496, 516

volcano

ash, 318, 368

causes and effects of eruptions, 237–238, 366, 368–369

gas from, 364, 366, 376

landslides from, 238–239

lava, 318, 364, 368

mapping locations of, 320, 322–327

minimizing impacts from, 378

in the "Ring of Fire"

warning signs of eruption, 376, 378

volume (of sound), 352

W

water. *See also* **ocean; rivers**

animal adaptations to, 224

aquadynamic testing, 34

boiling point of, 141

in canyon formation, 212–213, 218, 276

in deserts and rain forests, 223–224

erosion from, 216, 218, 220, 242, 244–246, 344–345

freezing and thawing, 221, 241

hydropower from, 180–181, 182, 184–185, 188

in natural hazards, 366, 369, 378, 379

in plants, 405–406, 408

steam, 81

water vapor, 81, 141

weathering by, 216, 217–218, 220, 221, 242, 244

waterfall, 243, 246, 264

"the wave," 346

wave carpet, 92

wavelength, 350–351, 352–354, 356, 533–534

waves, 344. *See also* **ocean waves; sound waves**

amplitude, 350–352, 354, 356–357

canceling, 356–357

in crowds of people, 340, 346

definition of, 344

energy direction in, 346

energy transfer in, 144–145, 147, 149, 344–345, 348

erosion from, 218, 220, 242, 251, 345

harmony and, 355

hearing the beat in, 358

interactions in, 355–357, 358

light waves, 144–145, 347

making, 340, 342–343

microwaves, 144–145

modeling, 313–315

parts of, 350–351

radio waves, 144, 531

seismic waves, 349

size of, 344

surfing, 341, 354

that move side to side, 346

that move up and down, 346–347

weathering, 217. *See also* **erosion**

definition of, 217

in deserts, 224

fossils and, 276

by freezing and thawing, 221, 241

by living things, 224–225, 240

rate of change, 242–244, 246

by water, 217–218,

220– 221, 240, 242, 244

by wind, 222, 244, 252

weather map, 293

wildfire, 366, 368–369, 376 –377

Williams, Geisha, 151–152

wind

energy from, 79, 180–181, 182, 184, 188, 222

in hurricanes, 369

plant reproduction and, 450, 451

rock erosion from, 218, 222, 240, 244–245, 252

sand transport, 222, 240, 245, 252

solar energy and, 146

waves from, 345

wind barrier, 252

wind farm, 184

wind turbine, 182, 184

wing, 431, 434

world map, 287

X

x-ray, 58, 144–145

Xiang, Jenny, 415

Y

Yosemite Half Dome (California), 240

You Solve It

build a wave pool. 311

crash course, 67

developing renewable energy guidelines, 123

evidence of change, 215

keeping it warm and cool, 1

species research, 487

structures and functions, 391

Z

Zewail, Ahmed Hassan, 173